THE ECONOMICS OF TOTAL QUALITY MANAGEMENT

THE ECONOMICS OF TOTAL QUALITY MANAGEMENT

Clashing Paradigms in the Global Market

William E. Cole
University of Tennessee at Knoxville

John W. Mogab
Southwest Texas State University

First published 1995

Blackwell Publishers, the publishing imprint of
Basil Blackwell Inc.
238 Main Street
Cambridge, Massachusetts 02142
USA

Basil Blackwell Ltd
108 Cowley Road
Oxford   OX4 1JF
UK

Library of Congress Cataloging-in-Publication Data

Cole, William E.
    The economics of total quality management : clashing paradigms in the global market / William E. Cole, John W. Mogab.
        p.   cm. — (Dimensions in total quality)
    Includes bibliographical references and index.
    ISBN 1-55786-504-3
    1. Total quality management.   I. Mogab, John W.   II. Title.
III. Series.
HD62.15.C58   1995
658.5'62—dc20   94-28079
                                                                            CIP

ISBN 1-55786-504-3 (pb)

British Library Cataloguing in Publication Data

A CIP catalogue record for this book is available from the British Library.

Typeset in Times Roman by Compset, Inc.
Printed in the USA

This book is printed on acid-free paper

TQM SERIES FOREWORD

In August of 1991, six US corporations with substantial global operations, American Express, Ford, IBM, Motorola, Procter & Gamble, and Xerox, sponsored The Total Quality Forum. The Forum was an annual gathering of academic leaders and corporate executives. Its purpose was to discuss the role of Total Quality Management in the United States and its role on US campuses, especially in business and engineering schools.

The chief executive officers of the six sponsoring companies summarized the importance of the topic in the November-December 1991 issue of the *Harvard Business Review,* "An Open Letter: TQM on Campus."

"We believe business and academia have a shared responsibility to learn, to teach, and to practice Total Quality Management. If the United States expects to improve its global competitive performance, business and academic leaders must close ranks behind an agenda that stresses the importance and value of TQM. Working together, companies and institutions of higher education *must* accelerate the application of Total Quality Management on our campuses if our education system and economy are to maintain and enhance their global positions." (94 – 95)

In 1989; 14 leading European corporations founded the European Foundation for Quality Management. By 1993 the membership had grown to nearly 300 European organizations (corporations and universities). The September 1993 Membership Information brochure included the following objective and vision.

"The European Foundation for Quality Management (EFQM) believes that, through Total Quality Management, Western Europe will become a leading force in the world market. Our objective is to create conditions to enhance the position of European industry by strengthening the role of management in quality strategies. EFQM's vision is to become the leading organization for promoting and facilitating Total Quality Management in Western Europe. This vision will be achieved when TQM has become an integrated value of the European society, and European management has achieved a global competitive advantage."

The commitment of the Japanese to quality management is legendary. Herein lies the theme of this series of books on TQM. As a system of management, whether in the Americas, the Pacific Rim, or Europe, TQM has become important for global competitive positions. Therefore, learning about TQM models and practices is relevant in universities, in corporate training centers, and in individual development.

CONTENTS

Contents

LIST OF FIGURES

PREFACE

This volume is concerned with an emerging new paradigm that serves to guide the design and management of economic organizations. The paradigm has its intellectual origins with W. A. Shewhart, who pioneered in the application of statistics to manufacturing. His ideas were expanded by W. Edwards Deming and Joseph M. Juran and placed within the framework of a managerial philosophy that was at once optimistic and egalitarian. It is, therefore, a decidedly American paradigm. And yet, today if it is most often identified by such terms as "Japanese management system," and "Toyota production system," that is because the ideas of Deming, Juran, and others first took root in the recovering economy of post–World War II Japan, whose firms desperately needed some way to make their products acceptable in the world markets, especially in the US market. Although we make many references to Japanese firms, and to Toyota in particular, and often cast them in a positive light, our intent was not to write yet another book in praise of Japanese firms. Nor was it our intent to bring forth another volume that bashes U.S. or Western management.

The number of books that treats the emerging new paradigm or parts of it is legion. Two terms from these works, surface as comprehensive descriptions of the new phenomenon: Total Quality Management (TQM) and the Continuous Improvement Firm (CIF). For us, these may be taken as different perspectives on the same phenomenon. From its viewpoint, TQM focuses on the beliefs and practices required of management to bring about and perpetuate the new type of firm. The CIF perspective, in its turn, is the new organization, itself, full-blown and operating. We use the terms interchangeably throughout. In our efforts to isolate and affirm the economic principles underlying the new paradigm, we endeavor to construct a Weberian "ideal type" as the working model of the CIF – in other words, a description of a firm whose dominant organizational rationale is the internal generation of improvements in the product and production process.

Our dominant concern is with the underlying economic logic of the emerging paradigm. In pursuing that concern, we range beyond the usual borders of economics into other disciplines, taking up topics that are typically reserved for engineering and the various business-school disciplines. In the course of our presentation, we try to make it clear that the behavior of the new form, the continuous improvement firm, cannot be understood when the standard textbook model of the theory of the firm is the analytical tool of choice. Indeed, there are things about this new firm that simply do not make sense if we insist on examining it through the lens of that traditional approach. We do not suggest, however, that the standard textbook model should be relegated to the dust bin of history; it has not lost its power to explain the market performance of firms that are organized according to the dominant paradigm of this century, what we call mass production-scientific management (MP/SM). Where it does fail is in the effort to make sense of the organization and management of the new firms and in the effort to understand the current head-to-head competition between firms organized according to the new principles and those grounded in the old ones.

Opinions as to the ultimate importance of the new paradigm are varied and contradictory. Some take the position that the new paradigm will replace the MP/SM paradigm because of its logical superiority. Others take it as a special case, appropriate to a certain time and place, specifically the postwar Japanese "hot house" in which it took root, grew, and blossomed. Still others see it as having potential almost anywhere but currently constrained by the idiosyncrasies of particular management cadres or other firm-specific characteristics. Whether it is destined to become a universal ideal or to have only limited application, we need a new economic approach to make sense of it. It is sometimes said in economics that "there is nothing new under the sun," the implication being that the current literature is comprehensive enough to account for any eventuality. We certainly have found no unturned stones in our investigation of this subject. Almost every issue that we take up has been studied in one form or another. We do believe, however, that the present work provides the basis for a heightened understanding of the differences between the old ways and the new. Furthermore, we believe that a rationale for embracing change emerges when these differences are analyzed together rather than left for separate study, as has been the case to date. The synergies that produce a distinct competitive edge for the CIF do not clearly emerge until the blinders of the old paradigm have been peeled away and that requires a comprehensive approach.

One question that we do not tackle is the extent to which the "ideal type" of CIF is related uniquely to the cultural milieu of Japan. We do work around the edges of it enough to show that versions of the CIF have found a place in various Western settings and even in some developing countries. Whether any of them will be as effective as the paradigmatic progenitors is left undetermined. What does emerge clearly from the analysis, however, is that some capability for continuous improvement may be better than none. In other words, there are many situations in which a firm does not have to approach the "ideal type" in order to gain a competitive edge from TQM. As we shall see, the firm just has to be better at TQM than the competition. In looking at the possibilities for the transfer of continuous improvement technologies, we do suggest the likelihood that it is the MP/SM paradigm rather than our culture per se that makes it difficult for Westerners to design and operate CIFs.

There is no doubt that elements of the MP/SM paradigm are compatible with some Western cultural attributes. Yet, we submit that it is the paradigmatic view, itself, that is more the culprit than the broader cultural aspects. For example, the old paradigm leads us to view just-in-time manufacturing as a system for eliminating inventories, but it simultaneously blinds us to the more fundamental advantages of that system. Indeed, we go so far as to submit that an understanding of TQM and the CIF does not require the assimilation of any aspect of Japanese culture. What is required is an understanding of the internal logic of the new paradigm, especially its economic implications. For some, that may require an arduous journey because the MP/SM paradigm that restrains them is the result of a lifetime of learning, in both the academy and the "real world." The journey, we believe, is worth the effort because the new paradigm represents a significant set of ideas that will probably be with us for a long time to come.

Once the logic of the new paradigm is understood, we see no reason why it cannot serve as an effective guide to Western firms. Most likely its implementation will cause changes throughout the culture within which it operates, as was the case with the advent of mass production and with the factory system that preceded it. In their times, those incipient new manufacturing technologies wrought major changes in society. If the internal logic of the new paradigm constitutes an instrumental imperative, the culture will not only accommodate it; it will change in ways to actively support it.

This work has grown out of the efforts of many people. The inspiration for us to move into the arena of Total Quality Management originally came from Warren Neel and John Riblett, who proposed that someone try to reconcile the new paradigm with received economics principles. All of the faculty associated with the Management Development Center and the Center for Advancement of Organizational Effectiveness, both at the University of Tennessee, were helpful in many ways. The same is true for members of the Carlos Vanzolini Foundation at the University of São Paulo. We owe an ultimately unpayable debt to Richard Sanders and Harlan Carothers whose stimulating ideas opened new horizons for us and often nudged us away from error and whose unflagging encouragement kept us going. Special thanks go to Antonio Bos and Steve Wilson who contributed research results from Brazil and Mexico, respectively, and who also provided us with original ideas and feedback beyond their research. Discussions with Stella Schramm on the topics of "learning" and technology were also invaluable. We express our gratitude to Hans Jensen, Melvin Cymbalista, Jim Schmidhammer, George Peeler, Dale Truett, Michael Best, Dilmus James, Robert Ballance, Feng Yao Lee, Sidney Carroll, Eric Blankmeyer, Joni Charles, and Lewis Hill for comments on various aspects of our work. Finally, we acknowledge the encouragement and guidance of Mike Stahl, the editor of the Total Quality Management series. We absolve all of the foregoing, of course, from blame for any errors that remain.

We wish to recognize the courtesy and cooperation of several firms that allowed us to tour their facilities and whose personnel responded to our queries. They include Toyota (Kentucky), Nissan (Tennessee), Saturn Corporation, Nippondenso of North America, Phillips Consumer Electronics, Aluminum Company of America, and certain facilities of Ford, General Motors, and Chrysler. We also offer a collective thanks to the many firms in Mexico and Brazil who participated in our studies of their efforts to transfer TQM technologies.

CHAPTER 1

INTRODUCTION

> The ideas of economists . . . , both when they are
> right and when they are wrong, are more powerful
> than is commonly understood. Practical men . . .
> are usually the slaves of some defunct economist.
>
> *John Maynard Keynes, The General Theory of*
> *Employment, Interest and Money*

The cover of a recent issue of *TIME* asked "What ever happened to the great American job?" The accompanying story concluded that persons entering the US job markets of today and those of the future should "forget any idea of career-long employment with a big company." The article predicted that there would be no rebound from the corporate "downsizing" that has been going on unabated for several years. Instead, it offered that the big companies will more and more look to temporary sharpshooters to solve special problems. It pictured the professionals of the future as "lone rangers," "computer and E-mail jockeys [who] will work mostly on their own at home . . ." (Church 39). That story was not a solitary voice in the night, sounding the alarm to an unaware citizenry. Rather, it was just an addition to the many accounts that have chronicled the attempts of US corporations to become "lean." Downsizing represents the latest response of some US and other Western firms to the global competition that has besieged it. The downsizing strategy was preceded by a strategy of out-sourcing the labor intensive aspects of manufacturing to low-cost overseas locations. From the viewpoint of many observers, the drastic cost-cutting measures were required to avoid a further loss of markets to an aggressive foreign competition. That the competition is fearsome was manifest in the destruction of much of the US manufacturing base in consumer electronics and the loss of market share in such basic industries as automobiles and steel.

More than a touch of irony lies in the fact that the most successful foreign competitors seem to gain their comparative

1

advantage from a dedicated work force that views its association with the firm as more a marriage than employment. Time after time analysts of the successful firms have argued that a dedicated, educated, and empowered work force is a major factor in their recent global successes. How, then, can we account for the fact that some Western firms prepare themselves for the next round of competitive wars by rejecting the very market weapons that dealt them such severe blows? Although many Western firms have tried to adopt some of the technical methods of their foreign competitors, such as just-in-time manufacturing (JIT), they still show ambivalence about developing the human capital that might produce innovations of magnitude comparable to JIT as a normal part of day-to-day business.

It would be amiss to imply that all or even most major Western firms have ignored the human element. There has been much talk about empowerment, for example, and considerable training in analytical methods, such as statistical process control, in addition to efforts here and there to form work teams. The approach of most Western firms has been schizophrenic, however, juxtaposing downsizing of the work force alongside the efforts to nurture it. Obviously, the anxiety and loss of loyalty associated with downsizing more or less cancels out the expected benefits of training and attempted empowerment. Moreover, during the past year or so it has become apparent that downsizing has been gaining momentum as the dominant of the two approaches, as if many firms were in a final rush to divest themselves of any possible "fat," whatever the consequences, the impact on worries about worker morale have apparently been pushed aside by the preoccupation with cost reduction. With this effort, they have returned completely and comfortably to their intellectual heritage, which, outdated and inappropriate, sees the goal of "lean and mean" achieved through a diet regime. That is a prescription for certain failure in a market environment where competitors will have become "lean and mean" through exercise. For both groups, exercisers and dieters, the scale for lean and mean is productivity of the work force.

We should note that it is management that initiates and implements the diet regime, while the work force in general implements the exercise approach. The diet approach reduces the work force, sometimes in conjunction with a retrenchment in those product lines that feature low productivity. Sometimes the downsizing is a straightforward cut in employment, accompanied by the hope that reorganization will allow the level of production and sales to be maintained. In the exercise approach of the continuous improvement firm (CIF), however, the members of the general work force initiate improvements in productivity. Furthermore, productivity in the CIF is broadly defined to include all facets of product quality as well as output per worker. In other words, not only does output per worker increase, but also the nature of the output improves. Indeed, we shall see subsequently that a basic operating principle of the CIF is that improvements in product quality often produce simultaneous reductions in cost. It does not follow, however, that the reverse is true. A focus on cost cutting via work force reduction will not, of itself, produce simultaneous improvements in product quality. Indeed, management will have its hands full trying to ensure that the reductions in payroll are fully realized in the "bottom line." The conclusion of this scenario will likely be that the improved and less costly products of the CIFs will gain market shares, return greater profits, and force their Western competitors into more and deeper cost-cutting regimes. The CIF's ability to continually improve on the value that customers perceive in its products places a value wedge between its price and its competition's price. As we shall see, products that are perceived to offer lower value must reflect that fact fully in the price differential. Indeed, it is that fact more than anything else that accounts for the frenzy of cost cutting in the form of work force reductions that we are witnessing currently among Western firms. Logically, then, the preferred method for producing a highly productive, lean and mean work force is through exercise. Carrying the metaphor to its logical conclusion, we can say that diet alone, or downsizing, produces a "skinny" or emaciated firm; whereas, the result of exercise will be a firm that is trim and fit, ready to continually improve on its product's perceived value to customers.

How do we account for the apparent "head in the sand" reaction of some Western firms to the "new competition?"[1] How can we make sense out of a situation in which the two sets of firms approach the role of labor so differently? We can view the two sets as equally rational when we realize that each interprets the world through its own theoretical principles. Theoretical principles that function as the dominant interpretation of behavior can be called a paradigm. Some of the principles comprising a paradigm are based upon science, the most fundamental of which may be called laws. Other principles are based upon observed repetitive behavior, representing attempts to find the logical roots of human decisions. When behavior seems pervasive enough, it may be called a "law," as in the case of the "law of demand." Sometimes, a principle derives from logical argument and is only later endorsed by practice. Such was the case with the principle of economies of scale which is rooted in the logic of Smith's argument for specialization and later validated by the mass production assembly line.

In its heyday, a paradigm furnishs a vision to guide progress; past its time, it serves as a set of blinders that prevents the consideration of alternative modes of understanding. These blinders are fitted to practical businessmen as well as academicians. Indeed, to paraphrase the words of Keynes presented at the opening of this chapter, men of current affairs, academic and business, are the slaves of defunct academics.

We call the paradigm that Western firms use to make sense of reality the mass production-scientific management (MP/SM) paradigm. It is made up of principles and laws from various academic disciplines and is reinforced by the experience of decades of real-world operations by firms whose names are household words in much of the world today. Along with the business disciplines and engineering, economics is a contributor to the MP/SM paradigm. Indeed, economics may have been the principle contributor. If so, it may be forced to accept the lion's share of the blame for the myopia caused by an outmoded paradigm. Indeed, we shall argue shortly that many long-held economic truths, such as Smith's principle of specialization are turned on their heads when applied within the context of the new paradigm. Consequently, firms operating on the basis of the new paradigm often appear to be violating many of the rules of good sense that flow from the old logic.

If the competition we see around us truly involves the clash of two very different paradigms, we should not be surprised to find that the emerging paradigm features some superior attributes. Indeed, we may be witnessing something akin to the replacement of craft manufacturing by the factory system and its culmination in mass production. It is, therefore, disconcerting that the adherents of the old paradigm are unable to get a clear hold on the logic of the new one. Most of the old-line managers, not unlike old-line academicians, insist on analyzing the "new competition" through the lens of the MP/SM paradigm. That should come as no surprise, however, given that paradigms, by their nature, are past-binding; they are the quintessence of conservatism. The new competition cannot be understood except in the context of the paradigm within which it operates. The only way to find the real meaning of "lean manufacturing" is to study it through the special lens of the new paradigm.

A New Competitive Force

The essence of continuous improvement is the utilization of the human resources of the firm to produce a constant stream of improvements in all aspects of customer value, including quality, functional design, and timely delivery, without sacrificing low cost. The key factor in this process of endogenous, incremental technological change is the organization and management of the firm in such a way that all members are motivated to promote change and are supported in their efforts to do so. A broadly skilled work force and production flexibility are hallmarks that contrast with the narrow specialization of labor and large volume of homogenous output extolled by the MP/SM paradigm, wherein a firm focuses efforts on minimization of production costs. The irony is in the fact that for the CIF flexibility in output mix goes hand-in-hand with low unit costs. Indeed, based on the logic of its customer-value focus, the ultimate competitive goal of the CIF is the ability to produce consumer goods on a custom basis for almost instantaneous delivery at costs lower than those featured by standard mass production firms. The key to achieving this flexibility and lower unit cost lies in the generalization of the work force. This difference in approach to labor utilization must be understood if the nature of the current competition is to be appreciated. That which is anathema to one paradigm is a hallmark of the other paradigm. Thus, mass production thrives when the product mix changes little, whereas the CIF uses flexibility as a major competitive strategy. Scientific management is forced to forecast demand; the flexible CIF ideally produces to customer demand. For the scientific management firm, success depends largely on the quality of management; its ability to plan and to direct the implementation of those plans is crucial. In the CIF, strategic advantage is based upon the ability of the entire work force, not just management, to constantly improve both the product and the processes whereby it is produced.

This new innovative form, the CIF, almost seems to have sprung straight from the mind of Joseph Schumpeter. In his famous discussion of the prospects for capitalism, Schumpeter (1962) argued that "the fundamental impulse that sets and keeps the capitalist engine in motion comes from the new consumers' goods, the new forms of production, the new markets, the new forms of industrial organization that capitalist enterprise creates." It is activity of this sort "that incessantly revolutionizes the economic structure *from within,* incessantly destroying the old one, incessantly creating a new one." (83) As did mass production before it, continuous improvement "strikes not at the margins of the profits of the existing firms but at their foundations and their very lives." (84) What is most remarkable about the CIF is its ability to operate simultaneously in all of the innovative arenas delineated by Schumpeter: new products, new technology, and new organizational forms. It is, in effect, a machine for continuous innovation. From that perspective we can see the continuous improvement firm as constituting an even more revolutionary change than that brought about almost a century ago by emergence of the mass production-scientific management firm.

The MP/SM Response

Mass production and scientific management are the common terms used to describe the production paradigm that has dominated most of the twentieth century. They represent two sides of the same coin. The mass production side represented by

Adam Smith reflects the belief of economists that efficiency flows from the increased specialization that is in turn a function of the scale of operations. The principles of the industrial engineering side of the coin, represented by Frederick Taylor, are put into practice through a fine division of tasks and the use of time and motion studies. "Fordism" is another popular term for the mass production/scientific management (MP/SM) paradigm.

Mass production in its time was effective at promoting productivity and pushing down unit costs, but at the cost of an inflexibility that is put in relief by the statement attributed to Henry Ford that a customer could have any color of Model "T" desired so long as it was black. One style, including one color, was consistent with, and indeed considered to be a requirement for, the low-cost approach to developing mass markets. One of the continuing organizational challenges for the MP/SM paradigm has been to create product diversity without losing the advantage of the economies of scale inherent in mass production. The emergence of General Motors as a leading force in the automotive market was due to its ability to solve that problem. The solution involved creating a multiplant organization that, in turn, required the conquest of a huge market share and the development of forms of effective coordination for the huge organization. New areas for economies of scale were discovered in the form of specialization in administrative services, marketing, and other areas. Thus, the *mass* in mass production became ever larger and the need for scientific management even greater.

Because the traditional strategic advantage of mass production has been low cost, it should not be surprising that the response of mass production firms to the new competition has relied upon measures to reduce costs. We have seen firms based in developed countries attempt to stem the decline in profits by moving parts of their operations to less developed countries that feature very low wages. Likewise, cost cutting through reductions in the size of the labor force have been prominent in the competitive arsenal. The higher quality and more diversified products coming out of the CIF are, nevertheless, ineffectively countered by the MP/SM firm that concentrates on finding ways to cut costs. Cost-cutting focuses on a single aspect of customer

7

value, whereas the CIF addresses all aspects of customer value simultaneously.

MP/SM firms have not been oblivious to quality – quite the opposite. Some have been consumed with a concern for it. For most, however, the problem has been the attempt to address product quality issues through their traditional paradigm. The consequence is that quality becomes another cost factor. While MP/SM firms are choosing between improved quality and lower costs, the CIFs are accomplishing both simultaneously, and the CIF's production process is becoming more and more flexible in terms of its ability to vary its output mix. Within the continuous improvement paradigm, better quality does not cost more, it costs less, and it promotes flexibility.

For some MP/SM firms, other trends are afoot. Many Western firms are attempting to adopt attributes of the CIF. Sometimes the attempt is superficial, and sometimes it is aimed at a fundamental renovation. The problem of technology transfer is often compounded greatly by the fact that the view of the transfer agent can be distorted by the paradigm employed. When one's productive life has been based upon the application of such principles as specialization of labor and profit maximization, it becomes difficult to make sense out of the CIF. For example, viewing the just-in-time manufacturing system adopted by CIFs as a response to unusually high inventory costs associated with real estate scarcity in Japan is a major mistake. It misses the point that inventory reduction is the by-product of the more fundamental process of reducing production defects to near zero, which in turn allows the firm to turn away from mass production and toward flexibility. More important, it misses the crucial point that the just-in-time manufacturing mode was not adopted in the usual sense, but came about through an evolutionary process.

At a more basic level there is a paradigmatic contradiction between the development of continuous improvement firms and the emerging concept of the *global factory*. In the context of the global factory, the manufacturing location for each and every component of a product is said to be selected on the basis of international comparative advantage. The World Bank (1987), for example, calls the European version of the Ford Escort the product of a global factory, its constituent parts being manufactured in no less than fifteen countries. As the logical culmination of the MP/SM paradigm, this trend runs strictly counter to the basic logic of continuous improvement. As we shall see, CIF firms work most effectively with a small number of suppliers. They develop very close relationships with those suppliers, a feat that would be difficult at best, and probably impossible, under global factory conditions. Furthermore, global dispersion of component manufacturing would make just-in-time manufacturing nearly impossible. In comparing these two trends later in the volume, we will argue that as an ideal type, continuous improvement should win over global manufacturing. Political trends will be noted, however, that could affect the process, especially in the short run.

Toward a New Manufacturing Paradigm

There are some who argue that the Western mass-production firms are in resurgence, pointing to the performance of the U.S. automotive industry in 1993. Such a perspective may lead one to conclude that the recent acclaim given to TQM and the CIF was just another fad in management whose time has past. A closer look at the issue, however, leads to a very different conclusion. Yes, some US automotive manufacturers have become more competitive, but others continue to suffer financial losses and declining market share. The observed resurgence of some automotive firms is not attributable to a revival of mass-production principles, but rather comes, at least partly, from their attempts to introduce some features of TQM.[2] For example, Ford Motor Company and Chrysler have implemented major restructuring in the way they manufacture automobiles, including incorporation of some of the TQM features of their foreign competitors.[3] As a result, quality is up for some models, relative costs are down[4], and they are more competitive today than they have been in many years. On the other hand, General Motors has relied much more heavily on its standard mass-production approach. The results have been frequent financial losses and decreased market share, despite huge investments in new equipment and facilities. Thus, the competitive threat to many Western firms is still very real in the mid-1990s. The outcome will depend upon how they respond – will they continue to view the world from the old mass production perspective or will they adopt the viewpoint of the new paradigm?

A paradigm gives us a way of conceptualizing a mass of phenomena, sometimes of apparently disparate nature, in a way that reveals basic cause-and-effect relationships. That is what we mean when we say that a paradigm shapes the way we see the world. The economists' version of the MP/SM paradigm is found in the textbook presentations of the theory of the firm. Specialization, economies of scale, and profit maximization are at the heart of the analysis. Product characteristics are given, as is the technology used to produce the good. Price, therefore, becomes the only relevant competitive variable, and product quality is of little analytical interest.[5] The ability to produce quality, in the sense of meeting standards, is assumed to be largely implicit in the technology. The technology is embedded in forms of capital, human and machine. Better quality requires the improved technological forms that produce it, and improved technology requires investment. In other words, quality costs. All of this is implicit, however. It is not spelled out in economics texts because technology itself is almost always taken as an exogenous factor.

The theory of the firm assumes that if a new technology is available in the market, managers (decision makers) will acquire that technology if doing so will result in maximizing the net present value of the firm. Production engineers and accountants will have provided management with analysis and data to make that decision. Economics generally takes it for granted that a firm's engineers will design correctly and that accountants will count accurately, at least for those firms that survive into the long run. Given a profit maximizing focus by management and full availability of pertinent information, the proper decisions will take place over the long run. If better products or better production processes emerge somewhere in the world, they will be adopted if appropriate to the firm's resource base, and if not appropriate they should not be adopted. In short the economist's version of the MP/SM paradigm assumes that any decisions about technology transfer, hard or soft, will be subject to benefit-cost calculations. Those that will improve profits will be adopted.

If we are to understand the CIF, we must put aside the mass production/scientific management paradigm because it only serves to distort our view of the new phenomena. The world of the new manufacturing paradigm requires that we view it through a new lens. To begin that task, we must plunge into the literature on technological change. Only after putting aside the view that technological change is largely exogenous to the production process can we begin to understand how the CIF's improvement process produces internal technological change that cannot be explained by the learning-by-doing metaphor. Furthermore, the role of specialization can then be seen in a new and different light. Whereas in mass production the specialization of tasks is mirrored in the parri passu specialization of workers, in the CIF tasks are specialized but workers are generalized. This conceptual uncoupling of task description and worker capacity is a crucial element in the dynamics of continuous improvement. In order to elaborate on the importance of this new view of the role of labor, an expanded view of the concept of technology is also required.

The old and inadequate view of technology as something developed externally to the firm has led to the assumption that there is some optimum organization of the firm around the imported technology that permits the most efficient operation. *Organizational learning* is the term used to describe efforts to get the best fit between the internal organization of the firm and the externally developed technology. The concept of learning-by-doing is all about getting each of the members of the organization proficient in their tasks to the point of optimum efficiency in the use of that technology. Those concepts of learning make sense within the confines of the MP/SM paradigm. Within the continuous improvement paradigm, however, improvement does not mean learning how to use an externally developed technology; rather, it is the essence of technological change itself. With the rising tide of recognition that the management systems and organizational structure peculiar to the CIF are crucial in explaining its improvement process, the obvious question is whether we should consider those systems and structures, themselves, to be forms of technology. Indeed, if those systems and structures yield more effective competitive outcomes than others (based on greater customer value), then, we believe, they must have a technological character.

An equally perplexing contrast arises from a comparison of the value foci of the two types of firms. It is often and strongly argued that the effectiveness of the CIF is based largely upon the fact that most members of its labor force focus upon the provision of customer value in its varied forms. Put simply, the continuous improvement firm reputedly exists to provide value to customers, and the firm is organized and managed so that this aim is internalized by the firm's members. This strategy contrasts with the value focus of the MP/SM firm – profit maximization. Indeed, the raison d'etre of the MP/SM firm is to provide profit for the shareholders. A fiction has been elevated to myth by equating the shareholder-investor with the traditional entrepreneur-owner. Consequently, decisions are taken in both the short run and long run based on their contributions to profit. The CIF, however, views shareholders merely as persons who have evaluated the full range of portfolio possibilities and who happen to have bought shares of the firm in question. As such, they constitute only one of several important stakeholders. The stakeholders, for their part, buy into the idea that everyone, including the shareholders, will be better off if customer value is the goal of the firm's management and of its employees, at least, according to the Japanese version of the CIF. This suggests a crucial paradox: The firms that subject each and every decision to a profit-maximization test will be unable to provide as good a return on investment in the long run as those firms that put the customer first and treat profit as a residual.

This difference in value raises some very interesting questions. If the ability to focus the work force on the provision of customer value helps to account for the competitive edge of the CIF, is that ability an aspect of technology as much as the machines and equipment are? If so, should that ability also be evaluated from the point of view of technology transfer? That question begs another. If the CIF's raison d'etre has a technological component, to what extent is it culturally specific? In other words, to what extent, if any, will the cross-country transfer of continuous improvement technology require cultural change within the host firm and host society to be successful?

Continuous Improvement and Technology Transfer

Major problems arise for those that attempt to copy features of prominent CIFs. Crucial among them is the problem of distinguishing between the process of change and change per se. Take, for example, the technique known as the *single minute exchange of dies,* which was the culmination of a long string of improvements made inside the Toyota manufacturing plants. A MP/SM firm might seek to copy the end result, the current method of changing dies. We could analyze such an effort through use of the standard paradigm for technology. In that context, technological change occurs exogenously to the firm, which will employ a benefit-cost approach to determine the appropriateness of the change for the tasks at hand. Consultants will help implement the transfer, and the host firm will go through a period of learning to use the new technology. The trouble with such an approach is that learning to change dies the way Toyota currently changes them does nothing in and of itself to turn a MP/SM firm into a continuous improvement operation. That is to say, it does not show the firm how to generate its own future improvements in die changing or in anything else. In fact, the MP/SM firm that tries to compete with Toyota by attempting to adopt Toyota's major improvements relegates itself to the role of a permanent follower. Furthermore, it would have to pay for what the leader generated as a normal part of its day-to-day operations.

There is also the question as to whether a follower firm could effectively transfer the major improvements made by a CIF competitor to itself, even if it tried. If the process operations of the CIF at any point in time reflect an accumulation of almost countless incremental changes, can this process be captured with a "snapshot" of the present? This is an especially troublesome question given the fact that many of the incremental improvements apparently are not documented. Take the Toyota production system as a case in point. A snapshot by a camera fitted with a mass production lens would record the system as one that featured just-in-time inventory management. The management of a putative host firm might with effort and expense adopt some elements of a just-in-time system into the otherwise MP/SM operation. The expected benefit to the MP/SM firm would be in the form of lowered inventory costs, but the paradigmatic lens would have filtered out the other major benefits that accrue to Toyota, including that of flexibility in the production process. Within the CIF paradigm, major innovations, such as the just-in-time manufacturing system, are the cumulative by-product of the incessant efforts by employees to improve the customer value content of the goods they produce. In addition to reduced costs, net customer value is enhanced in such areas as improved quality, timely delivery, and new functional product features. Over the long run, it could well be fatal to the MP/SM firm to concentrate on inventory costs while overlooking the increased flexibility enjoyed by its continuous-improvement rival. Evidence of such myopia abounds. Because follower firms are always lagging in terms of competitiveness and because they are paying for something that the CIF obtains without specific investment, following is a losing proposition. In mixed competition between the CIF and the MP/SM firm, the likely outcome is clear: the demise of the MP/SM firm.

Obviously then, for such an MP/SM firm to be successful it will have to convert itself into a CIF. Such a transformation is the essence of what we are treating as technology transfer in this volume. The task is not easy. One problem has already been mentioned; conceptually separating the improvements produced within the system from the process of improvement itself. A crucial and related problem is the tendency to confuse substance with form. In this study we focus on substance. As we shall see, even prominent observers of the CIF fall into the trap of mistaking form for substance so that the essence of a quality circle is thought to be reflected by the formal design and written procedures of the circle. This distraction with form is a little like trying to find the distinguishing characteristics of championship football teams in the size, weight, and deployment of their players. Indeed, the factors that distinguish winners from losers are likely to defy quantification, which also may be true in the mixed competition between mass production and continuous improvements firms. A MP/SM firm that took on such major organizational features of continuous improvement as quality circles, suggestion systems, cross-functional teams, job rotation, and permanent employment might fail to motivate the system to achieve a high level of internal improvements because it failed to articulate a customer-value approach. By adopting the forms of continuous improvement but retaining profit maximization as its raison d'etre, it would operate poorly as a continuous improvement firm, analogous to the football team whose technically astute coach did not inspire or otherwise motivate the players. The functional forms alone, without the proper motivation, may not be able to generate the desired improvements.

Are TQM Valves Transportable to Other Cultures?

Raising the questions about the productive content of corporate philosophies and value systems leads us again into another area of fundamental concern. Are the major components of continuous improvement culture specific? The question is more trenchant when we remember the priority of substance over form. For example, workers may be formed into teams or quality circles and equipped with identical analytical techniques without regard to culture. Their form in a US manufacturing facility might be the same as that in a Japanese factory. Furthermore, the value system articulated by management might appear to be very similar, for example, customer value. However, just as certain sports give the impression of fitting more appropriately in some cultures than in others, is it possible that the forms of continuous improvement may operate more effectively in certain cultures than in others? This point is controversial in the literature and may ultimately have to be resolved as an empirical question as Japanese firms themselves attempt to transplant the continuous-improvement mode to various parts of the world. As we shall see, the results of those efforts, thus far, have been mixed.

The questions raised here put a new slant on the topic of appropriate technology. Heretofore, the question of appropriateness was raised in the context of relative factor mix and/or the availability of complementary factors. Traditionally, we would refer to a technology as inappropriate if, say, it were capital intensive while the factor endowment featured surplus labor, if the host economy's labor force did not feature the educational and/or skill levels required for effective operation. Is the technology appropriate to the culture? Does it fit well with the religious, philosophic, political background within which it will operate? These questions go beyond simple compatibility. Even if the technology seems compatible across cultures, can the cultural differences make a crucial difference in the rate of change and, therefore, in the long-run competitiveness? "Putting the customer first" might seem to fit with Christian ideals, for example, but perhaps it might be more effective in a Confucian or Buddhist setting. That argument has been put forward before. Conversely, one might raise the question of appropriateness of the top-down MP/SM system for an ostensibly democratic society such as the United States. In that regard, we might speculate that over the long haul the basic values implicit in the continuous-improvement firm might be more appropriate for the current US culture than is the MP/SM paradigm. Later, in the course of this work we will argue that what is needed for the successful adoption of the continuous improvement mode in the West is not so much a change in culture as a change in the paradigmatic view of the business world.

International Trends That Clash with Continuous Improvement

The continuous improvement firm does not exist in a ceteris paraibus analytical vacuum. It exists in a world where political factors often weigh as heavily as economic ones and where currently several trends spell trouble for it, including the tendency for protectionist reactions in both the United States and Europe against the onslaught of the CIF, especially in automobiles and some consumer electronics. The pressure to protect domestic firms often has been based on allegations of unfair trade practices. Four decades ago, the exploitation of cheap labor was thought to be the basis for the competitive edge of the CIF. Later, "dumping" was given as the explanation for the ability to sell higher quality products at lower prices. In any event, it is a fact of life that an emerging superior method inevitably faces its own versions of the Luddites.

Not surprisingly, then, the progenitor CIFs from Japan have faced protectionist pressures that have greatly affected their long-term global strategies.[6] In automobiles, for example, pressures in both the United States and Europe have led to the establishment of Japanese subsidiaries that operate inside the protective walls. Later in this work, we suggest that the CIF forced into operation with global subsidiaries faces a reduction in efficiency. We will present analysis suggesting that the more geographically fragmented the firm, the lower the rate of improvement generation and the greater the cost of maintaining the improvement process. This analysis will go beyond a straightforward "cost of coordination" statement to show that certain synergies are lost in the fragmented format that no amount of coordination can recapture. This will be just one of several examples of how geopolitical factors can force the real-world CIF to diverge significantly from the ideal type.

The fact that the CIF is hobbled when forced into a subsidiary mode may prove useful to firms in the West and in less developed countries (LDCs). Western managers may come to view protectionism as a ticket to continued operation in the MP/SM format. Some, on the other hand, may view the foreign CIF's handicap as a boon providing a breathing space while they and their organizations develop their own versions of continuous improvement. Those able to develop their own effective versions of the CIF might be in a better position to fend off foreign CIFs, vanquish their domestic competition, and successfully compete in the global markets.

The results of several research efforts in LDCs offer interesting, if tentative, insights into the global prospects for transferring the components of the continuous improvement paradigm. From the point of view of the Brazilian and Mexican settings alone, Japanese firms trail both domestic firms and the subsidiaries of US transnationals in certain key features in the development of a local continuous improvement capacity. The Japanese subsidiaries are apparently hampered in their transfer efforts by their dependency on their home operations. They transfer key improvements that emerge within the context of their home operations without developing any significant improvement mechanism within the subsidiary. Although the strength of their home operations has been sufficient to carry the subsidiary to date, the question of long-run viability remains. Equally interesting is the finding that Mexican subsidiaries of US transnational firms are often more adept at assimilating continuous improvement characteristics than are the home facilities of the same firms.

While there is no doubt that product quality and productivity are greater in Japanese transplants than in the facilities of national companies, there are genuine questions about the ability to maintain that difference. More specifically, there are some strong reasons to believe that the continuous improvement mode might have better long-run prospects within the national firms of, say, Brazil or Mexico than within subsidiaries of Japanese transnationals. Furthermore, we will explore reasons why the experiences of Japanese transplants in the United States are apparently different from those of the subsidiaries of those same companies in an LDC setting. We will find that some of the explanations for their having made greater continuous improvement efforts in the US are rooted in the logic of the CIF paradigm and that some have political roots.

Focus of the Analysis

Large economic organizations are incredibly complex, whether our interest is in Japanese, US, European, or Mexican firms. Most of the CIFs studied are multidivisional, multiproduct and multinational. Accordingly, a large body of literature in economics, management, and other academic disciplines treats the problems of coordination, both internal and external, for such organizations.[7] Depending on the products involved, the markets in which they compete, and the nationality of the home base, "[d]ifferent organizational structures achieve coordination in different ways and with differing results." (Milgrom and Roberts, 1992, 26) Sometimes the focus of analysis is on coordination that is internal, as with the case of the several business units of a giant firm like General Motors. Other times, the analyst may be looking at external coordination, as in the case of Toyota and other member firms in its *keiretsu*. Though important in themselves, these aspects of coordination will not be of much interest to this study.

Our interests are more in the design, production, and sale of a good than in such matters as conglomeration strategies. For analytical purposes, therefore, our ideal type of CIF is composed of one business unit that produces and markets one basic product that may come in a number of varieties. To further trim the complexity and get to issues that are crucial to our goals, we will depict the firm as one simple organizational pyramid with a CEO at the top, operatives at the bottom, and a few layers of managers in between. (International subsidiaries are considered as a special case.) In contradistinction to the typical approach, we often will focus our analysis on the lower echelons of the pyramid. In terms of product design, we will focus at the level of the drawing board and in terms of manufacturing, inside the factory, including the operations of suppliers. It is in those settings that the myriad incremental improvements in product and production process emerge.

This narrow concentration of effort does not indicate a failure to recognize the importance of broader considerations inside and outside the firm. Indeed, in most cases the Japanese version of the CIF operates as a member of a formal business group called a *keiretsu*, and its efforts are supported and channeled by an active national industrial policy. Both the *keiretsu* and the government are sources of competitive strength as well as constraints on freedom of action. Though these broader features play significant roles in the competitiveness of the Japanese CIF, there is no logical reason why the continuous improvement mode cannot operate independently of them. It is certainly worthy of study, in and for itself.

NOTES

1. Best (1990) first used the term "new competition" to refer to the Japanese firms that feature continuous improvement.

2. The US auto makers were given a major competitive boost by the rapid appreciation of the Yen during 1993 that has forced large increases in the dollar price of Japanese cars.

3. Similar changes have been made by some automotive parts supplier firms. For example, Cummins, which supplies engines for Dodge trucks, reopened a plant south of Columbus, Ohio, which earlier had closed when Cummins reduced its production capacity. A condition of reopening the plant was that Cummins be able to run the factory based upon teamwork, a system they had been implementing in other plants. (Rose 1994, 4)

4. Probably most of the improvement in cost relative to Japanese automakers was tied to the rising value of the Yen.

5. While there have been a few works in economics that treat the topic of quality, their analysis has not penetrated the world of the economics textbooks.

6. In making this statement, we are fully cognizant that Japan has erected all manner of protective barriers against products and commodities from other countries.

7. The management literature tends to focus on intrafirm coordination while economics places emphasis on interfirm coordination.

CHAPTER 2

MASS PRODUCTION/SCIENTIFIC MANAGEMENT: An Old-Fashioned Paradigm

Thoughtful persons from outside the discipline of economics may be surprised to learn that in the theory of the firm, the firm itself is usually treated as a "black box." The assumption that technological change is an exogenous factor in most economic analysis may also be perplexing to the outsider. Regarding the internal operation of the firm, Jensen and Meckling (1986, 216) indicate that "the firm is a 'black box' operated so as to meet the relevant marginal conditions with respect to inputs and outputs, thereby maximizing profits, or more accurately, present value." Rosenberg (1982) also tells us that economists treat technology as a black box. Thus, textbook models give no consideration to the economic impact of alternative organizational structures or management practices, nor to the origin and nature of technological change. The boxes have remained closed because economists have assumed that each firm's management will be led to choose the most appropriate organizational structure, management system, and technology for its situation by its need to maximize profits.[1] If appropriate improvements in any of those elements emerge somewhere in the global economy, the firms that remain as producers in the market will eventually adopt them. It is all automatic; improvements follow if and when the discounted stream of future net benefits deriving from the change is positive. Apparently, then, we do not need to open the boxes in order to explain how resources are allocated and prices formed.

Although economics rarely concerns itself with the internal operation of the firm, economic theory is part and parcel of what we are calling the mass production/scientific management paradigm. Indeed, venerable tenets of economics furnish the foundation for both legs of the paradigm: economies of scale as the basis for mass production and specialization of labor as the rationale for scientific management. Those two concepts are related to each other, and both find their inception in Adam Smith's *Wealth of Nations* (1957). After tracing for the reader the major features of mass production and scientific management, we will return to the discipline of economics and highlight its important role in the development and perpetuation of that paradigm.

Mass Production

A mass production system manufactures products with interchangeable parts by means of specialty machines and specialized workers that together are organized according to the principles of flow. Henry Ford is often credited with adding the principle of flow to the preexisting features which together were referred to as the American system of manufacture.[2] The principle of flow refers to the sequencing of machines and associated tasks according to their logical order in the progressive elaboration of the product. Best (1990, 53) describes it as follows:

> The idea of a flowline is to lay out the machines in the order of the machining operations. Thus, instead of transporting batches from department to department, the machine operations would be laid out in a series that corresponded to the sequence required for production. A flowline held out the promise of less transport and handling time as goods moved directly from machine to machine rather than from department to department. Furthermore, intermediate inventories declined as the operations were streamlined.

One example of the flowline concept is the production of an old-fashioned toy, the spinning top. The logical steps in the top's production include (a) cutting the wood into pieces of the proper length, (b) turning each piece on a lathe to get the basic shape, (c) sanding each piece to smooth it, (d) painting, and (e) attaching the metal point at the base. Prior to the flowline concept, specialist work was largely accomplished by batch production within departments. This is represented in the floor plan presented in figure 2.1.

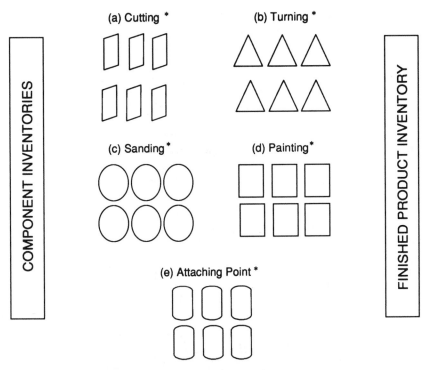

Figure 2.1. Organization by functional department for batch production of toy tops. *Each geometric shape represents an individual work station.

The output of each department would go by batches into inventory, and each department would draw all of its inputs in the form of batches from inventory. Thus, each item of the product went in and out of inventory many times during the process of elaboration. With the flowline, the machines are broken out of their respective departments and organized in a logical sequence of tasks to be performed as shown in figure 2.2.

Hence, the throughput does not itself go in and out of inventory. It merely travels downstream, directly from one work station to the next.[3] The reductions in handling time and inventory are obviously great.[4]

The production of more complicated products such as automobiles requires a large number of flowlines. The chassis and drive train, for example, are put together on separate lines, as is

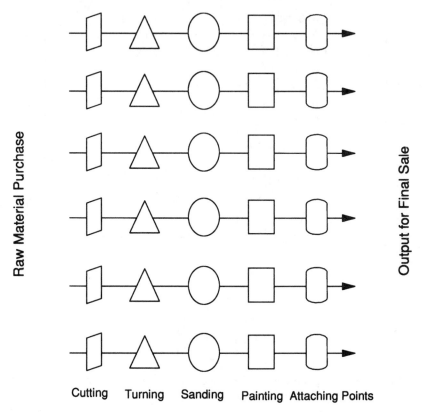

Figure 2.2. Flowline organization for manufacturing tops.

also the case with the starter, the alternator, and so on. Within each assembly line, the more specialization that takes place, the greater the level of labor productivity, at least up to some point. Ford not only introduced the principle of flow to factory organization; he also took specialization of tasks to dizzying heights. A description of one minuscule aspect of his Model-T plant shows the extent to which he exploited the economies of specialization.

> In the spring of 1913, Ford engineers broke the production process of the magneto coil down into 29 complementary operations by 29 different workers. Workers stood in a row along a sliding surface performing the same operation on each product and then hand

pushed it two or three feet along to the next worker for the next task. The time taken to make a magneto dropped from 20 to 13 minutes (Best 1990, 54).

By applying this same technique to other major components and to final assembly, the Model T's production time and cost per unit were reduced considerably.

Not all the rationale for scale derived from specialization and organization of production into a flowline sequence. Sometimes the efficient meshing of machines with different capacities would require overall plant capacity to be very large in order to avoid excess capacity at some work stations. The importance of balanced capacities can be illustrated by carrying our present example forward. In figure 2.3a, we truncate the top-making process in order to simplify the arithmetic. The figure shows only three work stations: cutting, turning, and sanding. The hypothetical machine capacities represent the amount of output that can be produced during an eight-hour work shift. Thus, a cutting station can provide enough pieces of wood to make 600 tops, a turning station can handle 400 pieces, and a sanding station 200. If we make the simplifying assumption that the total cost of each work station is $95 per shift, we can make some interesting cost and productivity calculations.

We immediately discover that turning is a bottleneck. If we put one of each work station in the line, then obvious excess capacity will result: Only one-third of cutting capacity is required to supply inputs and only 50 percent of turning capacity is utilized. That is, the output for the shift would be constrained by the 200 units capacity of sanding. The total cost would be $285 (3 × $95) and the cost per unit $1.425. If we balance our processes in a way that eliminates excess capacity, however, we find each flowline organized as shown in figure 2.3b. The total output per shift would be 1,200 tops and the total cost would be $1,045, yielding a cost per unit of 87 cents. The difference in cost between balanced and unbalanced flowlines is obviously overwhelming, but so is the difference in volume of production.

Given all these factors, it is not surprising that the economics of mass production were compelling in many markets. The firm that could amass sufficient size to feature minute specialization

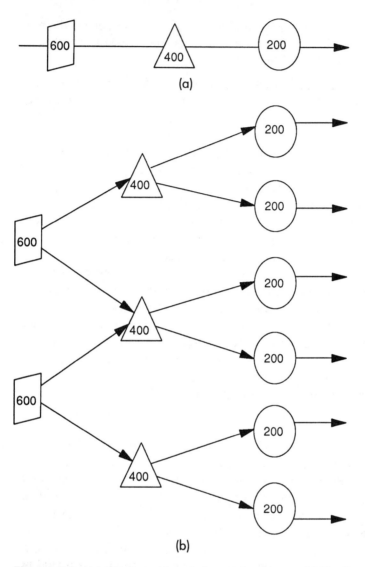

Figure 2.3. (a) Flowline without balance of processes. (b) Flowline with balanced processes. Numbers indicate shift capacity of a work station. For example, each cutting station could do the cutting operations for 600 tops.

of tasks and balance its production to avoid any excess capacities would have overwhelming cost advantage over smaller firms. There are, however, additional compelling reasons to think that economic efficiency increases with the scale of operations. The larger the firm, the more likely it can utilize administrative specializations such as personnel, purchasing, logistics, and so on, and the more likely that crucial operations such as marketing and product design be given over to full-time experts. Furthermore "with large operations, a firm may be able to afford more specialized equipment, more distribution outlets located nearer to customers, . . . training programs for its employees tailored to particular cicumstances, etc." (Milgrom and Roberts 1992, 106) We therefore see the compelling rationale for developing mass production as a prerequisite for success.

Scientific Management

The revolution in production was matched by similar drastic changes in the ways firms were managed. In Adam Smith's pin factory, for example, the owner-manager was literally within eye sight of the specialists. Over time, as the size of operations and the degree of specialization increased, the ownership group became separate from managers, and both became increasingly removed from the operators on the plant floors. Viewing the organizational structure as a pyramid, we see that as the base of manufacturing operations grows in size, the peak of the structure tends to move upward proportionately, with the intervening distance being filled with increasing layers of middle management. Smith's law of specialization was apparently as useful to management analysts as it was to production engineers. Business firms were organized hierarchically and divided into functional specializations such as purchasing, marketing, logistics, manufacturing, accounting, finance, and design. This organizational specialization by functional units was thought to improve productivity for reasons similar to those used to explain the division of the tasks among workers within each of those functions.

A glimpse at an ongoing firm in the process of trying to develop and market a new product may help to illustrate the operation of a mass production/scientific management (MP/SM) firm. Let us imagine a situation in which basic research has opened up new product possibilities in the area of consumer electronics – digital recording, video cassettes, or almost anything you wish to conjure up. The product design department would be the functional specialization with the assignment of coming up with a prototype capable of manufacture. In the course of design, this department probably will solicit information from other functional units, marketing and manufacturing, for instance. While that outside information may be useful and sometimes essential, it in no way detracts from the fact that the product design department has responsibility for the job. To think otherwise would be like advocating that firemen routinely do the work of policemen.

After the new product prototype is designed, manufacturing will have to make it and marketing sell it. Furthermore, to get production up and running, purchasing will have to exercise its function of acquiring the necessary inputs at a relatively low cost. Logistics must maintain the inventories of inputs and outputs and move them efficiently. Accounting, in its turn, must keep track of costs and audit the entire operation. And marketing and sales is delegated the task of moving the product to the consumer and monitoring consumer reaction to it.[5]

How does an organization know how to make a new product and how does it go about disseminating that knowledge? In what sense is the work of the functions coordinated? (Often, the coordination is implicit, through the budgeting process.) How do managers at the various levels of each function know what their job is on a budgeted project and how do they know how to do that job? The answer is that the technical and professional personnel are trained in universities and professional and technical schools, and they maintain external contact with their specialties through professional organizations. Thus, they keep up to date about practices in their respective fields and subfields of specialization. We can picture each of the firm's functional units handling its activities through the use of "best practices" as taught in leading schools of business and carried out in leading firms. Instead of being one pyramidal structure, the MP/SM firm is composed, in reality, of several pyramids, each representing one of the several basic functions. Those several pyramids are supposedly coordinated by a chief executive officer (CEO) who usually has training and experience in only one of them.

Functional Specialization in the MP/SM Firm

It may be helpful to view the functional specializations as silos with production workers on the floor and functional executives at the top. The hard walls of the silo reflect the reality that persons initially enter employment based upon an educational specialization and then proceed up the promotion ladder within that specialization. This analogy makes it easier to see that communications move vertically – information going up and instructions coming down. Below the levels of top management, there is relatively little horizontal movement of information and, as a result, relatively little opportunity for learning across the functions. Effective coordination of functional activities comes from the top management of the organization. At that level, above the functional silos, general plans are made and from there assignments distributed downward, becoming more and more specific the further down the silo they travel. Indeed, the finely divided division of labor requires that work flow be planned carefully, with the consequence that both the planning and implementation periods are unavoidably long. At the actual level of manufacturing, minuscule details of the work are based upon time and motion studies in a fashion that has become known as Taylorism. Chandler refers to the managerial structure that accompanies mass production as coordination by the "visible hand of management" and credits it with sweeping aside the "invisible hand of market forces." (Chandler 1977, 1) This is another way of saying that large-scale business operations have a commanding competitive edge in many industries.

The rationale for functionalism in business firms stems from the seminal idea of the division of labor. We might view the basic functions as the first, or proximate, cut in the division of labor.

If all of the work of producing and selling a product (or service) is pictured as a pie with each function represented as a slice, the basic underlying assumption is that if each of the functions performs well, an effective product will be efficiently produced. The whole is, therefore, thought to be the sum of the parts.

Each of the basic functional divisions of the firm allow further specializations to be developed. A division such as marketing, accounting, or manufacturing is subdivided into, say, departments, and departments into sections, and sections into groups, and eventually into the ultimate units that are represented by individual workers. As pointed out earlier, the belief is that the finer the division of tasks at the level of the individual, the greater the productivity of the organization and the lower the cost per unit. With maximum specialization, if each individual performs his/her task properly, supposedly the organization as a whole will prosper. This happy scenario stands or falls, of course, on how well the various tasks have been designed to fit into the job that the company as a whole has undertaken. It also follows from the logic of division of labor that the design of jobs starts at the top and moves sequentially downward. In that context, each level in the pyramid is responsible for the performance of the level below it and implicitly responsible for the design of the several tasks performed at the next level below that.

A manager of a functional division is a specialist in the division's activities who supervises the several types of activities among departments, which are also headed by specialists, who each manage several specialist sections. Finally, at the bottom, are the work groups, called by various names, and each managed by a supervisor or foreman. This process of job design and governance is decidedly top-down. Clearly, everyone has a specified job to do and is expected to do that job and not someone else's. This kind of system results in a proliferation of job descriptions, often thousands in number. Personnel specialists hire people for those positions and train them to do the work.

It is usual to view the organizational structure of modern manufacturing corporations as pyramidal in form. Those at the bottom of the pyramid are only concerned with carrying out routine tasks. Upward communication is mainly routine as well and is directed to an immediate supervisor. Any horizontal communication between functions is usually in the form of prescribed reports. The presumption is that the employees at higher levels of the organization have a broader understanding of the organization than do those at lower levels. Thus, the foreman is more knowledgeable than the production workers he/she supervises. The section chief has a broader view of the process than the foreman, and the department head more than the section chief, and so on, upward through the firm. Carried to its extreme, the CEO should be the person who best understands how the parts fit together in one integrated, smooth functioning process. This is not to imply that the CEO is supposed to understand the details of all of the jobs. What he/she understands is supposedly the big picture, and the shareholders undoubtedly hold the CEO responsible for the performance of the entire organization.

Often, however, there is a fundamental disconnection between the responsibility of the CEO and the abilities of the CEO. There is often little background or training to prepare the CEO for the responsibility of the entire firm. Before they reach the top, CEOs usually come up through the ranks to the position of operating vice president in one of the functional divisions. The CEO's understanding of the organization is, therefore, limited to or otherwise colored by experience in one of the functional divisions. This narrowness is a natural by-product of the specialization that is said to be the special strength of the MP/SM firm.

Accompanying these structural developments in the business world, especially in manufacturing, was the emergence of professional schools of business associated with major universities. University faculties studied the emerging new systems, conceptualized them, and applied the scientific method to the study of business activity. In their own organizational structure, the business schools largely replicated the functional structure of the dominant business firms. Marketing, accounting, finance, logistics, and personnel management became academic disciplines intended to prepare young labor-force entrants to operate successfully in their counterpart functions in business.

Oddly, manufacturing per se was not taken up as one of the business disciplines, perhaps because Frederick Taylor, the person originally associated with the manufacturing side of scientific management, was an engineer by training. The scientific organization and operation of actual manufacturing activities consequently became known as industrial engineering. The omission of production from business school curricula also might have had something to do with the fact that economics is the mother discipline for the several functional business departments. As we shall see shortly, economics is not concerned with the mechanics of technological change or with the internal dynamics of production. As emphasized by Barney and Ouchi (1986, 180), "Buying and selling is the fundamental process studied in economics."[6]

In both real-world and ivory-tower contexts, the assumption is that if each professional function does its best, the organization as a whole will excel. The reputation of a business school depends upon professional recognition for research and teaching in its individual departments. It should be noted, however, that the end product of the business school, say, a marketing major, does not have a counterpart in the business world. In the realm of the firm, no identifiable independent product for marketing, accounting, logistics, finance, or purchasing exists. There is an overall measure of success for the firm and that is the "bottom line." It is one thing to say that each of the firm's functions contributes to the profit position, but it it another thing entirely to try to say how or why those contributions fit together. Can we usefully picture these specialized functions working as a team to accomplish firm goals?

With a team as the metaphor, let us find out how a basketball team would operate if it were to follow MP/SM principles. If we picture each player as a separate function, we would have a situation in which players do not communicate with each other. Furthermore, no coach would have drawn up a master book of plays showing how the separate functions should relate to each other to make up a system for scoring points or a system for defending against scoring by the opposition. The MP/SM version of basketball would assume that each player should practice separately with his/her own specialized coach. The head coach would communicate such general information as scheduling to the specialist coaches who would relay it to the players. If each specialist came to master the knowledge related to his/her position, the five specialists would comprise a de facto masterful team for producing victories. This strategy might work only if all other teams operated in the same manner. However, once a team comes along in which players communicate with each other, occasionally swap positions in practice sessions, and practice with a book of plays drawn up by a coach who views the players as an integrated system for scoring, the old paradigm goes out the window. The resulting game of mixed competition between an aggregation of five "pure" specialists and genuine organic team would be bewildering, to say the least – and yet, that is more or less what we are witnessing in the "mixed competition" between MP/SM firms and continuous improvement firms. Mixing our metaphors for a moment, we find, for example, that the CIF team is able to put new products on the market in one-half to one-third the time of the MP/SM team. In the new form of competition, that between firms from different paradigms, the former strength of the MP/SM firm, specialization, is now seen as a major source of weakness.

Economics and the MP/SM Paradigm

Most of the functional departments of colleges of business consider economics to be their mother discipline. It is, therefore, useful to trace the strategic links between economics as an academic discipline and the development of the MP/SM paradigm. In this exercise, we are particularly interested in what economists call the theory of the firm and the theory of consumer behavior as presented in the textbooks used by undergraduate business majors and MBA students. These are the works that help to fashion and support the standard paradigmatic view that has been and is still dominant in North America and Western Europe.

Specialization and Economies of Scale

The productivity improvements associated with the earlier emergence of mass production were said to derive from increased specialization of the work force. According to the founding father of economics, Adam Smith, productivity growth is to be realized through three mechanisms. First is an "increase of dexterity of every particular workman." Second is "the saving of time which is commonly lost in passing from one species of work to another." Finally, Smith recognized the role of technology by including as the third mechanism the introduction of "machines which facilitate and abridge labour, and enable one man to do the work of many." (Smith 1957, 4) Smith illustrated the role of specialization by comparing a pin factory with pin making as a craft in which one skilled workman performed each of the required operations. Smith suggested that productivity per specialized factory worker would be hundreds or even thousands of times greater than the productivity of individual unspecialized craftsmen.

Smith's discussion of the gains from increased specialization of labor has come down to us in modern economics textbooks almost unchanged. In reference to economies of scale, it is typically said that "when workers and equipment are expanded together, very substantial gains may be reaped by division of jobs and specialization of workers. . . ." (Maurice and Smithson 1988, p. 290) The same authors write that "[a] larger plant with a larger work force may permit each worker to specialize in one job, gaining proficiency and decreasing and eliminating time-consuming interchanges of location and equipment." (290) Finally, echoing Smith, they add that "technological factors constitute [the other] force contributing to economies of scale." (290)

In addition to the arguments that are derived from Smith, current textbooks advance two other reasons for economies of scale. One is the fact that the balancing of machine capacities becomes easier as the level of output increases. Another concerns what might be called organizational economies of scale. As the firm's market grows larger, the volume justifies internalizing such specialties as marketing and accounting that were formerly purchased in the market as needed.

The textbooks usually mention diseconomies of scale, too. The concept is almost always presented in passing and is explained as a situation in which a firm becomes too large to be managed effectively. Bureaucratic arteriosclerosis sets in. However, because emphasis or analysis is rarely given to this concept, the focus remains clearly on the positive aspects of economies of scale.

The upshot is that large scale translates into high levels of labor productivity and, therefore, low cost per unit. In turn, the size of investment required to achieve economies of scale in itself constitutes a barrier to the entry of potential competitors.

Agency Theory

Agency theory is as close as economics comes to studying the internal operation of the firm. As should become clear, however, that is really not very close. Agency theory is part and parcel of the MP/SM paradigm and is a topic of discussion by each of the several business disciplines. The agency perspective evolved out of Arrow's (1974, p. 224) work on the theory of risk bearing. Arrow hypothesized that each organization is a group of individuals seeking to maximize an objective function and each member has objectives that are not coincident with those of the organization. Stockholders, as principals, are said to hire management as their agents to supervise the operation of the firm. As principals, the stockholders desire to maximize the present value of the firm, but management as agents, have additional, sometimes contradictory, objectives. Top management, in turn, hires others to assist it. These agents, at all levels of the firm, have individual goals somewhat inconsistent with the interests of both top management and the stockholders. The thrust of agency theory is the identification of contract alternatives and the stipulation of conditions under which alternative contract forms are most effective for monitoring the agents to ensure that the instructions of the principals are carried out (Eisenhardt 1989, 59–61). Effective contracts are designed to guarantee that organizational efforts come as close as possible to maximizing profits for the owners. Because profit maximization is the cornerstone of most economic models, the development of agency theory may be seen as a means to salvage the relevancy of economics in what was once the world of mass production-scientific management.

The fact that agency theory entails top-down control of the firm fits with and reinforces the central characteristics of mass production-scientific management. Indeed, agency theory is now a key part of the paradigm.

Transactions Cost and Information Cost

Transactions cost and information cost are also attempts to explain some of the internal operation of the MP/SM firm. They recognize that modern economies feature large bureaucratic firms rather than the atomistic entrepreneurial firms that purchase inputs and sell outputs in perfectly competitive textbook markets. The less than perfect markets of the real world mandate costs for obtaining the information necessary to make decisions and costs involved in effecting a transaction. Thus, successful firms appear to be the ones that can minimize the cost of making transactions, that is, the ones that can function efficiently as bureaucracies.

These concepts are sometimes removed from the context of their mother paradigm, MP/SM, and misapplied to explain certain aspects of continuous improvement. From one perspective, the advantages of the CIF's horizontal or cross-functional coordination might be properly couched in terms of savings in information cost and/or transactions costs. However, the usefulness of the transactions-cost approach is compromised by the fact that it is an ex-post rationalization of the perceived change. It gives us a plausible rationale for change but says nothing about how the change took place. Furthermore, because it is paradigmatically inappropriate, the rationale is often misleading. For example, we may try to explain the emergence of just-in-time manufacturing as the result of firm's having compared the costs of effective contracts with suppliers against the cost of holding inventories. In such a case we could arrive at an ostensibly credible explanation without ever realizing that the key determinant was the improved quality of throughput and not the cost of holding inventories. Because it does not look inside the process components that are being coordinated, the transactions cost approach overlooks the fact that a significant proportion of the cost reductions are the result of internally generated technological change. Moreover, because its focus is cost, it overlooks the crucial role of improvements in other areas of customer value, especially quality.

Finally, the implication is that any MP/SM firm can obtain and use the same information as CIFs or complete the same kinds of transactions as they do if it were willing to incur the associated costs. As we shall clearly see, however, the CIF's cost functions decline relative to those of the MP/SM firm, not because its outlays for information are somehow more effective than those of the standard firm, but because it often is able to generate and apply technological information costlessly that the MP/SM firm does not normally generate and may not be able to effectively appropriate in the market.[7]

Both the transactions cost and agency theory approaches get us beyond the market for the finished product or service and into the intrafirm and interfirm buy-sell relationships for factors of production, intermediate products, and raw materials. In both approaches, however, these relationships are no more than interfaces in which stylized contracts affect only buying and selling behaviors. Such things as the relative dynamics of alternative information gathering systems are never mentioned, much less studied. For that reason, extremely important aspects of the CIF are entirely overlooked, for example, the facts that technological change is endogenous to the production process and that it is largely costless. If we are to understand the new form of competition, we must get beyond the transactions cost approach, or, at least, develop that approach much more fully.

Learning-by-Doing

Learning-by-doing is another standard tool of economic analysis that has been used and abused in sporadic attempts to explain several continuous improvement phenomena. This tool is popular enough for some observers to refer to the CIF as "the learning firm," which is usually interpreted through the standard paradigm to mean that the CIF sometimes has the ability to move up a learning curve more quickly than its competitor. While the learning-curve metaphor may lead one to ask some useful questions, it tends to blind the user to important implications that may come into view only after relinquishing the constructs of the old paradigm.

To better understand the limits of the "learning curve" metaphor we must see it in the broad context of the MP/SM paradigm. In that setting learning is only one aspect of instrumental change, and possibly the least important. Its position in the hierarchy of instrumental change is shown in figure 2.4. By

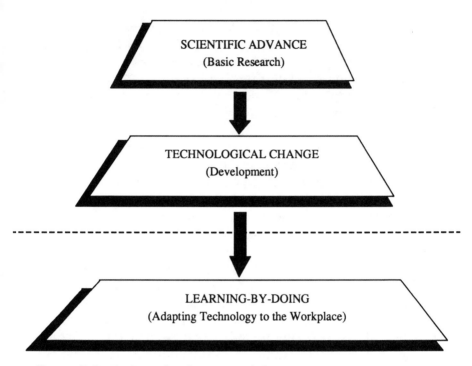

Figure 2.4. The hierarchy of instrumental change.

instrumental change, we refer to all advances in our objective knowledge of the universe and the application of that knowledge to processes for producing products, services, and devises or anything that supports, sustains, and/or otherwise responds to human wants. Figure 2.4 represents what purports to be a generally accepted hierarchy among the basic elements of instrumental change. For these purposes science is defined as a branch of knowledge concerned with establishing and systematizing facts, principles, and methods according to experiments and hypotheses regarding nature and the physical world. Science is engaged in basic research to enhance our understanding of the big and the small facts of the universe. In the words of Feibleman (1961, p. 308), "pure theoretical sciences are concerned with the discovery of natural law and the description of nature, and with nothing else." Technology, on the other hand, is interested in more practical questions of day-to-day existence. Thus, we have the widely accepted view that technology is applied science. It is involved in making use of the knowledge provided by science to produce sustenance, shelter, protection, and so on. Where "the goal of science is to gain more knowledge . . . that of technology is greater effectiveness." (Smolinowski 1966, 376) Science and technology are related to each other in a cause and effect manner. Though technological advances do enable scientists to better perform their work, scientific principles per se do not have a technological base in the same sense that technology derives from scientific principles.

At the bottom of the hierarchy, far removed from both research and development is learning-by-doing. The common setting for learning-by-doing is the firm and its efforts to utilize a new technoloy in the production of a good or service. For this scenario, the view of the economist and the industrial engineer coincide: Productivity growth is a function of cumulative output. Up to some point, the more output that is produced, the more proficient the labor force becomes in using the new technology.

Within this hierarchy of instrumental activities, the university and semi-independent laboratory are often pictured as the domain of basic research, especially in the United States. Development, or technology change, on the other hand, takes place within engineering departments of universities and within the business firms themselves. Within the business firm, development work, which often goes to a specialized department or function, may refer to new product or to new production process. Sometimes new product and new production process go hand in hand; sometimes they proceed separately. New products can derive from old processes or new processes can make established products. The important fact for analysis within the MP/SM paradigm is that technological change is exogenous to production processes.

Once the new product, with or without a new production process, is transferred to the production facilities, the instrumental change that occurs is called learning. Learning is not considered to be technology change. It is a separate and derivative phenomenon that constitutes a response to a new technology that is brought into a firm's manufacturing division from outside. Whether the R&D took place within a separate functional unit of the firm or in a university or special laboratory, the perspective is the same; the manufacturing unit is learning to use a technology developed elsewhere. Within the context of scientific management, top management must make the plans to assimilate the technology and communicate them downward through the organization. As the plans move downward, they change in degree of specificity, reaching the scope of time and motion studies at the lowest organizational level. All members of the manufacturing work force thereby learn to do their part. Learning-by-doing is summed up by the phrase "practice makes perfect." (Tirole 1988, 72)

This process of technology assimilation is complicated by the likelihood that the initial attempts will be imperfect. Feedback about problems and "glitches" from the lower echelons serve as the basis for changes in operating instructions and job descriptions. In this iterative fashion, the organization as a whole learns to assimilate the new technology (organizational learning) and the members of the organization, from top to bottom, learn how to perform their respective assignments (learning-by-doing).

Note that whether we are talking about rote learning-by-doing or the more complex organizational learning, the curve that describes the process is asymptotic. That, of course, is implicit in the conception of learning as "getting it perfect." Because the technology comes from outside of the organizations that utilize it, each manufacturing organization has to adapt it to fit its own idiosyncrasies. Implicit in this form of learning is the idea that each firm has an ideal organizational fit for the new technology, both in terms of organizational design and the individual abilities of employees. Once that fit has been found, the firm has "run up the learning curve" and has no more room for productivity growth until it puts another new technology in place. As we shall see, however, the continuous improvement paradigm suggests the inability to differentiate between technological change and learning. In the CIF, they are often one and the same.[8]

The MP/SM Firm as an Ideal Type

The ideal type of MP/SM firm described in economics textbooks produces and markets directly to consumers. Technological change being exogenous, analysts assume both the product and the process that produces it to be given. Within the model, the only leeway for improving productivity is through learning, which has strict upper limits. The sheer size of the firm provides it with economies of scale that generate its major competitive weapon, relatively low costs of production. The system of decision making is strictly top-down in nature, and the organizational form and incentive systems chosen are the ones that minimize information and other transactions costs. The information to be purchased concerns the "givens," such as technology, resource availability, and even organizational form. Although these factors affect the firm's ability to compete, they largely remain in analytical black boxes, unopened by economists. Economics assumes that through the process of weighing the associated benefits and costs, firms will choose the technologies and organizational forms that will provide the greatest return on investment. If not, the firm fails and exits the market. The implication is that if the organizational form of the CIF is superior, it will prevail in the market and that if the mass production firms do not convert, they will lose out in the marketplace and disappear. What actually transpires on the floor of the factory may be of interest to the production engineer and what happens in the offices of the firm's managers may be of interest to management scientists, but neither is of interest to economists.

Given that the product, the technology, and the internal organization of the firm are exogenous to the analysis, the remaining decision variables are quantity to be marketed and price at which to sell, which are determined by profit maximization rules.[9]

Competitive Weaknesses Inherent in the MP/SM Paradigm

With the evolution of a new production paradigm (the continuous improvement firm), characteristics which had previously been considered the strengths of the MP/SM firm now can be shown to be competitive weaknesses. First off, economies of scale require large production runs of a relatively homogenous product mix. The additional need to provide some product variety immediately multiplies the minimum required size of organization. If we look to the history of the first real-world MP/SM firm, we see how these two factors support each other in compounding the requirements for scale. For a number years Henry Ford operated large facilities for producing one standardized automobile, so standardized that it came in only one color, black. Eventually, customers' desire for variety presented General Motors with an opening, which it exploited to emerge as the world's dominant producer of automobiles. General Motors produced a variety of automobiles and produced each variety in large enough volume to allow full economies of scale. The new requirement was for a multiplant firm.

An organization that sells a wide variety of products in large volume must plan its activities carefully. Such planning logically begins with forecasts of demand. In the case of automobiles, the forecast must take place at least a year or more in advance of actual production, and it must specify brands, models, styles, and so forth. The production decisions determine which plants will produce how many of which vehicles. The various plants are then re-tooled to carry out their respective production assignments. Thousands of competing parts suppliers are asked to submit bids to produce components. Contracts are let and production of components commences many months prior to official introduction of the automobile to the market. Thus, inventories of both parts and finished products begin to build up. One result is the accumulation of huge inventories of automobiles in retail dealers' show lots across the country. Those huge inventories are not a way to show the customer a wide range of choices so much as they are a requirement of the MP/SM system.

If the volume and variety of automobiles that consumers purchased matched the MP/SM firm's forecast, it would be off to the races. Of all of the aspects that are planned, however, demand forecasting is the most likely to fail. It is the Achilles heel of the MP/SM paradigm. The state of the economy and the unpredictable actions of competitors can be counted on to affect the outcome. For example, if the economy's performance is more sluggish than anticipated in the forecast, not only will sales volume not live up to the forecast, the mix of sales will probably be different. Consumers will demand fewer luxury cars, for example, and more low-priced ones. Even if the economy performs better than forecast, the mix of demand still might present problems. In either case, some plants might have to shut down or run at less than capacity and others might have to be "gear up" with overtime. All of that means higher costs per unit and increased problems related to quality. Forecasting mistakes often show up in the form of unsold inventory. Sales gimmicks, such as rebates, are market evidence of such costly mistakes.

We must note, however, that getting better forecasts is not the answer to the competitive problem of the MP/SM firm. Though a perfect forecast means that all inventories clear the market at planned prices, the problem of carrying large inventories through much of the model year still remains as a normal part of doing business. As we shall see, the CIF offers greater variety to the customer without the necessity of accumulating inventories.

An important area of competitive weakness that derives from the nature of the MP/SM firm is in the area of new product design. Because design is a specialization, there is a need for a great deal of back-and-forth iteration of the prototype, especially between design departments and manufacturing. The magnitude of competitive difference is illustrated by research showing that for a similar design project, MP/SM auto firms require up to twice as many design drawings as CIFs do. CIFs also feature short product-development cycles and the ability to add new functional features to products almost as they are developed.

As we shall see, the prototype CIF operates with very little inventory cost, producing a large variety of models, styles, sizes, and so on. It bases production on actual demand and not on forecasts. Lead times are as short as one week, and they are getting shorter. On top of all that, the production processes have improved to the point of near zero defects. The systems have become so flexible that there are production runs in some auto plants, for example, in which no vehicle is similar to any of those immediately preceding or succeeding it in the production line.

All of that flexibility is achieved without sacrificing economies of scale. Furthermore, many of the improvements that enhance product quality and impart flexibility are achieved without investment cost. We cannot understand this new type of firm if our thinking remains mired in the constructs of the old MP/SM paradigm. We must, therefore, try to understand the internal logic of the continuous improvement paradigm.

NOTES

1. More specifically, as agents of stockholders, management will adopt those organizational forms and process technologies that maximize the present value of the business, given full information and relevant market prices.

2. According to Hounshell (1984, 16), the use of the term "American system" to apply to the use of specialty machines to make interchangeable parts dates to the 1850s.

3. Differences across work stations in operating speed and capacity may necesitate accumulation of some in-process inventories. Inventories are also held to cover situations in which a work station may be down or performing flawed operations.

4. Note that this flowline organization of work does not eliminate the need for inventories of raw materials (wood), intermediate products (paint) and components (metal points).

5. Sometimes these two functions are combined, but just as often they are separated.

6. The impact of this deprecation of manufacturing was reflected in the widely circulated cartoon depicting the revolt of MBA students during a lecture titled Production. "I'm not interested in making things," one student said, "I'm interested in making money."

7. We acknowledge that all of the information generated is not costless. Nevertheless, the distinguishing feature of the CIF is the ability to generate improvements as a normal pert of day-to-day operations. For development of this argument see chapters 5 and 6.

8. The authors are greatly indebted to Stella Schramm for her insights into the learning process.

9. In most models, the price is derivative, having been determined by selection of quantity to be sold. That quantity, in turn, is determined by equating marginal cost and marginal revenue.

CHAPTER 3

ON THE NATURE OF THE CIF:
TQM in Action

Nippondenso of North America is a Japanese transplant that produces alternators, starters, and other auto components. A tour of their production facilities reveals that manufacturing operations are almost totally automated. Robots perform most operations with the labor force seemingly acting as monitors. More than one observer has been prompted to conclude that the plant's blue-collar labor force has been relegated to a caretaker role by the advent of high technology. Indeed, a US academic was heard to say: "the Japanese have 'foolproofed' this production line" with a tone that implied that the management had little respect for local labor. This reaction is certainly understandable for anyone who refracts that situation through the prism of the mass production/scientific management paradigm. Within that view technological change comes from outside the production facility and is installed within a top-down system of management. To assume that blue-collar workers have rote assignments without significant responsibility is as natural as assuming the CEO has a relatively large and plush office. At Nippondenso, however, neither of these assumptions is appropriate.

If the observer touring the Nippondenso facilities is able to view the world through the lens of continuous improvement, a radically different perspective emerges. For one thing, robots are being built in house which suggests that at least some aspects of technological change are internal. The key observation is the fact that the new machines are designed in response to suggestions for improvements that are intended to enhance quality and/ or reduce cost and/or improve output flexibility. Also worthy of special note is the fact many of the suggestions are coming from the very workers who are monitoring the production line. Furthermore, the CEO, who is at least nominally responsible for the observed processes, is sitting at his desk in the same open office space as the several vice presidents, the design engineers, accountants, and the entire clerical staff, including mail clerks.

The analytical tools of the mass production/scientific management paradigm are of limited service when one tries to understand the apparently strange things at a Nippondenso or a Toyota. Indeed, it is those tools that lead us to misinterpretations.

The Continuous Improvement Process

The continuous improvement firm (CIF) is particularly adept at incremental change. This is not to say that it does not engage in radical change, but rather that incremental change is its hallmark. Within the CIF, "gradual, constant, and incremental improvement" emerges as a normal part of day-to-day operations (Imai 1990, 45). Incremental improvements are small changes in the day-to-day process of work, improvements that, for the most part, would not likely emerge in the setting of a research laboratory. Such improvements, taken individually, often have a minuscule impact on the production process or product and would often go unnoticed by an outsider. Over time, however, the incremental improvements may alter the system to such an extent that the operation as presently viewed would resemble a manufacturing breakthrough compared with a snapshot of that same operation several years earlier.

Matsumoto provides some examples of continuous improvement as an evolutionary process. The "single-step system" in which the changeover time for the die on a press was reduced from several hours to only a few minutes was achieved with "no particular epoch-making technological innovation. It [was] simply the result of the accumulation of innumerable small improvements made within the factory, . . ." (Matsumoto March 1982, 43)[1] Similarly, he recounts the development of the so-called "one touch joint" system, and the "parallel changeover system." Just-in-time manufacturing is another good example of what is now called an innovation but which resulted from the build-up over time of innumerable incremental improvements.

One of the most widely acknowledged theorists on the concept of incremental improvements is Maasaki Imai. Imai refers to such improvements as *kaizen*. "Kaizen . . . is often undramatic and subtle, and its results are seldom immediately visible. . . . Kaizen is a continuous process." (1986, 23) In discussing the characteristics of Kaizen he explains that it "does not necessarily require sophisticated technique or state-of-the-art technology. To implement Kaizen, you need only simple, conventional techniques. . . . Often, common sense is all that is needed. . . . Kaizen does not necessarily call for a large investment to implement it, [but] it does call for a great deal of continuous effort and commitment, [which] brings about gradual progress." (Imai 24–5)

Reflections by Taiichi Ohno, a former vice-president of Toyota Motor Corporation and the person most often associated with the development of the Toyota production system, make it clear that the new system evolved internally. He states,

> since the Toyota production system has been created from actual practices in the factories of Toyota, it has a strong feature emphasizing practical effects, and actual practice and implementation over theoretical analysis. As a result, it was our observation that even in Japan it was difficult for people of outside companies to understand our system; still less was it possible for the foreign people to understand it. (Monden 1983, i.)

Obviously, Toyota's transition from mass production to just-in-time manufacturing (JIT) was a hallmark case of technological change, but one that was brought about in unconventional ways and was peculiar to its place of origin. The foundation of this major manufacturing innovation consists of several breakthroughs in manufacturing techniques, each of which developed on the basis of a multitude of incremental improvements. The JIT innovation and its supporting breakthroughs are discussed in detail later in this chapter.

Seeking the Sources of Technological Change

The essence of the continuous improvement process proves difficult to comprehend for those who are accustomed to viewing economic phenomena through the lens of the MP/SM paradigm. A theory of technological change helps us understand the continuous improvement phenomenon and to differentiate it from the MP/SM paradigm. A satisfactory theory should produce answers to two basic questions: How does technological change occur and why does it occur more in some techno-cultural settings than in others? A good starting point for the first question is the discussion by C. E. Ayres in which he says that "it is now generally agreed that all inventions are combinations of previously existing devices." (1962, 112) Ayres's reference to "invention" is in the context of a discussion of technology, which he understands to include those categories that are variously called science, technology, and innovation. For Ayres, the term technology comprehends all activities that are instrumental in purpose, whether they are aimed at understanding or action. Furthermore, he often replaces the term "devices" with "tools," and uses it to refer to both corporeal and conceptual phenomena so that a mathematical equation, a pulley, the lever concept, or a pair of pliers are candidates to constitute a new combination of tools to effect a technological change.

In a pointedly relevant statement, Ayres says that "every [technological] innovation analysis reveals the combination of previously existing devices." (1962, 114) Given the general context of Ayres's work, the term "innovation" likely refers to a technological change of any magnitude. He gives no reason why a small change should originate in a process different from that of a larger one. Indeed, it would appear that any technological change necessarily involves the recombination of previously existing tools, broadly defined. The sociologist William Ogburn visualized the process in much the same way as Ayres did when he defined "invention as a combination of existing elements; as the existing elements increase, the number of combinations increases faster than by a fixed ratio." (Quoted in Westrum 1991, 54) Sean Gilfillan, a contemporary of Ogburn, likewise concurred in this view. He wrote, "invention is a new combination from the 'prior' art." (Quoted in Westrum, 58) Westrum, however, suggests that Gilfillan went further than either Ogburn or Ayres in his belief that "often the most important changes in technological capability are not revolutionary inventions, but rather small, incremental improvements." (58) Technological change, from that view, is an apparently serendipitous process in which man, endowed with natural curiosity, perceives new ways of combining existing elements or devices in ways that result in new scientific insights, new products, or new processes for producing the products. The changes may come in innovative leaps or small steps. In any case, the likelihood of change seems to increase with the number of tools or devices that are available.

If the potential for technological change is enhanced by the range of tools or devices at a given employee's disposal, we can see the CIF as having been designed to promote creativity. In the CIF, top executives manage transfunctionally rather than through specialized functions, middle managers are rotated across functions, and operators are crosstrained and rotated across a host of tasks and work in groups. These features enhance the prospects of any given individual conceptualizing new tool combinations. As should become clear as we continue, the CIF is intentionally structured and managed in ways that greatly increase the volume of critical information available to each employee.

We can put the crucial difference in approach to information into relief if we compare the CIF with a situation depicted in the *Wealth of Nations* where Adam Smith presents a unique and questionable theory of internal improvements. Very early in the first chapter we find division of labor and specialization linked to a theory of internal incremental change. Smith says

> Men are much more likely to discover easier and readier methods of attaining any object when the whole attention of their minds is directed towards that single object than when it is dissipated among a great variety of things. But in consequence of the division of labour, the whole of every man's attention comes naturally to be directed towards some one very simple object. It is naturally to be expected, therefore, that some one . . . in each particular branch of labour should find out easier and readier methods of performing their own particular work (Smith, 5).

If this were proposed as a theory of learning-by-doing, it would be worthy of consideration; it clearly fits with the MP/SM paradigm. Thus, we may interpret it to mean that the more narrow the specialization, the faster a given worker can move up the learning curve. Certainly, that view would fit with the definition of learning-by-doing as "practice makes perfect." The more narrow one's task, the sooner one can get it perfect; and therefore, the more narrow the specializations of all a firm's workers, the faster the organization moves up the (learning-by-doing) curve. (Recall that the learning curve derives from a given technology and is asymptotic.) However, the context leads one to suspect that Smith put this statement forward as an explanation for technological change. In that context, it clearly has shortcomings.

As it turns out, a critical flaw in the MP/SM approach is evident in Adam Smith's pin factory. It is summed up in Smith's argument that inventions are "much more likely . . . when the whole attention of their [workers'] minds is directed towards some one very simple object." The continuous improvement counterpart might be stated as follows: Workers are much more likely to improve parts of a process if they understand the process *as a whole*. The importance of this distinction is pursued with the help of figure 3.1.

Figure 3.1 presents alternative ways of organizing the work of manufacturing pins. According to Smith, there were some eighteen distinct operations involved in making a pin and he elucidated several:

> One man draws out the wire, another straightens it, a third cuts it, a fourth points it, a fifth grinds it at the top for receiving a head; to make the head requires two or three distinct operations; to put it on is a peculiar business, to whiten the pin is another; it is even a trade by itself to put them into the paper; and the important business of making a pin is, in this manner, divided into about eighteen distinct operations. . . . (3)

Figure 3.1(a) represents pin making as a craft in which all of the said operations are performed by one multiskilled worker. Alternatively, we find in figure 3.1(b) a version of Smith's pin factory in which one worker is assigned to each of the specialties. The question of interest is which of these environments is likely to produce more internal improvements in the pin-making processes?

Let us pursue this issue by taking a look at the cutting of the wire as a specialization. Two aspects are especially important:

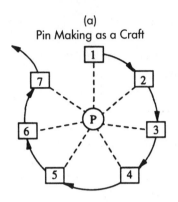

(a)
Pin Making as a Craft

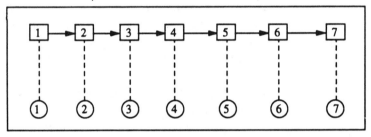

(b)
Specialization in Smith's Pin Factory

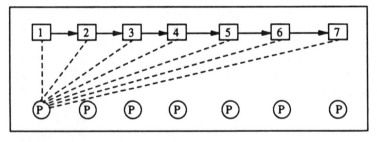

(c)
Pin Making with Job Rotation

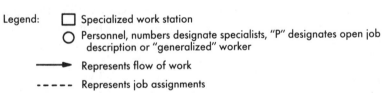

Legend: ☐ Specialized work station
         ○ Personnel, numbers designate specialists, "P" designates open job
           description or "generalized" worker
  ——▶ Represents flow of work
  - - - - - Represents job assignments

Figure 3.1. Specialization and generalization in hypothetical pin making.
(a) Pin making as a craft. (b) Specialization in Smith's pin factory. (c) Pin making
with job rotation.

the length of each cut piece and the squareness of the cut itself. If the length is too long, the piece has to be ground down enough to meet specifications. If too short, it must become scrap if quality standards are to be maintained. Because one end of the piece of wire has to be square in order to receive the head, the amount of grinding required increases the more a cut is out of square. If Smith had looked at (a) and (b) of figure 3.1 through the lens of the continuous improvement paradigm, he would have concluded that the craftsman would be more likely to discover improvements for cutting wire than would the wire-cutting specialist of the factory. Because the craftsman spends some of his time sharpening one end and fitting a head to the other, he would have understood the importance of square cuts.

Because the craftsman also inspects and boxes the finished pins, he appreciates the importance of having the correct length. By having a working knowledge of each component of the process, the craftsman has a better awareness of the important aspects of each work station. Because the craftsman performs the work at all of the stations, he has a special incentive to see that each station's work is performed as well as possible. By cutting the wire square, he facilitates his work at a succeeding station.

If the possibility of change depends upon the worker's ability to conceive of possible new tool combinations, the probability of change is severely restricted in Smith's factory. There each worker's specialization constitutes blinders that inhibit technological change.[2] Therefore, if we compare a factory made up of seven craft operations, as in figure 3.1(a), to one organized like Smith's pin factory, as in figure 3.1(b), the opportunity to perceive potential technological change should be much greater in the former than in the latter.

If we now take the basic factory situation shown in figure 3.1(b), seven job specialties and seven workers, and introduce job rotation to it, the perspective changes radically. As now shown in figure 3.1(c), the new situation has each worker enjoying the same expanded information horizon that was formerly available to the craftsman. It is obvious that compared to Smith's factory, the possibilities for new tool combinations have grown exponentially. Now we observe a situation in which the jobs are specialized, but the workers are generalized. The operation enjoys the economies of scale that derive from the factory system's use of specialized machines and full utilization of capital but, at the same time, reintroduces the advantages of the generalist's perspective. Furthermore, because there is a serendipitous side to the perception of new potential tool combinations, an increase in teams performing the same set of functions should increase the rate of improvement. For example, with the seven production lines shown in figure 3.1(c), the rate of improvement should increase sevenfold, ceteris paribus.[3]

The CIF is structured and managed to expand the possibilities for change. In order to facilitate the emergence of technological changes, management of the CIF makes conscious efforts to get as much information as possible to as many persons as possible. Consider the KAO Corporation whose president said that "the newcomer who joined [the firm] yesterday and the president share equal access to the same information pool, which allows both of them to develop the same kind of creativity." (Maruta, 1990) Likewise, consider the implication for information dissemination of replacing metal machinery covers with transparent plastic, as some plants have done, or the removal of interior office walls, or the replacement of opaque walls with glass. Furthermore, throughout the CIF hierarchy, job descriptions are much broader in conception and much less detailed than those of the MP/SM firm, and all employees are given greater access to information. Those approaches certainly comport with the Ayres/Ogburn/Gilfallan view of the sources of technological change.

If the process of technological change begins with individual perception, and it must, it follows that the more tools, that is, the more data, machines, materials, and operations, accessible to every employee, the more likely that potential technological innovations will be perceived. It is precisely in this arena of information provision that the CIF is said to excel. Furthermore, we may conclude that in the MP/SM firm, with its narrow specialization of labor, the workers at the lower organizational levels are actually obstructed from perceiving potential technological changes. As work becomes increasingly narrower in scope and more routine in nature, ennui rather than creativity might be the more likely result. We are, therefore, left with a broad contradiction between the Ayres/Ogburn/Gilfallan approach and Smith's approach to technological change within the firm.

It is also noteworthy that information exogenous to the firm plays an important role in the improvement process. In accord with the principle of recombination expounded earlier, "tools" can come from anywhere. Each employee brings to the workplace a unique set of ideas that influences his/her perception of potential technological change. While the core information tends to focus all the workers on similar problems and opportunities, the volume and variety of outside information brought to the workplace should influence the rate and nature of technological change.

The amount and variety of information available to the workers are not the only factors affecting the perception of potential technological changes. The number of employees performing a given set of operations is also positively related to it. In short, the perception of technological change in the CIF is subject to a form of economies of scale that is not available to the MP/SM firm. Because the conception of an improvement possibility is tied to individuals, there is necessarily a serendipitous element to technological change. But, ceteris paribus, the rate at which improvement opportunities are perceived for a given production process, is a function of the number of persons engaged in it and the amount of information available to them. Say, for example, a production process calls for a work station with six machines and three workers. If, as a result of the firm's growth, the production process is duplicated 19 times, there will be 19 times as many persons as initially capable of imagining new combinations of existing tools in the Ayres sense. Obviously, the rate of change should increase with the number of work stations, not only because of the increase in personnel but also because of the increased synergism among both workers and supervisors. Consequently, there are strong reasons to believe that the rate of perceived improvements is some function of the scale of operations.

Before leaving this topic, we should note that maintaining standardization of production processes is a foundation of the continuous improvement system in that it ensures that all workers begin with the same set of existing tools. As a matter of policy, the CIF must ensure across all work stations that employees performing the same tasks are always apprised of any improvement inaugurated at any one station. This standardization means that there is always a common information core consisting of the product itself and the process employed to accomplish the work station's part of the production.[4] Failure to standardize across all work stations performing the same task not only creates the potential for variations in output but also severely reduces the potential rate of technological changes.

The Urge to Improve

The material presented in the preceding section represents a first step in the development of a theory of technological change. It provides a working definition that relates technological change to information. If we could then assume that all valid perceptions of possible change would be implemented, we could stop here. Obviously, however, we have further to go. The next step toward a more complete understanding is to inquire about the reasons why this allegedly serendipitous activity occurs more in some socio-cultural environments than in others. Ayres's response is that some sociocultural or institutional settings are less resistant to change than others.[5] For him, the potential for technological change, in the form of a serendipitous perception, has an instrumental dynamic of its own, the realization of which depends on the tenacity of resistance to its implementation. Thus, differentials in institutional resistance are said to explain differentials in technological change. Bernhard J. Stern, another contemporary of Ogburn, likewise argued that "technological changes were often suppressed by economic interests set against their introduction." (quoted in Westrum 1991, 59) Westrum does not get us much further by arguing that "[a] number of features of society serve to channel and limit invention." (54)

All three theorists' emphasis is on the role of sociocultural or institutional factors in inhibiting the implementation of technological change. We can paraphrase their argument as follows: Because humans are naturally curious, they perceive change possibilities everywhere around them. Furthermore, technological change is instrumental; e.g., there are no doubts about what constitutes a better radio or a better way to produce a radio. Without the interference of sociopolitical factors, a perceived opportunity for instrumental advance would be promptly implemented. The most effective sociopolitical matrix, therefore, is that which offers the least resistance to progress, so defined.

It is at this point that we wish to diverge from Ayres and company and enter upon a different path. Evidence suggests that it is not simply sociopolitical factors that permit CIF workers to make technological changes; rather, the design of the CIF puts its employees in a better position to conceive of change possibilities and then propels implementation through expectations and incentives. The Matsushita employees' chant of the corporate values each morning is not the stuff of the Trobriand Island "bull-roarer" whose job is merely to lend ceremonial trappings to the otherwise technological activity of canoe building. It is not an exaggeration to say that at Matsushita "bull-roaring" *is* technology, in the sense that it helps focus employees on aspects of customer value and promotes an interest in making improvements.[6] Prudence and experience move us toward the view that the process of perceiving potential technological changes, though possibly serendipitous, is not random. We have to face the likelihood that some sociocultural settings expand the number of potential new combinations of tools or devices and give individuals incentives to perceive potential technological change while actively promoting its adoption and diffusion. On the other hand, some production settings may so dull the worker's sensibilities that they not only inhibit or abort such perception but perhaps also provide disincentives to the implementation of any perceived possibilities for technological change.[7]

We have arrived at a point where we may offer a theory of technological change. Technological change always results from new combinations of familiar tools, broadly defined. The process starts with an individual's perception of a potential change.[8] A particular perception might die, however, for any of the following reasons: (a) The perceiver lacks interest in pursuing the possible change; (b) further thought turns up logical flaws in the idea; (c) perceived benefits of the potential change are outweighed by expected costs; or (d) the immediate and/or more general sociopolitical environment discourages bringing it to fruition.

It also follows that the sociopolitical environment may enhance the rate of change. We see that, ceteris paribus, potential change perceptions increase with the amount of relevant information available and the number of people who obtain it. Furthermore, it is possible, through group psychology and specific incentives, to enhance the willingness and desire of individuals to spend time, both in and out of the work environment, looking for change possibilities. Finally, it is possible to enhance the rate of implementation of change through organizational design, management systems, and incentive systems.

While individual perceptions of potential technological changes may have a seredipitous element about them, there is nothing serendipitous about the volume, rate, or type of technological changes that occur in the CIF. These are the result of conscious efforts to build organizations that promote their emergence and implementation.

The CIF's Organizational and Management Structure

What organizational and managerial structures of the CIF are responsible for expanding the range of information available and for promoting its use in the continuous improvement process?[9] Those factors are to be found outside as well as inside the firm. Starting with the broad perspective, the CIF in Japan has evolved primarily within the framework of the *keiretsu,* a network of firms in which a large proportion of the stock shares are held by other firms of the *keiretsu.* This pattern of cross-holding stock shares among the firms is of particular importance because it gives the CIF a set of stable shareholders who are primarily interested in the long-term success of the firm. The *keiretsu* firms, as primary stockholders, prefer reinvestment of profits for long-term growth and stability rather than maximizing the short-term return on investment. This approach is reflected in the continuous improvement firms' organizational objectives, which "emphasize growth, such as increased market share and new product ratio" (Kagono et al. 1984, 36) as well as in a strategy tending toward long-term resource accumulation and a pattern of only slowly withdrawing from disappointing markets (40–1).

One consequence of the cross-holding of stocks is that the stockholders exhibit little interest in the day-to-day management of the firm. Decision making within the firm, therefore, is relatively unencumbered by stockholders' influences, as is evidenced by the fact that close to 100 percent of all institutional shareholders submit blank proxies to general shareholders meetings (Matsumoto 1991, p. 5). Corporate management is free to pursue the goals of internal stakeholders without external interference except in the case of crisis. Without such freedom, the Japanese firms might have been unable to develop such key features as employment stability or pursue such strategies as market-share growth through customer value.

Within the firm, a key goal of top management is to establish a strategic vision to guide the lower levels of the firm in their search for improvement possibilities. The strategic vision focuses every employee on the primary philosophy of the CIF, that is, continuously providing increased customer value, and it suggests the general vector for realizing the promise of that philosophy. We offer the example of Toyota president Kiichiro Toyoda, who, upon observing a US supermarket, conceived the idea of developing an automobile firm that produced in direct response to customer orders (Best 149).[10] In the supermarket, when customers purchase products they trigger the movement of cans from inventory to the shelves, which in turn triggers orders for replacements. In the automobile industry, on the other hand, traditional MP/SM firms customarily estimate annual sales by models, styles, and so on, and plan their production on the basis of those estimates. They then ship the planned mix of vehicles to dealers, hoping that customer choices will come close to matching demand forecasts.

When Mr Toyoda initiated work on the "supermarket" strategy, the implicit long-run goal became the ability to meet each customer's desire at the right time and at competitive prices. Wittingly or unwittingly, the Toyota management set the vector of change toward an ultimate target of customized production at costs commensurate with mass production. Henceforth, employee change efforts were to be directed by that focus. For example, the flexibility required by the supermarket approach suggested that die changes would have to be made much more quickly than before and quality defects would have to be drastically reduced. The Toyota supermarket vision, therefore, included the basic philosophy of providing customer value and the strategy for accomplishing it. While the ultimate goal of custom manufacturing is yet to be fully attained, the currently realized point on that vector of change is just-in-time manufacturing.

An effective corporate vision is more likely to be conceived and implemented if top managers have *cross-functional experiences* that help them to conceptualize the firm as an organic whole. Consequently, top managers in the CIF are almost always promoted from within the firm and across departments, so that each manager's career spans most of the operating functions of the organization. Top management personnel usually have followed much the same path as their subordinates, only to be identified as top management candidates relatively late in their careers. The selection for the top management positions, from among the most successful personnel in the management pool, is the result of an evaluation process that takes place during the entire length of managers' careers and involves all of their supervisors. Managers are promoted primarily on the basis of their interpersonal skills and their contributions to the various teams to which they have been assigned. As a result, they have become generalists, in the sense that they are uniquely fitted to take a *transfunctional view* of the firm's corporate systems.[11]

The creation of knowledge and the *horizontal and vertical flow of information* are crucial to the continuous improvement process.[12] The creation of knowledge takes place continuously at all levels of the CIF as an outgrowth of the problem solving in which all employees are engaged. Given the number of sources of new knowledge within the CIF, information expands at an exponential rate, which puts a substantial burden on management to channel the information to those areas of the firm that can employ it effectively. Within a traditional hierarchy, such as the mass production firm, information flows vertically. It travels from the bottom to the top, and only at the top does it flow horizontally. If necessary, the information then resumes its vertical course downward to the level where it is needed. In the CIF, information must flow vertically and horizontally at all levels of the organization. The importance of the horizontal flow of information is related to the continuous and incremental nature of the improvement process. Because the improvements are small changes that constantly emerge as a normal part of the day-to-day work situation, information about each change must be communicated directly to workers who are upstream and downstream of the point where it emerges, in addition to being communicated vertically to the appropriate supervisory level. To rely upon only vertical communications would act as a bottleneck on the improvement process and overwhelm the organization, which could result in organizational paralysis and a loss of information.

The loss of information would result not only from the inability of the organization to process the continuous vertical flow of information and direct it to all points needing access to it, but also from the fact that much of the information that emerges from the continuous improvement process is undocumented and undocumentable (Hattori 1986, 315). The information content in the small changes is often specific to individuals and operating units. Attempts to pass it through the organization vertically would require it to be codified so that others less familiar with the process would be able to pass it along to their supervisors and/or subordinates. In the process, much of the value would be lost in translation by the time it reached the level of operation. This type of loss is avoided when information flows horizontally from one worker to another at the level of operation, and flows vertically to higher levels of the organization only to the extent necessary.

The horizontal flow of information, however, puts unique strains on the CIF to coordinate it with the resulting actions. The responsibility for cross-department coordination in the implementation of improvements developed throughout the firm falls on middle management. The CIF relies upon *consensual decision making* to resolve conflict. This is largely accomplished by means of the *ringi* system in which written proposals circulate throughout the firm to the relevant personnel for comments and suggestions. By the time the proposal reaches management with the authority to approve or reject it, a consensus generally already has emerged. The *ringi* system is supplemented by *nemawashi,* informal discussion of a potential proposal to pave the way for its later approval. These two processes make adjustments in improvement proposals in order to obtain the necessary support for implementation (Matsumoto 1991, 146). The importance of information flows to the success of the CIF is evidenced in a report on the Japanese style of management by Audrey Freedman of the Conference Board. She states, "The pervasive theme was *information sharing* among all employees." (Freedman 1982, 31; author's italics)

Another CIF attribute that promotes continuous improvement is a corollary to the previously mentioned diminished role of the stockholders – namely, the enhanced role of employees. Faced with a largely immobile labor market, a long-term employment system provides job security for many of the CIF's workers. A large percentage of the workers who join a CIF after graduating from school or an apprenticeship program usually stay with the firm until retirement, enjoying what is known as *lifetime employment.*[13] Consequently, employees' interests are closely tied to the firm's interests. Each employee has a personal stake in the firm's policies, and employee initiative in decision making is not regarded as a problem by management. Production workers not only perform the typical production tasks, but also, in conjunction with management, take responsibility for planning and organizing production, quality control, maintenance of equipment and initiating suggestions for process and product improvements.

Employees are organized in work groups, each with a team leader. Team leaders in the CIF are, more or less, the equivalent of a foreman in a MP/SM firm. Like the MP/SM foremen, team leaders occupy the bottom rung on the management ladder. Unlike the MP/SM foremen, however, team leaders work alongside production workers and act as information conduits between the production workers and higher management rather than simply acting in a supervisory capacity. The work groups are given a set of assembly steps, assigned to a part of the production line, and told to decide together how to perform the necessary operations (Womack, Jones, and Roos 1991, 56). Workers' contributions in solving problems and making improvements come through such steps as quality circles and suggestion systems. Workers form *quality circles* on their own initiative to discuss product quality and other areas of production control. As of December 1988, 280,000 quality circles were registered with the Japan Science and Technology Association (Matsumoto 1991, 70–1). Such work groups nuture the development of workers as generalists because the members share among themselves useful insights about all aspects of the production process. *Formalized suggestion systems* also generate a large number of improvements. A survey of 643 companies by the Japan Suggestion Activity Society indicates that of almost 53 million suggestions submitted in 1988, 83.5 percent were adopted, with an average economic effect of almost 6,000 yen (Matsumoto 1991, 70).

The lifetime employment system also gives the CIF incentives to invest in human capital (for both managerial and blue-collar workers). Beginning with a well-educated work force typically hired directly out of high school, technical college, or the university, the CIF seeks to leverage their knowledge of theoretical principles by providing them all with ongoing training. Hayes and Wheelwright note that Japanese firms "encourage extensive *training and resource development . . .* to emphasize problem-solving skills, especially in small groups." (Hayes and Wheelwright 1988, 389) On-the-job training is perpetual along with periodic refresher courses throughout workers' careers to update technical knowledge, thus ensuring a workforce capable of highly specialized tasks. The CIF also employs *job-rotation schemes* to instill a generalist understanding of the production process. Referring to the annual spring personnel reshuffling that takes place in Japanese companies, Matsumoto concludes, "The fact that Japanese factory workers initiate improvements and display ingenuity of their own accord must be attributed in part to the broad vision and flexible thinking which results from having been required to work in a number of different positions." (Matsumoto 1991, 132)

In an effort to continuously provide customer value, the CIF employs a range of *analytical tools,* including statistical quality control (SQC), statistical process control (SPC), Pareto analysis, cause and effect diagrams, design of experiments (DOE), and more. These analytical tools were first introduced to Japanese manufacturers through the Union of Japanese Scientists and Engineers (JUSE), which was formed in 1946.

In 1949 JUSE established the Quality Control Research Group (QCRG) with members drawn from universities, industries, and government. Its aim was to engage in research and dissemination of knowledge of quality control. The members sought a means of rationalizing Japanese industries, of exporting quality products overseas, and of raising the living standards of the Japanese people. To accomplish this, they wanted to apply quality control to industry (Ishikawa, 16).

In 1950 JUSE held a seminar for managers and engineers in which Dr W. Edwards Deming lectured on SQC. The concept then spread among Japanese firms during later visits by Dr J. M. Juran at the invitation of JUSE. Dr Juran conducted seminars for top and middle-level managers to explain how to promote quality control and the importance of top management's commitment to making quality a priority of the firm. The CIFs not only implemented SQC but went on to adopt SPC, expanding and refining both procedures. Two of the most noteworthy contributions of Japanese theorists are included in the list of analytical tools, the Taguchi design of experiments and the Ishikawa cause and effect diagram. Analytical tools such as these help identify the causes of defects at all levels of the CIF so that defects can be reduced to a minimum. The tools can also help improve products and processes that are not considered to be defective. In other words, they serve to extend the state of the art, which is tantamount to saying that they promote technological change.

CIFs cultivate long-term relationships with supplier firms which, in many cases, are members of the same *keiretsu*. Interfirm cooperation with suppliers includes the exchange of ideas, as well as material orders, money, and products, within the context of a long-term relationship. The long-term reciprocal relationship is a means to facilitate investment in highly specialized activities and components and to spur the development of improvements. The CIF works with tiers of supplier firms.

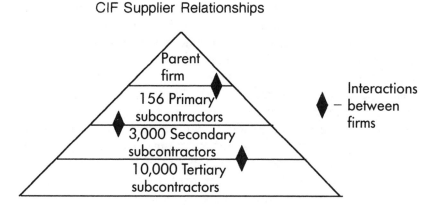

CIF Supplier Relationships

Figure 3.2. CIF supplier relationships.

Figure 3.2 illustrates the supplier-firm relationships of a Japanese automotive manufacturer, represented here as the "parent firm," which produces approximately 31 percent of its automotive components in house. The remaining 69 percent of the component parts are produced by supplier firms. The parent firm works directly with 156 primary subcontractors who are responsible for manufacturing entire component systems (e.g., the brake system). The primary subcontractors work with approximately 3,000 secondary subcontractors who manufacture many of the component parts (e.g., the brake pads) of the component systems. An additional 10,000 tertiary subcontractors work with the secondary subcontractors in the manufacturing of component parts (NHK 1987).[14]

The first-tier suppliers assign staff members to work with the CIF's product development team to provide input into the development of the product. The first-tier supplier firms have full responsibility for designing and producing the component systems to comply with the agreed upon specifications in the finished product. The supplier firms' development teams collaborate with the staff members assigned to the CIF's development team and with second-tier supplier firms to develop and engineer the component systems. Second-tier supplier firms provide the parts needed for the component systems and may work in a similar manner with third-and fourth-tier supplier firms (Womack, Jones, and Roos 1991, 146–7).

The long-term relationship between CIF and supplier firms is guided by a contract that also establishes rules for determining price, quality assurance, orders and delivery, proprietary rights, and materials supply. Within this system the supplier firm must share a substantial part of its proprietary information about costs and production techniques. The CIF and the suppliers establish a target price for the component systems (derived from the target price for the product), with a negotiated agreement that price will decline by some percentage over the life of the product. Throughout the production period the continuous improvement firm and the suppliers work together analyzing the suppliers' production process looking for ways to cut costs and improve quality. Supplier-derived cost savings that exceed the agreed upon cost reduction accrue to the supplier firm rather than resulting in a further lowering of the price of the component system (Womack, Jones, and Roos 1991, 149–50).

To summarize, the organizational and managerial characteristics of the CIF actively promote the development and introduction of process and product improvements. The organizational and managerial characteristics vital to the continuous improvement process include: cross-holding of corporate stock among a network of firms (a *keiretsu*); top management personnel internally selected to provide a strategic vision for improved customer value; cross-functional experience; transfuctional view by management; horizontal and vertical information flows; life-time employment system; work teams; voluntary quality circles; suggestion systems; job-rotation; ongoing training; the use of analytical tools; and long-term relationships with suppliers. These characteristics are a total package. The emphasis is that attempts to introduce some of the characteristics in the absence of the others may result in less than satisfactory results.

The Emergence of Just-in-Time Manufacturing[15]

The nature and development of the continuous improvement process can be illustrated by a study of the Toyota production system, which the Toyota Motor Corporation during the course of more than two decades beginning in the 1950s developed into one of the more prominent accomplishments of continuous improvement. Since 1973, the system has attracted the attention of other Japanese companies and, more recently, of companies outside Japan. Its most important initial objectives were to increase productivity and reduce costs of production in order to enable Toyota to compete with Western automotive manufacturers. Over time the vision expanded to include the enhancement of all facets of customer value. Various observers have placed Toyota's emphasis on productivity, quality, or flexibility, but the widespread impression is that Toyota and other CIFs have been successful because of their attention to quality. The fact is, however, that Toyota correctly saw productivity, flexibility, and quality as interrelated. It is true that the initial focus was cost, based on a strategy of trying to move into the U.S. automobile market at the low end. The low cost, however, which had been achieved largely through MP/SM techniques, was not enough. The first cars were of such shoddy quality as to be an instant failure. Toyota management then put the firm into a problem-solving mode, with everyone working in teams and utilizing statistical process control and other techniques to eliminate the production of defects. At some point relatively early in their efforts, the lessons of Deming became apparent to Toyota management: Total quality tools can help manage systems in ways that simultaneously improve quality, productivity, and flexibility, and therefore can serve as the basis for implementing a comprehensive customer-value strategy.

Emerging improvements are for the most part incremental in nature; they build upon each other in an evolutionary fashion. When coordinated and rationalized, a group of mutually supporting improvements may be taken as a whole to constitute a higher order of improvement. For analytical purposes, we will use three categories of improvements arranged in a hierarchy: (a) incremental improvements, (b) breakthrough improvements, and (c) internal innovations. The bedrock foundation of technological change in the CIF is the incremental improvement. As its name indicates, it is small in terms of impact, but because so many of them emerge over time, they serve as the basis for most of the technological change that takes place.

The breakthrough improvement is really the culmination of a series of incremental improvements directed toward breaking bottlenecks. Often it is the result of coaxing the incremental process along a certain vector, and possibly bolstering that process with one or more relatively sizable improvements. We shall discuss several of these in detail shortly, including the single minute exchange of dies (SMED) and autonomation. Breakthroughs are so called because they are the prerequisites for moving to a desired innovation level. Sometimes they are understood as such only in hindsight, because the potential for innovation was not perceived until after the breakthrough had been made. On the other hand, sometimes a bottleneck does not exist until the top managers announce a major strategic change. In the case of SMED, the existing state of the art turned into a bottleneck by the announcement of a new strategy based on gearing production to customer orders. With autonomation, however, the bottleneck did not exist until literally thousands upon thousands of incremental improvements brought the system to the point where the attainment of zero defects was a necessary and attainable goal. We will develop both of these examples more fully in subsequent pages.

Toyota's most significant internal innovation is the just-in-time (JIT) system, also known as the Toyota production system and "lean production." The JIT system is based on the "idea of producing the necessary units in the necessary quantities at the necessary time . . ." (Monden 1983, 4) a deceptively simple reference to probably the most advanced system of production devised to date. While JIT is popularly considered a system for eliminating inventories, its benefits go far beyond that to include zero defects. The popular names applied to the system may have made the understanding of it difficult. Indeed "lean manufacturing" has become a metaphor for cutting back on the work force and reducing inventories. The confusion is compounded by the mixing of paradigms, of trying to reinterpret JIT within the context of the MP/SM paradigm. Theoretically, JIT can be made to work for all stages of mass production except one; the finished product still has to go into inventory. Of course, the inventory may be forced on to dealers, but it is inventory nonetheless.

JIT must be understood within the context of customer value as a system for producing what the customer wants when the customer wants it, at a competitively low price. It then becomes apparent why it cannot be interpreted correctly within the context of mass production in which the firm cannot eliminate all inventories, including finished product inventories (and dealer inventories), unless it can produce and ship a daily output mix that matches customer orders. Furthermore, suppliers must be able to produce components to order and make deliveries to orders that fit one-to-one with the final customers' order mix.

Because production is based on customer orders, it is referred to as a "pull system," in contrast to the "push system" of MP/SM. In the push system, management makes long-term estimates of probable sales and then "pushes" long homogenous production runs through the system to be stored in inventory until actually purchased. The underlying logic of the "pull system" is evident in figure 3.3. Imagine that today's production is based upon orders recently received from automobile dealerships, which, in turn, are based upon restocking of items that consumers have been purchasing (supermarket approach). Ideally, that which is produced today will be shipped today. Furthermore, suppliers should deliver today the precise components needed to produce the order mix. Each work station determines its daily output requirements by consulting the needs of the work station immediately downstream and informs the suppliers what they must deliver. The separate order requirements are communicated with tickets known as *kanbans*. Imagine a situation in which a particular customer order mix calls for five models of an automobile, which require four distinct engines and five different sets of body panels. Then assume that there are eight different exterior colors and twelve distinct combinations of interior and exterior colors. To make things even more complicated, some customers want automatic transmissions and others want manual. If we are going to produce what customers want and also avoid the cost of inventories, the proper component must arrive at a work station at just the right time. For example, when a four-cylinder Corolla powertrain arrives at W_3 in figure 3.3, it must be matched by the arrival of a Corolla chassis, which

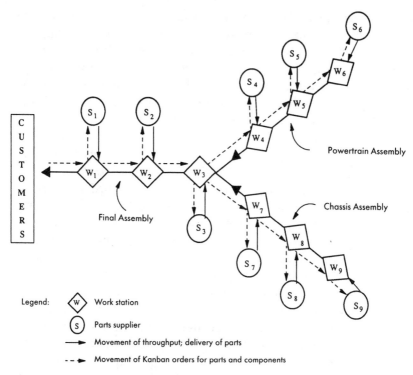

Figure 3.3. The "pull system."

means that the four-cylinder engine for a Corolla had to arrive at W_4 at the same time that Corolla body panels reached W_7. Finally, when this Corolla arrives at W_1, the proper seats in the required color must be there for installation. Ideally, the precise component needed arrives just at the moment of need.

It should be obvious now that flexibility of the production process is a key feature of the JIT system. Yet, the flexibility must not sacrifice economies of scale. It is also crucially important that input suppliers and internal work stations perform their work flawlessly. Without zero flaws, inventory requirements would have to be especially large to support a flexible production system. Ideally then, the system has three key features: zero flaws, zero inventories, and flexible production. The ability to closely approximate these ideals in practice required ten years of intensive improvement efforts by Toyota (Ohno 1988, 35). The magnitude of that effort belies the simplicity of the example presented in figure 3.3.

To better understand the complexity of the JIT system, we should look at the breakthrough improvements that serve as its foundation. JIT is coordinated by the *kanban* system, which we might properly label as a breakthrough improvement. At the time President Toyoda enunciated the supermarket vision, the extant coordinating system included demand forecasting and a top-down production schedule. A coordinating system designed to support the high volume-homogenous output approach of MP/SM constituted an obvious bottleneck to development of a system that would have to change its plans at the whim of actual customer choice.[16] The control mechanism which Toyota developed in response is referred to as the *kanban* system.

The *kanban* breakthrough is also complemented by a great many other improvements, some of which also were breakthroughs. Improvements in production smoothing, reduction of lead time, set-up time reduction, implementation of standard operations, and improved machine layout were developed prior to and/or concurrently with the *kanban* system. Without the tremendous reductions in defects at all areas of production, these breakthrough improvements as a whole would not have been feasible.

The *kanban* system of control looks at the entire production process in reverse and from the perspective of customer value. It starts with the order from the customer and extends sequentially back through the final assembly, intermediate assembly, and component production, including external input suppliers. This method proceeds through the use of a *kanban,* usually a card in a vinyl envelope. There are withdrawal *kanban,* production-ordering *kanban,* and supplier *kanban.* The cards circulate within the Toyota factories, between Toyota and its supplier companies, and within the factories of the supplier companies. The *kanban* system is essentially an information system to control the production quantities at every stage, both inside and outside the factory. The system itself has evolved on the basis of incremental improvements that include computerization of certain tasks, such as communications with key component suppliers. In essence the customer order is the first *kanban,* and it is repeated as it moves backward through the production process. Starting with the last work station, the use of parts by each successive station keys the production of the work station immediate upstream. "[T]he people of a certain process go to the preceding process to withdraw the necessary units in the necessary quantities at the necessary time. Then what the preceding process has to do is produce only enough quantities of units to replace those that have been withdrawn." (Monden 1983, 4)

Production smoothing made it possible for a line to manufacture many varieties of a product each day in response to the changing demand of customers. Production smoothing evolved to cover two levels, adaptation to monthly demand changes during a year, and adaptation to daily demand changes within a month. The workload on a machine was normally set at 90 percent of capacity when operated by a multifunction worker who would handle up to ten machines. When demand increased, production could be increased by 37.5 percent with overtime, and when necessary, by as much as 100 percent with the addition of temporary workers. When demand was slack, production would be decreased but the regular employees would be retained to perform maintenance and repairs on machines, devise improved tools and instruments, practice set-up activities, and meet in quality circles.[17]

In order to smooth production among the many models of automobiles, Toyota also had to solve the time-consuming problem of setting up for the different types of product. Switching from one model to another requires the changing of dies in the pressing process. The production line must stop while the die is changed. If the production line is to be smoothed by interspersing the production of the various models, changing dies used in the punch press must be done frequently. That was clearly uneconomical when the set-up time was 2 to 3 hours, as in the 1950s at Toyota. At that point, the time required to change dies emerged as a major bottleneck. By the 1970s Toyota had reduced it to only 3 minutes. Known as single minute exchange of dies, SMED, the system today accomplishes most die changes in a matter of seconds through a long series of incremental improvements based on the idea of separating internal and external set-up actions.[18] Matsumoto says of the development of the SMED breakthrough, "It [was] simply the result of the accumulation of innumerable small improvements made within the factory . . ." (1982b, 43)

Standardization of operations was another important improvement that was a prerequisite for production smoothing. A standard operations sheet, tacked up in the factory for all workers to see, specifies the cycle time, standard operations routine, and the standard quantity of work in progress. The cycle time is the specified number of minutes and seconds in which each line must produce a part or product. The supervisor of each process determines the number of workers necessary to produce each unit in the specified cycle time and repositions workers throughout the factory as needed. Each worker follows a procedure so that one unit is completed in the time necessary and only one unit is produced at a time.[19]

Another breakthrough improvement that preceded, and made possible, the just-in-time system is what Toyota refers to as autonomation. "Autonomation means to build in a mechanism a means to prevent mass-production of defective work in machines or production lines." (Monden 1983, 10) Sometimes called pokayoke, autonomation includes machines that have automated inspection units that shut down the machine if a defective part is introduced to it or is produced by it.[20] The machines also shut down if a worker fails to carry out the prescribed sequence of procedures. When one machine shuts down for whatever reason, all machines shut down. In addition, on the assembly lines where manual labor occurs, workers are required to stop the entire line whenever something abnormal happens. In either case stoppages elicit an immediate response by a work team to determine the cause of the problem, to fix it, and to prevent it from being repeated. Autonomation cannot be introduced into a system for which suppliers are not also producing zero or close to zero defects. Otherwise, the autonomation machines would have the entire system shut down most of the time.

Shingo (1988, 30–1) makes it clear that not until employee generated incremental improvements had almost eliminated product defects did Toyota engineers see either the opportunity or the necessity to develop machines that refuse the production of defects. The use of the various analytical tools for continuous improvement of the production process, had reduced defects significantly. However, once managers realized that it was going to be impossible to reduce defects below 3 or 4 per million hand operations, it became obvious that a breakthrough was required (Shingo 1988, pp. 30–1). Only by designing machines to block the system from accepting flawed components could that system be guaranteed to produce defect free output.

We should note that each of the breakthrough improvements discussed was the result of many smaller incremental improvements that have gone undocumented. In toto they represent the major innovation known as the Toyota production system. These incremental improvements have been continuous; today's Toyota production system is in many ways different from that of just a few years ago, and the system will change even further in the coming years. The incremental improvements that furnish the bedrock for technological change owe much to the quality circles that meet regularly to work on topics of their choice, related to solving problems or improving production processes or products. They transmit suggestions to sectional, departmental, and plant committees which, if adopted, result in commendations and rewards for the team. The importance of the quality circles to the incremental improvement process is reflected in the large number of suggestions made at Toyota and their high rate of adoption. In 1976 not quite 500,000 suggestions were made with an adoption rate of 84 percent and in 1980 more than 850,000 were made with a 94 percent rate of acceptance (Monden 1983, 130).

The breakthrough improvements that remove major bottlenecks usually require major participation by management and technical personnel. Bottlenecks materialize in otherwise perfect production systems after a change in the grand strategy. Before enunciation of the supermarket strategy, the ability to change dies in three hours represented the state of the art. If dies could be changed at night, between shifts, that kind of time did not affect the ability to operate on a mass-production basis. However, if the production mix were going to vary greatly during any given shift, three hours for a die change became an impossible bottleneck. Similarly, four defects in a million operations was once state of the art for mass production, but eventually proved to be a bottleneck for production on the basis of customer orders. When top management proclaimed a vision that forced lower-level managers to seek out the bottlenecks that prevented its realization, those lower managers then articulated the nature of the bottlenecks to the floor level so that the major thrust of the incremental improvement efforts could be directed toward them. Thus, the firm worked as an organic whole to reach a new level of Schumpeterian competitiveness by creating a major internal innovation.

The fact that JIT resulted from a process of change internal to the firm does not deny the investments in research and development of new products that were made or the capital goods that were purchased to replace worn out and outdated machinery and to build new factories. However, the basis of the new production system was developed on the factory floor as a result of a multitude of incremental improvements, many of which required little or no financial outlay. Furthermore, when investment was required to facilitate some step in the development of the JIT system, it was not the practice to base the decision on narrow benefit-cost studies. In the case of improvements related to each and every bottleneck, the firm's ability to move up to a higher and unprecedented plane of competitive competence was at stake. It would have been unthinkable to allow short-term cost-benefit considerations to preclude the realization of long-term strategic advantage.

Conclusion

The concept of total quality for the continuous improvement firm takes its meaning from the unifying goal of customer value. Quality applies broadly to all components of customer value, including functional features, performance, reliability, prompt delivery, and price, as well as aesthetic issues. Total quality management, therefore, refers to the efforts of managers to design systems and direct employees to pursue the enhancement of customer value in all its various forms. When successful, TQM results in constantly improved technology that yields new products, new features, enhanced performance, greater reliability, reduced costs, and prompt delivery. Furthermore, TQM promotes a flexibility in the production process that permits the CIF to develop a varied mix of products that more and more corresponds to the range of customer taste. In the next step in our study, we will explore the role of human capital investment in the implementation of TQM.

NOTES

1. The "single-step system" referred to by Matsumoto is more generally known as the "single-minute exchange of dies," or SMED. The latter terminology will be used later in the book.

2. The foreman or supervisor, it might be argued, would be the person with a view of the entire process and might be thought to add the element of generalization found in the craftsman. Nevertheless, in our comparative case, we have gone from a situation in which each worker (craftsman) has a firm appreciation of the entire process to one in which only one worker in eight has that capacity.

3. As we shall see later, this is the very reason why activities are standardized rigidly across teams: The process has to be standardized in order to improve it.

4. In Chapter 9, we take up the issue of whether the CIF should allow subsidiaries to develop based upon their own internally generated improvements without coordinating and standardizing with the home operations.

5. Ayres uses the terms "institutions" and "ceremonial patterns" to refer to the sociocultural factors. See chapters VIII and IX of *The Theory of Economic Progress* (1962).

6. Ayres (1962, 108–9) uses the example of a primitive canoe-building society in which workers carry out the technological activity of hollowing logs to make canoes while someone "rattles shark's teeth and roars what are obviously incantations." The general discussion that follows makes it clear that ceremonial aspects of such institutions as the "holy order" of canoe builders may be expected to resist progress if, for example, some members of the builders group attempted to introduce a technological innovation that changed the way canoes were built.

7. The view propounded here is distinct in its emphasis, but consistent with some recent theorists' views on innovation. For example, Bikjer and Pinch (1987) argue that the path of development of a technology is determined by a network of interested parties. Our emphasis here is not primarily on the nature of technological change as much as the rate of technological change in different types of firms.

8. Perceptions originate with the individual, even if the individual is part of a team.

9. We emphasize that the "continuous improvement firm" is a Weberian "ideal type" whose characteristics may not be fully reflected in any single firm (possibly the closest fit would be Toyota Motor Company). Certainly, not all firms in the Pacific Rim countries and Japan are of the continuous improvement type. Many firms in these countries deviate considerably from the continuous improvement mode. Significantly, however, many of the firms that are identified as "world class" performers in the automobile and electronics industries have adopted continuous improvement as their dominant strategy.

10. Taiichi Ohno (1988, 26) says that the US supermarket served as the inspiration for development of the *kanban* system of Toyota. The *kanban* is discussed in some detail shortly.

11. The difference between transfunctional management and a cross-functional management team is analogous to the difference between an interdisciplinary academic approach to a set of problems and a multidisciplinary approach. The interdisciplinary view has to come from individuals who each have training or insight into several disciplines. The multidisciplinary approach typically puts together several persons who individually are experts in only one discipline.

12. With respect to the CIF, Best argues that "a distinction be made between information, a core concept for the conventional theory of the firm, and knowledge and its refinement. Creating production knowledge by problem solving involves more than the flow of information: information is already existing knowledge; problem solving is the creation of knowledge" (1990, 13).

13. At the time of this writing, the Japanese economy has been in a prolonged recession, which has prompted some observers to predict the demise of the permanent employment system. We note, however, that as yet very few employees have been dismissed in Japan, a fact that stands in stark contrast to the massive downsizing in the US economy.

14. In comparison, a US automotive manufacturer (an MP/SM firm) as parent firm produces approximately 50 percent of the components in house and works directly with approximately 1,300 primary subcontractors and with as many as 25,000 secondary and tertiary subcontractors (NHK, 1987).

15. This section is largely based on *Toyota Production System* by Yasuhiro Monden (1983).

16. In some cases, and especially in the case of Toyota in the US, the dealer is in fact the customer. Dealer orders are placed on the basis of immediate experience and do not constitute a long-range forecast. In Japan, some orders are taken by door-to-door salesmen while other orders are placed with dealers. In either case, the order is custom produced. For example, the customer may place an order this week for delivery the next week. If convenient, the customer may actually see the vehicle come off the line with the colors and features that match the original order.

17. A bottleneck to production smoothing was the standard but long lengths of production lead time. As a first step in reducing the production lead time, Toyota refined the moving-assembly concept on the conveyor system. The conveyor system, in its standard form, is operated to equalize the operation time and conveyance time of each process. The assembly line is therefore divided to allow the conveyance time between each workplace to begin and end at the same time. This system was developed so that a finished automobile could be produced during each cycle time and that each unit of output of every process on the line could be sent to the next process

simultaneously. Toyota refers to this system as the single-unit production and conveyance and it has extended the single-unit flow to almost all processes including machining, welding, and pressing, in addition to the production of intermediate parts. In this manner, Toyota realized a firm-wide integrated single-unit flow of production that reduced the lead time for the production of all parts and final assembly.

18. By working with the punch press operators to clearly separate the two phases, and incorporating as much of the set-up into the external phase, much of the set-up now takes place while the punch press is in operation. The machine is inoperable only during the time it takes to make the minimal internal set-up changes. To accomplish this end, innumerable incremental improvements were made, like replacing round washers with u-shaped or oval washers for one-motion removal of the die, using spacers to standardize the height of all dies, installing limit switches on the punch press machines quickly to adjust the knockout stroke for different dies, and using a revolving table car to easily and quickly replace one die with another.

19. The standard quantity of work in progress is the minimum quantity of work in progress within a production line. This ensures that the predetermined sequence of machine operations can be run without inventories building up among the successive processes. Furthermore, to achieve the goal of single-unit production, Toyota devised a new machine layout that would allow for multiprocess holding, that is, for each worker to handle several types of machines at the same time. In multi-process holding a worker picks up a unit from the preceding process and sets it on the first machine. At the same time he removes from the first machine the unit already processed and sets in on the chute to be moved to the next machine. While he walks from the first machine to the second, he pushes a switch turning on the first machine. He then performs the same functions at the second machine before moving on to the third machine. He repeats this process until he has operated all the machines in his station and then returns to the first machine.

20. These machines have their counterpart on the assembly line in the form of line stop mechanisms by which a worker can stop the entire line if a defect is being produced at any location.

CHAPTER 4

HUMAN RESOURCES AS CAPITAL INVESTMENT

The term labor strikes a decidedly different chord when sounded in the context of the CIF paradigm than when used in reference to the MP/SM paradigm. In the former, labor is the principal stakeholder; in the latter, it is, in all its forms, an agent. The MP/SM paradigm makes a clear distinction between management as direct agents of the owners and labor as operators who are directly contracted to the management. The economics version of the paradigm, especially that found in the textbooks, has traditionally taken labor as a homogenous mass made up of managers and workers. This does not imply any belief on the part of economists that labor was in fact relatively homogenous. It reflects the belief that the marked differentiation that in fact exists is not important for explaining price formation. There was the obvious, but usually unwritten, assumption that efficient contracts would be drawn that spurred and guided management and their operating agents to promote the interests of stockholders. Whether explicitly stated or merely assumed, the key feature of the MP/SM paradigm is that stockholders as owners are the principle stakeholders and workers as agents are the secondary ones. Furthermore, because operators are secondary agents, a chasm is recognized that separates planners from doers.

Recognizing the emergence of a new paradigm, Odagiri proposes that the old and venerable neoclassical view that capital hires labor should be turned on its head. He suggests that "in the modern corporation, it may be that labor hires capital, in the sense that the level of human resources determines the speed and direction of the firm's growth and the capital required is then financed accordingly." (1992, 2) Here, the "level of human resources" carries qualitative as well as quantitative connotations.

Furthermore, Odagiri uses the term *labor* in the generic sense of including all persons on the payroll, including top management and even the board of directors.[1] From his viewpoint labor is the principal, and stockholders are in a secondary position. Labor, broadly defined, initiates action, guides and propels the firm along vectors that it has chosen while shareholders do no more than facilitate those actions by helping to finance them. This perspective helps to make sense out of some characteristic actions by Japanese firms. Within this framework, it is not surprising that in recessionary periods, dividends to shareholders are sacrificed so that permanent employees may be maintained. Indeed, within the context of the CIF paradigm, it would be irrational to sacrifice the foundation incentive of permanent employment for a "one shot" payment to a secondary stakeholder. To favor the shareholder would indeed be a case of misplaced altruism that would give away the strategic advantage of the firm. This is a reasonably realistic view of the role of the stockholder in a modern industrial economy. Share purchases are viewed largely as an alternative way of making a return on money. Shareholders should have no more interest in the operation of a corporation than they do in the management of a bank where they may have savings. Because Japanese shareholders accept this secondary role, the CIFs can maintain permanent employment, which is much more important for the long-term success of the firm, a success that may redound to greater profits than otherwise would be possible.

The current period of extended recession and sluggish growth in the US economy has furnished many examples that reflect the MP/SM perspective on relative stakeholder power. Again and again, we read of firms that have cut their work force so that the cost reductions will allow an acceptable level of dividend payments. That behavior is consistent with a paradigm that envisions the owner as initiator of the firm. That view of the shareholder is a holdover from an earlier time when the entrepreneur was a principal source of capital as well as the initiator of the business. The captains of industry made the major decisions and used hirelings to carry them out. Conceptually, the MP/SM paradigm tries to bridge the gap between the days of yore and modern times through the use of agency theory, which posits that management acts as proxies for owners.

A quarter century ago Galbraith (1971) argued that shareholder influence had been severely reduced, having been bought off by the management. Earnings for many firms were such that they could pay handsome dividends while still retaining sufficient funds to finance rapid expansion. Two factors unanticipated by Galbraith intervened to abort or reverse that trend. One was the sudden emergence of corporate takeovers financed by "junk bonds." Many corporate victims, weighted down with the debt, were no longer able to finance growth from internal resources and so chose to sell off assets. Under a threat of takeover, it is in the interest of management to ensure that the stock is not undervalued in the market – ceteris paribus, the higher the dividend rate, the higher is the share value. The other emerging factor was the rise of the CIF, which was able to grab market share from the US firms and compound their earnings problems.

Even for the period when Galbraith identified an apparent separation, albeit temporary, between ownership and control of the firm, no apparent change took place in the relationship of management to so called blue collar labor. The latter were still seen as hired agents of the former. The view that management is of a different and higher order has a long history. That there are higher and lower orders is implicit in statements such as that from Smith's description of a factory worker: "The man whose life is spent performing a few simple operations . . . becomes as stupid and ignorant as is possible for a human creature to become." (1957, 340) In more modern times the same view appears in the writings of the father of "scientific management," Frederick Taylor. Speaking of a pit-iron handler, he concluded that to do such work one "shall be so stupid and so phlegmatic" as to resemble an ox so that "it is obvious that a man more intelligent than him must school him in the correct manner of working." (quoted in Goonatilake 1984, 124) Taylor is credited with instituting "a radical separation between mental and physical labour, between thinking and doing, which he ingrained into the technology of a well-run factory." (Goonatilake 124)

Looking at the CIF, we find that management reduces or downplays ostensible distinctions between managers and workers to avoid the perception of a line between those who think and those who work. The operator on the assembly line is just as integral to the firm, in just the same ways, as management: as a stakeholder in the fortunes of the corporation and as a contributor of ideas to realize its success. Given labor as principal stakeholder, the concept of permanent employment is hardly surprising. Permanent employment, and the supporting role of labor as agent of change, is an indication of how the CIF invests heavily in promoting the capacity of its human capital. The concept of human capital is also in use within the context of the MP/SM paradigm. Much of the discussion, however, is directed to investment in the general education system. With regard to human capital at the level of the firm, the understanding is that the principal-agent problem limits the incentive of both the firm and the individual to invest in expanding the workers' capabilities. From the point of view of the firm, the mobility of labor makes it possible for the benefits of investment to be lost or even captured by other firms. From the point of view of the individual, any investment in the firm's specific capability will have severely limited market value, and the possibility of job loss greatly reduces the incentive to obtain firm-specific training. The broad paradigmatic view of labor as workers not thinkers also has a negative impact on human capital investment. The broad assumption is that the role of the worker is to operate the machine, much in the same sense that electrical power does, which rules out flexibility for labor because that would add variability to the process, which in the MP/SM paradigm would limit the ability of managers to control the operations. Thus, human capital investment is usually limited to the training of workers in the use of a given technology.

From the point of view of the CIF paradigm, however, human beings are crucial to the success of the endeavor and machines merely facilitate matters. It is the harnessed efforts of all minds that bring about the improvements in quality, cost, deliverability, and design that give the firm its strategic Schumpeterian advantage in the marketplace. Investment to enhance those efforts makes eminent sense; by providing employment stability, the firm is extending the period over which it will realize a return on that investment.

We must stress that investment in human capital makes much more sense for the CIF than it does for firms who operate in the world of MP/SM. It is a mistake, therefore, to single out this feature and advocate it as a sort of "magic bullet" for reviving competitiveness in the MP/SM firm. Why should management invest in people it may be laying off at any time? Why should individuals put extra time and effort into learning firm-specific information if they do not see a future with the firm? If the firm continues to otherwise operate within the MP/SM paradigm, an expanded approach to the investment in human capital would very likely be money down the drain.

Because human resources are viewed by the CIF as the most important factor in its long run success, a substantial number of the employees that are hired upon graduation from high school, technical school, or the university remain with the firm throughout their careers as permanent employees.[2] The firm recruits prospective permanent employees largely without regard to their specific job skills, focusing instead on trying to hire those graduates who they believe demonstrate a willingness and ability to learn. It is also crucial that the hiring process search out persons who are likely to function well in the continuous improvement environment and who seem capable of loyalty to the organization.

Some Western observers believe they have detected an incipient break-up in the system of permanent employment. For one thing, they point to the formation of a small headhunters market for executive talent that developed during the boom period of the 1980s. Additionally, they point out that the recession of the early 1990s has forced a few Japanese companies to reduce the size of their labor force through layoffs and early retirement. To conclude that this is evidence of the inevitable crumbling of the permanent employment system, however, may come as a result of viewing the situation through the MP/SM lenses. Indeed, it is more likely that the extended recession with its limited job creation has dampened growth of the headhunters market and the relatively few layoffs may emphasize the importance of maintaining a permanent employment base.

Given the importance of human resources in the CIF paradigm, we would do well to examine how the society, the individual workers, and the firm go about the many tasks of enhancing those resources.

Public Schooling in Japan

Education prior to employment is a significant determinant in the long-run development of human capital. It is the foundation upon which the firms themselves invest and upon which the investment by the individual can build. The stronger the foundation, the more postemployment investment it will support. A perceptibly weak foundation, on the other hand, may properly been seen as discouraging postemployment efforts at building human capital. The CIF's view of labor as a long-term investment is complemented by the Japanese belief that training and education of the labor force is the shared responsibility of the public, the individual, and the firm. In Japan public responsibility for education and training includes the provision of primary, middle (or lower secondary), and high (or upper secondary) school instruction, in addition to higher education.[3] The public cost of formal education in Japan is relatively low; approximately 16 percent of total public expenditures go to education, which represents slightly less than 6 percent of the GNP (Dore and Sako 1989, 1). Of the total public expenditure on education, approximately 70 percent is spent on preschool through high school (New York State Education Office 1992, 24). The family's responsibility for education and training includes paying for supplementary instruction for primary through high-school students who have difficulty keeping up with their cohorts or for those who aspire to enter the most prestigious educational institutions; paying for students to attend high school (approximately 30 percent of high school students attend private schools) and university (approximately 70 percent of university students attend private institutions of higher education); and paying for any correspondence course they may take throughout life to keep up with change. It is estimated that students and their families contribute approximately one-fifth of the 6.9 percent of GNP spent on mainline education in Japan (Dore and Sako 1989, 3). The firm's responsibility for education and training includes providing workers with on-the-job training as well as off-the-job training and reimbursing workers who have completed correspondence courses related to job skills certification.

"The Japanese educational system is highly centralized, fosters uniformity of standards and achievements, and emphasizes the mastery of school curriculum by all students. . . . The Japanese education system seems to serve its national interest and works efficiently for its country in providing universal basic education to all of its children and producing a broadly literate population and work force." (New York State Education Office 1992, 29) As a result, Japan has a very high percentage of its school-age groups enrolled in educational institutions, with the vast majority below the higher education level in public educational institutions. In 1989, 100 percent of the relevant age groups were enrolled at the primary school level, 96 percent at the secondary school level, and 31 percent in higher education (World Bank 1992, table 29, 275). The strong interest in education has a long history in Japan, dating back to the Tokugawa period (1603–1867) (see, for example, Kunio 1986, 89–91). Employers typically place a great deal of significance on the quality of the school from which the recruit graduates. Top firms recruit only from the top high schools and universities (Dore and Sako 1989, 5).

Education in Japan is compulsory through the middle-school level. The school year begins in early April and is organized into trimesters that run from April to July, September to December, and January to March. The school week is five and one-half days and the Ministry of Education requires a minimum of 210 days per year. Local school boards can add more days at their discretion and usually add as many as 30 days for activities such as field trips, Sports Day, cultural festivities, and so on (US Department of Education 1987, 10).[4] The average Japanese student spends 1,584 hours per year on school work (New York State Education Office 1992, 13). Classes are large. In 1983, the average class size was 34 students in elementary schools and 36 in middle schools, and a class could have as many as 45 students before being split into two smaller classes (US Department of Education 1987, 27, 34). The schools are well equipped, although relatively little advanced technology (e.g., computers in classrooms) is available. Discipline problems are relatively uncommon in Japanese primary and middle schools. Teachers work hard to achieve a cooperative, mutually supportive environment in classes of students with mixed ability. Though the pace is geared to the average student, considerable effort is made to feed extra material to quick learners and to give extra help to the slow learners. Consequently, international comparisons in mathematics, for example, show that the best Japanese students do as well as students elsewhere, and Japanese students in the lower half of the ability range do much better. We should note here that this basic facility with mathematics is especially supportive of the widespread use of statistical quality-control techniques.

Beyond the middle-school level, enrollment is based on a merit system. At the high school level, approximately 70 percent of the students attend public institutions. Entrance into the high schools and universities is based on rigorous examinations and competition is very stiff.[5] Entrance exams are weighted heavily in the subjects of Japanese language, math, and English language. Partly in recognition of the importance of entrance exams, there has been general acceptance of a uniform curriculum at the high school level that emphasizes math, Japanese literature, English, history, and general science. Even during the first two years of college, students continue to take a wide range of courses, specializing only during the last two years. At the high school level international comparisons again indicate that the quality of schooling is high. For example, in an international ranking of twelfth-grade students in thirteen countries, Japanese students ranked first in algebra, second in geometry and calculus, and fourth in chemistry and physics (International Association for Evaluation of Educational Achievement, Changing America, *The New Face of Science and Engineering* (Washington, D.C.: Task Force on Women, the Handicapped and Minorities in Science and Technology, 1988, 9; cited in Schnitzer 1991, table 6.1, 110).

In addition to the academic courses, Japanese high schools, colleges and universities offer a wide range vocational courses–all within the jurisdiction of the Ministry of Education. Vocational courses at the high school level are generally offered by schools considered below elite schools offer academic courses exclusively as preparatory schools for the best universities. The second and third tier high schools typically offer vocational courses but with a heavy reliance on academic courses, especially mathematics. A student choosing a vocational curriculum in a second-tier high school does not automatically eliminate the possibility of going to college because he/she still will have taken all of the courses covered on the university entrance exams. Among the industry-related vocational courses offered are machinery, electricity, electronics, architecture, civil engineering, auto repair, metalwork, textiles, design, printing, welding, and information technology. Nonetheless, the vocational curriculum has a poorer image than the academic curriculum, and employers are less eager to recruit those who have taken this path. Of the 4.75 million full-time students enrolled in Japanese high schools in 1984, approximately 72 percent were in academic courses and the remaining 28 percent in vocational courses (US Department of Education 1987, table 8, 79).

During the third and final year of high school, a joint decision-making process takes place in which the schools, parents, and students determine whether each student should go on to study in a university or seek a job. Those students seeking a job can use the intensive job referral system operated by the schools, employers, and the Public Employment Security Office (a government agency).[6] Within the job referral system, schools and employers try to establish and nurture long-term relationships through ongoing "courtesy visits" to each other. The employers submit recruitment cards to the Public Employment Security Office (PESO) for PESO's approval and send the cards to the schools. The schools process the employment data, make it available to students, consult with the students and parents on employment possibilities, and refer students to prospective employers. In addition, the school acts as an intermediary between the employers and its students to support the students' efforts. According to one study of the job referral system,

> The Japanese schools' major emphasis was not on specific skill acquisition but on the provision of an extensive network with employing companies, and of large amounts of information pertaining to them. Career guidance was conducted not only in relation to what kind of work would suit a particular individual, but with more emphasis being given to choosing an appropriate company using an abundance of accumulated information. The process of transition was *gradual:* it took place over one year (Okano and Claridge 1992, 52, authors' italics).

The author of this study viewed the job referral system as both maternalistic and paternalistic – paternalistic in the sense that the system could be viewed as depriving the students of their independence and autonomy and controlling their decisions, and maternalistic in the sense that it could be viewed as caring and protective of the students. Okano believes the former view is likely to be held by outsiders (Westerners in particular), and the latter view by insiders (Okano and Claridge 1992, 57).

Given the accomplishments of the Japanese system, it is interesting to note that investment in education in the United States is slightly higher than that in Japan. In 1988, the United States spent approximately $335 billion on education – $185 billion on K – 12 schooling, $125 billion on higher education, and $25 billion on continuing education (Bowsher 1989, 7) – representing approximately 6.6 percent of GNP, and excluding continuing education, 6.1 percent. These figures compare favorably with the rate of expenditure in Japan. However, the United States spends a lower percentage of its GNP on K – 12 education than Japan and a correspondingly larger percentage on higher education. In a study of 16 countries, the United States ranked second in percentage of GNP spent on education, but twelfth in percentage of GNP spent on K – 12 education. In the same ranking, Japan was sixth in percentage of GNP spent on K – 12 education (New York State Education Office 1992, 24).

The school year in the United States begins in September and ends in May, with a lengthy Christmas holiday and three-month vacation during the summer. The school week is five days and the average length of the school year is 180 days. Thus, by the time of high school graduation, American students have been in school the equivalent of one year less than Japanese students. Moreover, the average American student spends just 720 hours per year on school work compared with over 1,500 hours for the typical Japanese student. Decisions on curriculum in American schools are made at the local or school level, and, as a result, vary according to academic progress and ability. In general, the philosophy of American schools is that curriculum should be based on the needs of the individual students as perceived by educators, which has resulted in a plethora of courses being offered. One researcher estimated that the typical American high school offers about 200 courses over two semesters compared to only 25 to 30 courses in the typical Japanese high school (Cummings 1986, 70). As a result, American students spend less time in school studying mathematics (17 percent versus 23 percent in Japan) and on mathematics homework (79 minutes per week for American six-year olds versus 233 minutes for their Japanese peers, and 256 minutes for American 10-year olds versus 368 minutes for their Japanese peers) (New York State Education Office 1992, 13). On the other hand, American schools spend a greater proportion of class time teaching the national language and social sciences.

A number of studies indicate, however, that the United States does not get as high a return on its investment in education as Japan does.[7] Despite the greater emphasis on teaching English, approximately 20 percent of the US population is functionally illiterate, and despite the attempt to individualize the curriculum, 30 percent of American students drop out of high school before they graduate. The lower quality of US education in math and the sciences is shown by the twelfth-grade students' relatively low ranking in international comparisons among 13 countries. The United States ranked among the bottom three countries in geometry, biology, algebra, calculus, and chemistry; only in physics did the United States rank in the top ten (at number 9) (International Association for Evaluation of Educational Achievement, Changing America, *The New Face of Science and Engineering* (Washington, D.C.: Task Force on Women, the Handicapped and Minorities in Science and Technology 1988, 9; cited in Schnitzer 1991, table 6.1, 110).

Public Higher Education in Japan

Between high school and university there are five-year technical colleges, special training schools, and two-year junior colleges. The two-year junior colleges are primarily public institutions that serve almost exclusively as finishing schools for young women (90 percent of the students are female); they place less emphasis on education and training in preparation for entering the labor force. The special training schools were first established in 1976 and offer three-year courses to middle school students, two-year, post-secondary level courses to high school graduates, and continuing education courses open to anyone. Approximately 90 percent of the special training schools are private and many of the courses are designed to help students meet occupational qualification and certification (US Department of Education 1987, 57). The technical colleges, dating from the early 1960s, recruit students out of high school and provide an intermediate level of technical training. In 1985 there were 62 technical colleges; more than 90 percent were public institutions, which enrolled approximately 48,000 students (US Department of Education 1987, 57). They offer courses in all the main branches of engineering but maintain a substantial proportion of general subjects (especially during the first two years of study). The technical colleges also arrange work experiences at local factories, although typically only for a few weeks during the summer break. The high proportion of general academic subjects taken during the first two years makes it possible for a student to transfer to a university for the third and fourth years to earn a university degree. The majority of students, however, remain at the technical colleges and after graduation go directly into industry. The quality of the technical college curriculum has achieved some recognition within industry, such that "a number of the larger companies have made a special career provision for College of Technology graduates, creating a salary scale which puts them a cut above junior college graduates who have nominally the same number of years of full-time education." (Dore and Sako 1989, 46–7) Graduates of the colleges of technology are employed increasingly by firms in research, development, and design and, to some extent, they even have opportunities to move up to managerial positions.

At the university level approximately 30 percent of students are enrolled in national public (established, funded, and operated by the national government) and local public (prefectural or municipal) universities. The national public universities generally have more prestige and more resources and so are able to provide a better education at a lower cost. The Ministry of Education, which has a high degree of control over university curriculum, sets the total number of hours required for a degree as well as the number of hours in each discipline (e.g., foreign language, math, science). The curriculum during the first two years concentrates on general academic studies, and the last two years are devoted to the student's chosen specialty.

Vocational curriculum (e.g., engineering) at the university level does not suffer from the inferiority complex that it has at the lower educational levels, as is reflected in the direct correlation between the ranking of a university and the proportion of its students majoring in engineering. Approximately 20 percent of university students study engineering, as compared to 7 percent in the United States, allowing Japanese universities to produce as many engineers as the United States despite the fact that they confer only 40 percent as many bachelor degrees as the United States (U.S. Department of Education 1987, 49–50). Engineering education at the university level is more theoretical than practical and leans more toward the basic sciences. Research conducted within the engineering departments of the universities also tends to be more basic rather than applied. This seems to be consistent with the desires of industry. "Japanese companies do not expect engineering graduates to possess substantial mechanical skills on graduation. . . . Since the early 1960s there has been no pressure from corporations to make Japanese engineering education more explicitly practical" (E.H. Kinmouth, quoted in Dore and Sako 1989, 54). One may interpret this emphasis to imply that the ties between the university engineering departments and industry are rather weak. While this may be true in terms of the transfer of technical information, it is not true in terms of recruiting by the central research labs of the firms. Almost all recruits to the firms' central research labs are new university graduates.

> These graduates are brought into the firm by highly routinized paths. Key professors in the major Japanese universities routinely allocate their students to the major companies. Although student desires are consulted to some extent, the professor in charge of placement will usually write only one letter of recommendation for each student, and that will be to a major company that will accept without question that recommendation. For a company to disregard the recommendation would be to forfeit the opportunity to obtain future graduates from that professor (Westney and Sakakibara 1985, 322).

It is worth noting that this permanent working relationship with university professors closely emulates the relationship of firms to input suppliers. The hallmarks of both types of relationship are permanence and trust. Because the competitive market search by both parties, which characterizes the MP/SM paradigm, is conspicuously absent here, the cost of job searches is greatly reduced for both buyer and seller.

The work load for Japanese university students is quite the opposite of that of Japanese middle and high school students. It is widely accepted that the Japanese universities are "hard to get into, [but] easy to get out of." (Dore and Sako 1989, 51) That is, overall failure rates in the university are low, and there is no accumulation of grades. Because students only have to pass the required courses and accumulate the requisite number of course credits, they have little incentive to do more than the minimum work required to pass the course. For many Japanese students the period of university study represents a break between the high pressure of high school and the corporate world. "It is frequently said that the four years of university life represent the 'moratorium period' in the Japanese middle-class male life." (51) Dore and Sako also point out, however, that this generalization does not apply to engineering students who want to go on to earn a graduate degree, nor to those "in the vocational subjects of engineering and science, [where] employers are interested in substantive learning accomplishments and less predominantly influenced by the university-rank ability-labelling effect than when recruiting arts or social studies graduates." (52)

Private Sector Education and Training in Japan

The Japanese acknowledge early in life that education and training are an individual responsibility. Though only a very small percentage of students attend private primary schools – in 1985, approximately one-half of one percent and in middle schools approximately three percent (Dore and Sako 1989, 3) – the infamous Japanese private cram schools (*juku*) have flourished for students in these age groups. These schools offer supplementary instruction to mainstream education in the basic subjects in after-school and Sunday classes. The cram schools serve as "catch-up" and "keep-up" classes for students struggling to stay up with their class and advance classes for students trying to improve their chances of securing a place in the elite high schools and universities. At the national level, *juku* attendance by primary school students rose from 16.5 percent in 1985 to 44.5 percent in 1990, and from 18.6 percent to 52.2 percent in middle school students (do Rosario 1992, 21). The cost of *juku* to a family with only one child in elementary school represented approximately 2 percent of the family income in 1985 (New York State Education Office 1992, 13).

Individual responsibility for education and training is even more extensive at the high school and university levels. Approximately 30 percent of all secondary students are enrolled in private high schools (Dore and Sako 1989, 3), which are either elite preparatory schools for students anticipating entering the top universities, or schools at the lower end of the spectrum for students unable to gain entry into any of the public high schools. To some extent these schools receive public subsidies, but the individual pays a majority of the cost of education. Nevertheless, the curriculum is subject to the requirements of the Ministry of Education and so is similar to that in the public school system. The school year is also the same as that for the elementary and middle schools, divided into trimesters of up to 240 days per year. In the first year of high school all students take the same set of courses. From the beginning of the second year of high school, students enter into either the literature or the science curriculum, which stresses considerably more mathematics.[8] Approximately 70 percent of university students enroll in private universities (Dore and Sako 1989, 3). The private universities also receive subsidies from public sector, but the tuition and fees are still considerably higher than those of the public universities.[9] They too come under the jurisdiction of the Ministry of Education with the same framework and curriculum as the public universities discussed earlier. The private universities fall into two groups, elite and lower-level institutions, but the majority are at the lower end of the spectrum.

Individual responsibility for learning extends beyond formal education and continues throughout the lifetime of many Japanese as they sign up for correspondence courses in a wide range of subjects. To some extent correspondence courses are simply a replacement for formal education (i.e., correspondence classes for high school and university subjects) but also include a large number of supplementation courses (e.g., English) for students still in school. A third category of correspondence study is in the arts, and those courses are mainly taken by housewives.

The fourth and largest educational category comprises the business and technical courses taken by employees to improve their knowledge and skill levels. To some extent these courses are reimbursed by the firm (which may, in turn, apply for a subsidy from the government), but the individual bears a substantial portion of the cost. Many individuals take correspondence courses simply to improve their knowledge, but another major incentive is to prepare for national qualifying exams or skill tests given by their employer. In a survey of the correspondence courses approved by the Ministry of Education, 45 percent of the respondents indicated they took courses for fun, cultural improvement, or for the chance to make a hobby profitable, while 17 percent responded the courses were necessary for their work, and 31 percent indicated they were for qualification. Only 7 percent took the courses in hopes of getting a job or changing jobs (Dore and Sako 1989, 100).

Qualifying exams and skill tests are ubiquitous in Japan in both the private and public sectors. Dore and Sako (1989, 119–120) have analyzed the Japanese system of qualifying exams and skill tests and concluded that

1. the central and local governments play a much greater role than occupational associations in setting and enforcing the standards
2. the definition of the public interest, which permits the public authorities to insist on state-certified competence, is rather broad
3. the national interest has justified government leadership in defining levels of competence

4. where private associations do play a role, associations of organizations that employ skilled people are more important than associations of skilled people

5. the Japanese tend to resist delegating certification responsibilities to training institutions and

6. where new training needs are identified the Japanese government tends to set standards and establish testing systems as a means of catalyzing private training efforts.

The four broad types of qualification exams administered by the central government typify the types of numbers of qualifying exams administered in Japan: (a) qualifications legally required as a condition for exercising certain professional functions (146 different exams); (b) qualifications legally required as a condition for assuming certain self-descriptions (31 exams); (c) qualifications required for appointments to government posts (23 exams); and (d) qualifications designed to certify and encourage high levels of occupational performance (563 exams) (Dore and Sako 1989, p. 121). The use of an exceptionally large number of exams to cover occupational performance is indicative of the national importance given to the education and training of the labor force. This policy, in combination with the government's preference for setting standards and establishing testing systems to catalyze private training efforts, reflects the widespread acceptance of individual responsibility for education and training in Japan.

Correspondence study is also a means by which American workers seek certification in a wide range of subjects and skills. The courses are offered by public and private institutions of higher education (many accredited by private associations), each with its own requirements and procedures (see, for example, *The Macmillan Guide to Correspondence Study* (1985) for information on institutions, requirements, and subjects). Many people take correspondence courses for fun or personal edification, but a substantial proportion take courses toward a college degree in hopes of getting a promotion or a new job. Certification of general skills achievement, through such means as the General Education Development (GED) tests, is a second route to skill certification in the United States. The responsibility for GED testing is shared among the GED Testing Service and the state, province, and territory departments or ministries of education. GED tests, administered for a fee locally throughout the United States, most US territories and commonwealths, and in ten Canadian provinces and territories, certify skills in writing, social studies, science, reading, and mathematics. GED tests are intended as high-school equivalency tests, and the content and performance level required are based upon representative samples of graduating high school seniors (Patience and Whitney 1982, 2–3).

A third means of worker certification of skills in the United States is through various professional associations. Workshops, seminars, tests, and other forms of communicating skills are administered by many professional associations, each setting their own standards and requirements, in a variety of fields. Unlike in Japan, the United States shows a complete absence of national standards and testing systems, and certification of skills and education belongs exclusively to private associations and educational institutions. In fact, the US government plays no role at all. Moreover, individuals in the United States are more likely to seek certification for general skills and education in hopes of getting a promotion or a new job than in Japan.

The CIF and Human Resources

Human resources are the most important factor in the long-term success of the CIF. A substantial proportion of the firm's employees are hired upon graduation from high school, technical school, or college and anticipate becoming permanent employees. As stated previously, the firm recruits prospective permanent employees largely without regard to their specific job skills, focusing instead on those graduates who demonstrate a willingness and an ability to learn. This view of labor contrasts with that of the MP/SM firm, in which labor is considered one of many factors of production that can be substituted at the margin in response to changing market conditions. Workers are hired in the market, either as recent graduates or as experienced hands, based on the specific job skills that they can bring to the firm.

The expectation on the part of the MP/SM firm is that the duration of the employment will last as long as the firm has a specific need for the worker. Changes in labor employment can follow short-term decreases in demand for the product (resulting in layoffs with a probability of rehiring when demand increases) or can follow when capital is substituted for labor in response to changes in relative factor prices and productivity (resulting in structural unemployment with little likelihood of rehiring).

As a key private-sector institution, the CIF represents another source of private responsibility for the education and training of employees. Lifetime employment and seniority wage and promotion characteristics make it possible for the CIF to assume a greater proportion of the investment in human capital than is rational for its MP/SM competitors. Investment in human capital formation by the CIF takes the form of both off-the-job training and on-the-job training. Off-the-job training (Off-JT) takes place away from the workplace; it may take place instead of work (during work hours) or after work hours and may be undertaken partly at the individual's expense or fully paid for by the company. Off-JT is generally characterized by group learning and presented as a series of lectures. The first off-the-job training takes place immediately after an employee is hired, in the form of an induction training course.

> The purpose of this course is twofold. The first task is to familiarize the employee with the firm and give her/him a feeling of belonging and identification. Thus he may learn the history of the firm from the president, the market situation from the sales manager, the organization and personnel policy from the personnel manager, the production system from the production manager, and so forth. The second task is more technological. Although technological training in the induction course is confined to general matters, such as the basic technology of the firm's products or an introduction to computers, the participants may be separated into groups on the basis of the jobs they are to be assigned, and given more specialized training, such as the use of particular machines (Odagiri 1992, 65–6).

Induction training courses may last from a few weeks to a few months, longer for university graduates and shorter for high school graduates.

The CIF also provides mid-career Off-JT either at fixed intervals, for example every three or five years, or upon assignment to a new position. This training may last only a few days or several months. Experienced managers, engineers, and technicians of the CIF often serve as Off-JT trainers at various times during their careers. The extent of this practice is indicated in an interview with a personnel manager for one large Japanese company who estimated that more than 80 percent of experienced engineers and managers in his company taught at least one off-the-job course during their careers (Stern and Muta 1990, 81). Occasionally workers may get mid-career Off-JT outside the firm, for example, when they have to pass qualifying exams in order to be licensed for a particular job, or when managerial candidates have to attend an executive course in a private school or, in rare case, enroll in an MBA program in a foreign or domestic business school.

Investments in human capital by the CIF are, however, most often associated with on-the-job training (OJT). The emphasis on OJT is a reflection of the belief that employees can learn only so much from formal education, which is believed to be best suited to acquiring a logical system of knowledge. It must be supplemented with OJT which supplies the information that cannot be codified and that is firm-specific. OJT within the CIF takes place at the workplace while employees are working and is conducted at all levels of the organization. It can take the form of cross-department lectures, education and training within the quality circles, one-on-one training of junior workers by senior workers, and job rotation. Cross-department lectures take place frequently within the CIF, especially when a new product or production process is introduced. Dore and Sako state, "a taken-for-granted part of the production engineering involved is for the engineers and work study experts to hold formal sessions to explain the changes, and to instruct – as hands-on as necessary – those who have to do something new just how that new thing is to be done." (1989, 90) This type of OJT extends beyond the CIF's employees. When products or production processes change engineers are dispatched to the suppliers to make sure that its workers understand the changes they will need to make on subassemblies. This training and education process, what

Okuda calls "sociological engineering," is not just a one-way transfer of information. In addition to the engineers providing production workers with technical information, "engineers must try to encourage and help operators to develop their own ideas and present them in the form of specific suggestions." (Okuda 1983, 26) In this manner the production workers not only learn about changes that have developed elsewhere within the firm but also provide feedback to further improve the product and production processes.

Education and training within the CIF is a central function of quality circles. All quality circle groups study a standard set of analytical techniques, including simple operational research methods of defect analysis, tree diagrams, Pareto cumulations, statistical process control, and so forth, as a basis for further training. Beyond this basic education, a group chooses a problem area to explore that has a potential bearing on improving products, processes, or systems. This strategy may include purchasing books to be studied, discussions with quality circle groups from other departments, and inviting someone on the engineering staff to come and present a lecture on some aspect of the topic. These activities usually take place at the workplace, but sometimes elsewhere, and they may take place during or after work hours (for example, when workers meet to have drinks together in the evening).

One-on-one training between a supervisor and his subordinate and between seasoned and junior level employees is another important source of training and education within the CIF. The role of a supervisor as a trainer is considered a long-term responsibility that counts heavily in the evaluation of a manager. Supervisors are expected to be good teachers. They must be willing to give each subordinate a job that demands more of employees than they are initially capable of doing so that the employees can extend their abilities. Because the subordinate may fail, this approach holds a potential risk for the supervisor. If the supervisor is to be held accountable in the short term for the failure of his subordinates, he will be less likely to challenge them and, thus, their training will be less meaningful. However, even failure in the short term can provide useful lessons for the subordinants in the long term. To ensure that supervisors are willing to engage in this mentoring process, the CIF evaluates managers' performance over time. Workers with seniority are expected to take responsibility to pass on to their juniors what they have learned during their years of experience. To encourage this type of training and education, the CIF bases its salaries primarily on seniority rather than skill level. Senior workers are less likely then to keep their knowledge from junior workers out of fear junior workers may encroach upon their wages. Moreover, since all permanent workers are multiskilled, sharing knowledge and skills with other workers does not represent a threat to one's job.

The creation of multiskilled workers is achieved through what is probably the most extensive form of OJT within the CIF, that of job rotation. Job rotation is practiced not only with managers and technicians, but it is also utilized extensively with production workers.

> For the training of graduates and of potential high-flyer technicians and foremen, deliberate rotation around the firm is a standard part of the learning-teaching process. It happens at two levels: induction rotation–the process already described of having recruits spend their first six months, say, working in various departments a week or two at a time–and more long-term rotation, when people are given regular eighteen month/two-year postings, but the posts are chosen so as to make up optimal packages of useful experience–with the greater care, the greater the promise shown of being potential senior management calibre (Dore and Sako 1989, 91).

For production workers the job rotation is more likely to be limited to the performance of tasks within a single department or two, but it is equally important at this level for several reasons. It gives the employee a view of how several work stations fit together as part of a system and, importantly, it reduces boredom. It also reduces the number of injuries that derive from repetitive tasks.

Despite the costs associated with job rotation, it is a vital form of training within the CIF. When workers shift to a new job, they enter a learning stage, and their productivity may be low. Though the reduced productivity is a cost that the firm must incur until the worker has mastered the new task, it is more than offset by the advantages of the multiskilled labor force that comes from job rotation. The first is that the CIF achieves a flexible work force, which makes it easier for the firm to cover for absent employees (a relatively minor problem for the CIF, but not completely inconsequential). More important, job rotation provides all workers access to a general knowledge of the production processes and their interactions, which enables them to be much more effective at offering suggestions for improvements. Having an understanding of the various production tasks provides workers with information they can use in the quality circles to solve production problems. Job rotation also facilitates the knowledge sharing needed for the important function of horizontal communication within the CIF. Job rotation familiarizes workers with the various jobs and enhances their ability to process and communicate information necessary for all workers to effectively participate in the continuous improvement process (Aoki 1990, 11).

Multiskilled workers (with lifetime employment) are less likely to resist technological changes because of a fear that they will lose their jobs. Since their employment is not tied to a specific job they are more likely to accept new technologies and make direct contributions to the production process. Carmichael and MacLeod have analysed this relationship and state, "multiskilled workers will cooperate with labour-saving technical change in cases where singly skilled workers will not." (1993, 143) Furthermore, they argue that where workers are multiskilled " 'Innovation' skills, such as general mathematical and engineering training, should be distributed farther down the hierarchy than at single skilling firms. Finally, multiskilling firms will exhibit a comparative advantage in 'process' style innovation, which makes it possible to produce given products more cheaply . . . . " (144)

Job rotation is also an important factor contributing to the experience of engineers and their success in the design of new products. Maruyama refers to it as "experience looping."

In experience looping, the inventors, researchers and designers (IRD) themselves accumulate their own experience in various aspects of the production process, distribution, use and service. Before being assigned to R&D departments, the IRDs spend two or three years actually doing what the assembly line workers, retail store salespersons, users (customers), and repair technicians do on the actual site of production, retail and service. . . . Having worked in the various aspects of the production process, retailing, use and service, the IRDs become able to invent and design products which are fast and easy to assemble with a minimum probability of errors, which adequately meet the customers' specifications and preferences, which are convenient to use, and easy to repair with a minimum of machine down time." (Maruyama 1985, 385–6)

Job rotation was likewise reported by Westney and Sakakibara (1985) in their analysis of the engineering personnel at the central research labs of the major Japanese firms. Engineers are recruited directly from the university (usually with a masters degree) and, after they go through the firm's introductory training program, they are assigned to the central lab where they spend the first two years on a succession of projects. For the next four to five years the engineer becomes more and more active on a succession of projects and eventually takes a major role. After this period, the engineer transfers to another division of the firm (very few engineers spend their entire career at the central research lab), usually as the principal carrier of a research project in which he or she has taken the major role.

The general knowledge of the production process and products resulting from job rotation is especially important for those managers who ultimately rise to the top of the managerial ranks. Their broad experience provides them with the background necessary to express a meaningful vision of leadership. This vision spans the specialized functions of the organization and ideally enables the manager to discern the organization's cross-functional suprasystems that link the various specialized functions in a chain that begins with the customer and spans all the way back to the supplier.[10] The broad experience of management personnel expands the pool of potential candidates for higher-level positions and makes it more likely that the firm will select individuals with the greatest potential for success. This situation also creates incentives for candidates who have not been promoted to continue to contribute to the firm's success because of the large number of positions for which they may eventually qualify. This contrasts markedly with the MP/SM firm in which one's promotion ladder is largely limited to the functional unit into which one was initially hired. A manager who rises through the ranks of a single function to become president of the firm has experienced a career that has put blinders on his/her vision. In an analysis of Japanese firms' investment in human capital and its relationship to lifetime employment and seniority wage and promotion systems, Imaoka says that the firm and the trainee share the costs and benefits of OJT investment.

> In these systems, the trainee bears part of the initial OJT cost but is afterwards guaranteed its benefits. Those benefits give the employee an inventive to stay with the company that trains him. In this way the corporations employment structure gains its cohesiveness and rationale. A large part of the skills is most often passed on by employees embued with the corporation's work customs, thus making skills uniform throughout the corporation (Imaoka 1989, 417–18).

The employer bears the expense of the resources allocated to the training and education of its workers, while the employees share the cost by foregoing the possibility of getting an immediate wage increase as compensation for improving their skills. The benefits accrue to the firm over time in the form of product and production process improvements that flow from a permanent labor force that is highly trained and educated. As the firm grows and prospers, the employees also benefit in the long run as their salaries increase with their seniority, and as more management positions open up to increase the probability for promotions. Consequently, the costs of training and education to the CIF are held down in the short run, and the long-term benefits are secured for the firm that maintains a permanent labor force using its skills to advance the firm. The result is a high level of investment in human capital by the CIF.

By comparison, MP/SM firms have less incentive to invest in human capital. The MP/SM firm that hires its employees in an external labor market where pay is based on the employee's skill level and tied to a specific job has to differentiate between general skills and firm-specific skills that the employee will acquire through education and training provided by the firm. If the skills are general, there is the possibility that employees' newly acquired skills will increase their marketability and result in them taking positions with other firms. In such a case, the firm will have lost its investment in human capital. Alternatively, the MP/SM firm may be in a position where it must increase employees' remuneration in order to keep them in its employ, thus reducing the firm's return on the human capital investment. Both of these factors reduce the incentive for the firm to make human capital investments. If the skills are firm-specific there is less concern that employees' marketability will be enhanced, and the probability increases that the firm will recoup its investment via higher productivity. However, the higher productivity may also necessitate a pay increase for the employee and reduce the return on the firm's investment. Again, the ultimate effect is to reduce the incentive for the MP/SM firm to invest in the human capital of its employees. This proposition is supported by a study of private-sector training in the United States using data from the National Longitudinal Survey youth cohort to reconstruct the entire formal training history of individuals. The conclusion is that "on-the-job training with the current employer increases wages with the current employer, [and] this type of training seems to be quite firm-specific." (Lynch 1992, 311) The author notes that this finding is consistent with recent findings by the Hudson Institute that only 8 percent of 645 US firms had any sort of general on-the-job training programs.

Where labor is mobile and wages are related to workers' job skills, investments in general skills usually come at the employees' initiative and expense, but only if they think they can sell their improved skills in the market by receiving a higher compensation. An important factor in employees' expectations of being able to reap the benefits of investing in general skills is the ability to communicate the improved skill level to prospective employers. As noted by Katz and Ziderman (1990, 1, 115), in a mobile labor market, employees' desires for certifiable training and the employers' interest in minimizing the information in the labor market about workers' training contributes to the MP/SM firms' providing a low level of training in general skills. The authors further note that this results in a heavier burden on workers to finance such training and education.

Conclusion

The CIF views human resources as a capital investment and the key to the long-term success of the firm. This perspective complements the importance the Japanese people and government attach to education and training. The Japanese tradition and the lack of natural resources have induced Japan to focus on its human resources as the primary means to improve its economy. The CIF builds upon this heritage with its emphasis on incorporating all of its employees (production workers, engineers, and managers) in the continuous improvement process. To achieve this end the CIF has made significant contributions, along with individuals and the general public, to the education and training of the labor force. The organizational and managerial characteristics of the CIF create incentives for extensive education and training of its labor force, beyond what is feasible for its MP/SM competitors. As a result, employees at all levels of the CIF have training and skills, both general and specific, that make them especially adept facilitators of the continuous improvement systems.

As a final note, we reiterate that we cannot isolate any of the specific types of education from the context of the continuous improvement paradigm. Without the customer value focus for all employees and without the incentives to collect and utilize firm-specific information to support it, the investment would be relatively unproductive. To single out for adoption elsewhere what the Japanese do in terms of public education is of limited utility. The same can be said for on the job training; training in MP/SM techniques will not yield the kind of generous returns that the CIF is accustomed to enjoy. Nevertheless, it is obvious that education and training play important roles in the apparent success of firms operating within the continuous improvement paradigm. In succeeding chapters, especially ten and eleven, we shall return to this topic and explore some problems and prospects associated with adapting the American education system to the needs of a Western version of the CIF.

NOTES

1. In some major Japanese firms, all members of the board of directors are from the ranks of the firm's employees.

2. A person who is employed with the same firm for a period of six consecutive months is generally treated in Japanese labor relations as a permanent employee. In addition to permanent employees, some persons are hired on a temporary basis when short-term increases in demand necessitate it. However, temporary employees normally represent a small percentage of the CIF's work force.

3. The Japanese Ministry of Education has authority over the public and, in some respects, private educational system. The educational institutions are generally based on the 6-3-3-4 system; six years of primary education, three years of middle (or lower secondary) school, three years of high (or upper secondary) school, and four years of college. These institutions are complemented by two-year (junior) colleges and five-year colleges of technology.

4. Adjusting for the half days on Saturday, the Japanese school year has the equivalent of about 195 full-time days of classroom instruction per year.

5. The high schools and universities are ranked in a hierarchy, based largely on the individual school's record in sending its graduates to the prestigious universities (in the case of the high schools) and companies (in the case of the universities).

6. By law, employers and students can communicate only through the Public Employment Security Office (PESO) or, more likely, the high school. While a few students may find employment through personal connections, the employers who hire them will usually go through the formality of sending recruitment cards to the high schools.

7. See for example US Dept. of Education, National Commission on Excellence in Education; *A Nation at Risk: The Imperative for Education Reform* (Washington, D.C.: Government Printing Office, 1983). and Carnegie Foundation for the Advancement of Teaching; *An Imperiled Generation: Saving Urban Schools* (Princeton, N.J.: Carnegie Foundation for the Advancement of Teaching, 1988).

8. Literature majors also take mathematics and science courses but take only 4 to 6 hours per week rather than the 14 to 19 hours per week that the science majors take (US Department of Education 1987, 43 – 44).

9. The public sector also provides special grants to private universities, aid to students in the form of loans, and research grants to the faculty of private institutions.

10. The terminology "suprasystems" is credited to Carothers and Adams (1991) In general, it refers to the major cross-functional systems of the corporation as they relate to the provision of customer value.

CHAPTER 5
PRODUCTIVITY AND COST IN THE CIF

The concept of productivity is narrowly defined in both economics and the MP/SM paradigm. For both, the most popular measure of productivity is output per worker over a stated time period, or in other words, the number of hours of labor time required to produce a unit of output. As an illustration, data show that for the United States in 1981, the assembly of one automobile required 20 hours of labor time; whereas, a comparable auto in Japan required only eight hours.[1] Although productivity is always stated in terms of labor units, we should not infer that labor is thought to be responsible for productivity growth. Whether the viewpoint be from economics textbooks or the MP/SM paradigm, the origin of productivity growth clearly derives from a change in the capital stock. The change may be in the form of more capital per worker, an improvement in the technology embedded in the capital stock, or a combination of both. In any case, it is clear that increases in productivity necessarily require investment. Investment, therefore, is the driver of productivity growth.

If productivity growth requires investment, firms are left without recourse to improved efficiency in the short run.[2] While a possible recourse is learning-by-doing, we should recall that the conventional learning curve is derived from new technology and is viewed as asymptotic, so that the period of gains is relatively short. Hence, the textbook models take learning for granted in the sense that all firms in the analysis are considered to have peaked on their respective learning curves. We see, then, that in the day-to-day operations of the firm, the nature of the product, the capital stock and its embedded technology, and even learning are all given. Furthermore, when any or all of those aspects change over the long run, the changes necessarily ride on the back of investment. From the perspective of individual firms, therefore, productivity growth is discontinuous, occurring only in conjunction with major changes in capital equipment. That is the situation for the firm in the textbook models that reflect the world of the MP/SM paradigm.

Customer Value and Productivity

When the concept of productivity is refracted through the lens of continuous improvement and customer value, new dimensions open up. In this context nothing is fixed or given. Through continuous improvement, productivity changes on a day-to-day basis without necessarily requiring investment, and where the standard textbook analysis takes product characteristics as given, the customer value approach assumes that several crucial product attributes are changeable in the short run and that those attributes may serve as the basis for competition. More to the point, the quality of the product or service may improve in one or more of its dimensions, or delivery of the product may coincide more closely with evolving customer needs. Furthermore, new functional features may appear in the short run. They do not have to wait for new designs to become incorporated in new technology. Indeed, improvements in quality, new functional features, and improvements in delivery times all emerge on a day-to-day basis as a normal part of the production routine.

Another important characteristic of the CIF's process that distinguishes it from the MP/SM firm modeled in standard textbooks is its increasing flexibility of production. The improvements that increase quality often add flexibility to the output mix. The same is true of improvements that enhance deliverability. Indeed, improvements in any one area usually act synergistically with all areas. Flexibility imparts an ability to the firm to vary its product mix without a significant loss in the economies of scale usually associated with mass production. Perfect flexibility would be a situation in which a firm could produce on a custom basis for immediate delivery and at a unit cost identical to mass production.

How does the concept of customer value relate to productivity? Is it not an improvement in labor productivity if the quality of the product is enhanced, especially if the improvement is due to activities of the labor force? Is it not an improvement in productivity when the day-to-day routine results in the ability to deliver the finished product to tighter and tighter schedules? Surely, a labor force that contributes ideas and assistance for the development of new functional features is also exhibiting enhanced productivity – and yet, economics has developed no robust method of thinking about productivity in these terms. Surely, a meaningful concept of productivity must recognize that improvement in any aspect of customer value is an increase in productivity.[3] We must also recognize that within the context of the CIF, improvements in all aspects of customer value go hand in hand. This means that improvements directed at quality and deliverabilty usually result in lower unit cost, and vice versa. Importantly, then, even productivity as conventionally measured improves in the short run for the CIF.

Opportunity Cost Approach to Product Quality

The argument that improvements in process and product quality come without cost is counterintuitive for those who interpret the world through the MP/SM paradigm. The standard approach to the question of improvements turns on the concept of opportunity cost. In other words, any improvement in the quality of the process or of the product is held to involve some cost to the producer. For example, greater conformance to quality standards could be obtained through such devices as more inspection, better materials, more maintenance, training, etc., each of which requires a financial outlay. On the other hand, the improved conformance to standards would reduce certain costs associated with poor quality, for example, scrap, rework, repair under warranty, and cost of litigation resulting from poor product quality. According to Juran and Gyrna (1970, 47 ff.), firms taking this opportunity-cost approach will invest in improved quality so long as the additional benefits, for example, cost reductions due to improved conformance are greater than the additional expenditures required to improve comformance. Figure 5.1 puts the matter in the parlance of economics.

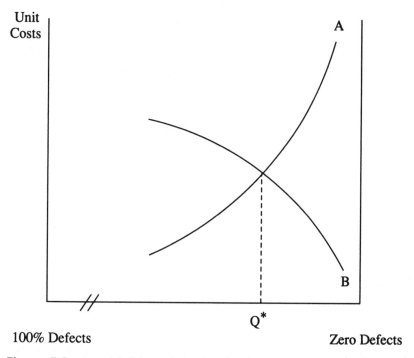

Unit Costs

A

B

Q*

100% Defects

Zero Defects

Figure 5.1. A model of the traditional quality decision. "A" represents the marginal cost of defect reduction. "B" represents the marginal saving from defect reduction. Graph adapted from Juran and Gyrna (1970, 47ff).

Line A in the figure represents the marginal cost of improved quality, for example, the outlay required to reduce the number of flaws per production run by one unit, and line B represents the commensurate marginal reduction in costs that derives from reductions in scrap, rework, repair under warranty, and/or reductions in the cost of litigation. In that light, initial efforts to reduce defects are relatively easy (i.e., have low marginal costs) and result in high marginal savings. As the defect rate is reduced and the zero level approached, marginal costs increase significantly while incremental savings become minimal. It follows, then, that in a competitive market the firm utilizing the opportunity cost or benefit-cost approach would operate where the marginal cost of quality equals marginal saving (represented by Q^*).[4] In theory, decisions about the level of product quality and the size of the production facility are made simultaneously so that the short-run cost function incorporates the quality decision. Thereafter, any short-term decision to change quality would result in an upward shift of that cost function.

The Deming-*Kaizen* Approach to Product Quality

Eschewing the oportunity cost approach, Deming and others argue that downward shifts in the cost function and improved product quality should be expected to go hand in hand (Deming 1986, 180–1). For example, when internally generated improvements in production result in a higher percentage of throughput meeting engineering specifications, scrap and rework rates will be lower, and the requirements for in-process inventories and inspection will be reduced as well. The crucial points to note are that the improvements in product and process are achieved by the continuous improvement firm as a part of the day-to-day operations and that their implementation often does not require special expenditures. Put in the terms of figure 5.1, the CIF often achieves cost reductions (benefits) similar to those represented by line B without incurring the costs represented by line A.

We can illustrate the Deming-*kaizen* approach by use of a simplified case study. A firm we will call Acme Paper produces unfinished paper within a MP/SM organizational and management structure, while its competitor, Japonica, operates as a CIF. Figure 5.2 shows the basic elements of the production process for both firms.

The process starts with the purchase of logs from suppliers. Then follows the production of wood chips, the combining of the chips with a chemical solution to make pulp, the pouring of the pulp onto a conveyer-dryer, and finally, the winding of the paper onto a parent roll. The parent roll is then sold to a firm that converts it into finished paper. From the customer's point of view, quality is conceived in terms of tensile strength, consistency of the finish, width of the roll and thickness of the paper.[5] As far as consistency of finish is concerned, for example, the

(1)
Purchase logs

(2)
Chipping

(3)
Pulp preparation

(4)
Conveyer/dryer

(5)
Accumulating paper
onto parent roll

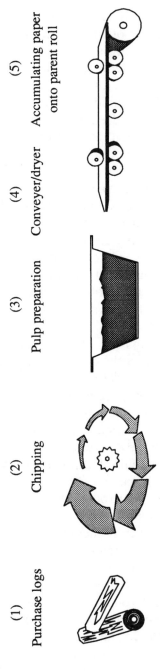

Figure 5.2. Basic processes of Acme Paper, Inc.

entire roll should consist solely of paper; no bits of undigested wood or other extraneous material is acceptable. As for width and thickness, the customer provides the specifications, including a statement of the amount of variation permitted. Such a parent roll, if perfect, may be expected to weigh, say, 10,000 lbs.

We should note that the firm cannot expect to produce perfect rolls. Deming's approach to manufacturing starts from the proposition that variation in output is always present. We could weigh an entire inventory stock of parent rolls and find the average weight to be very close to 10,000 lbs. We could also find, however, considerable variation around that mean. Variation across rolls could indicate differences in the average thickness of the paper. The underweight rolls could be made up of paper whose average thickness falls under the specifications for an average weight of 10,000 lbs. Furthermore, even rolls that happen to weigh 10,000 lbs. could show considerable variation in other respects. In other words, we could find areas of relative thickness and relative thinness within them as well as variations in width.

From the point of view of the customers, variation in the weight of the parent roll is a source of problems. Put in economic terms, variation leads to higher cost. To pursue these cost ramifications, we need to take a glimpse at the conversion process used by the customer who purchases the parent roll, of which figure 5.3 is a simplified version. We ask the reader to visualize the basic conversion operation as moving unfinished paper from the parent roll through a finishing process and onto a roll of converted paper – ceteris paribus, the faster the paper moves from the parent roll to the converted roll, the lower the unit cost of conversion. To a certain extent, the time required to convert a roll is set by the nature of the process itself; for example, under optimal circumstances, a certain minimum time is required to make the conversion. Beyond that, however, variation plays a major role in determining the actual time required. If an underweight roll, for example, has relatively thin paper, the speed of the conversion line must be slowed to prevent tears in the paper. In the event of a tear, the line must be stopped and the paper restrung. Most likely, then, the converter firm would be interested in screening lightweight rolls from any incoming shipments. That screening process would entail the cost of in-

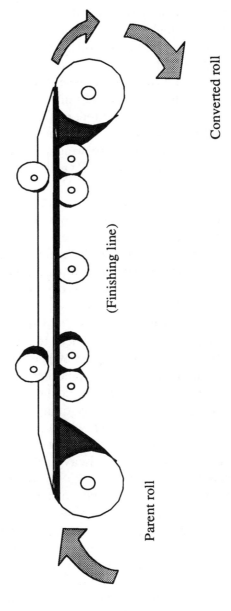

Converted roll

(Finishing line)

Parent roll

Figure 5.3. A glimpse at the conversion process.

spection (space, equipment, and personnel). Alternatively, the converter might refuse to purchase parent rolls from any firm that ships underweight rolls. That decision would push the cost of inspection back to the producer of parent rolls.

We can now begin to assess the impact of variation in product characteristics on the unit cost of production. Assume that the information presented in figure 5.4 represents production data for the two firms, Acme and Japonica, for which newly produced parent rolls were weighed and the respective data sets recorded.[6] The amount of variation is represented by the bell-shaped curves, labeled "A" and "J." Relative variation is expressed numerically by the standard deviation ($\hat{\sigma}$). We start with case "A," or Acme Paper, where the sample represents a production lot with a relatively wide range of variation, for example, $\hat{\sigma} = 1,000$ lbs. With the upper and lower limits of customer's engineering specifications shown by (x), we can see that many rolls are significantly overweight and many significantly underweight.

One plausible response to the production of underweight rolls would be for the producer to reject all rolls weighing under 10,000 pounds. That implies 100 percent inspection, a costly process. The rejected rolls would become scrap and could be sold at significantly less than the cost of production, recycled through the full process, or simply dumped. Any of these possibilities involve a loss of revenue, which constitutes an opportunity cost. Furthermore, if only rolls that weigh 10,000 pounds or more were shipped, the many heavy rolls would utilize more raw materials than required by the converter's specifications. Moreover, the converter would not necessarily be able to handle all of the heavy rolls. Heavier means thicker and a producer of magazine quality paper, for example, can tolerate only so much thickness. Therefore, some of the heavier rolls in the "A" distribution would also have to be scrapped. Finally, the shipping of heavier rolls adds to transportation costs.

It should be obvious by now that a reduction in variation reduces the cost of production for both the producer and the user. To visualize the discovery, compare Japonica's distribution "J" with "A" in figure 5.4. Let us assume that the upper and lower limits of "J" lie within the converter's specifications and

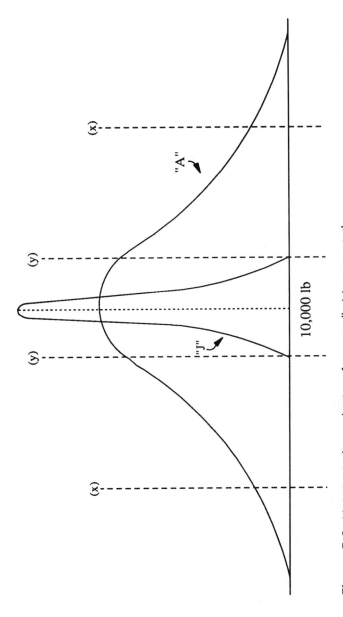

Figure 5.4. Variation in the production of parent rolls. (x) represents the upper and lower limits of engineering specifications for "A" and (y) the upper and lower limits of engineering specifications for "J." $\sigma_A = 1,000$ lbs; $\sigma_J = 100$ lbs.

that this distribution has been replicated several times to show that the new distribution is being maintained, eliminating the need to pay for inspection of the full output. Occasional samples suffice to ensure the satisfactory level of variation. Furthermore, there is no scrap or rework, and transportation costs drop due to the lighter loads. In addition, because a higher percentage of each log winds up as finished product, fewer logs need to be purchased and/or kept in inventory for a given output. Obviously the requirements for raw material purchase are significantly reduced.

Variation is, therefore, one important way to approach the topic of product quality. A reduction in variation is tantamount to an improvement in quality and, it also eliminates some of the costs associated with poor quality. So what? A MP/SM firm can also utilize statistical methods to find such problems; no problem solution originated by a CIF is forbidden to the MP/SM firm. What is the difference? Actually the differences are many and complex, with the result that the improved quality that invariably costs the MP/SM firm often comes free to the CIF. Whereas the MP/SM firm always asks if a proposed improvement will provide more benefit than cost, the CIF simply plows ahead with the benefits. Neither of these outlooks makes sense if viewed through the lens of the opposing paradigm.

To try to clear away some of the paradigmatic fog, we return to Acme paper where the CEO is meeting with top management to discuss the fact that several key customers are complaining about quality. Heretofore, those customers have considered what Acme produced to be generally equal to what they expected to find in the market. Now, however, they are being approached by overseas manufacturer Japonica who is ready to guarantee not only that their shipments would include only rolls that meet their specifications but also that those "specs" now could have a much narrower range. That new and narrow range is represented by (y) in figure 5.4. "All of this," says Japonica, "can be yours at very competitive prices." What is Acme to do?

Let us assume that the managers at Acme are aware that foreign competitors enhance product quality by using the statistical methods of an American named Deming who introduced them overseas decades ago. We would not be surprised if they decided to explore the feasibility of introducing statistical process control (SPC) techniques into Acme's operations. Furthermore, we would not be surprised that their understanding of the uses for SPC would be shaped and colored by the basic paradigm within which they have worked throughout their careers. They would quite naturally deduce that they need a quality control department in which they might employ specialists. They could head it with a good statistician, preferably one with a master's degree in statistics. Note that this first step obviously adds to the cost column.

Let us assume that quality department staff learn from management that many of the firm's customers use weight of the parent roll as a proxy measure of quality. The logical thing for them to do then would be to establish work stations to pull sample rolls, weigh them, and record the data. They could then work up distribution charts. The data might show interesting variations across production lines and/or across shifts. Let us say that they also find a considerable amount of variation around the mean on all production lines and all shifts. Is there anything concrete that the quality department can do with such data? After all, they are specialists in statistics and not persons knowledgeable in the production of paper. Of course, they could pass a summary of their statistical results to the top managers, letting them know that some lines are faring relatively poorly. But how do they get at the sources of variation that may be occurring all over the place?

A possible approach would be to put statistical capabilities "all over the place," in the hands of persons who understand the actual work. That would require that the quality department train members of the labor force, management, technicians, and floor workers in statistical techniques, which no doubt would entail a significant financial outlay, given the poor mathematical ability of the average high school graduate.

So at this point we have persons at various work stations and in various offices at Acme collecting statistics about variation in order to find ways for improving quality, and they might even succeed to some extent. The problem is that the level of discernment of all these workers is greatly limited by their individual specialty. Thus, their improvements will fall far short of potential, in both number and impact. To expect such a framework to produce optimal changes is to make the same type of error as Adam Smith did when he argued that the more specialized the worker, the more likely he or she is to find ways to make improvements. Each person's specialization constitutes a set of blinders. The purchasing agent says "tell me what's needed and I'll get it cheaply;" the maintenance manager says "let us know when a machine is down – or about to go down – and we'll fix it;" marketing says "you make it and we'll sell it;" production says "give us the customer orders and the raw materials and we'll produce what you need;" and logistics says "you sell the paper and order the inputs, and we'll move and store things as required," and so on.

According to Deming, the major benefit of SPC is to teach the managers to see the work of the organization as a unified system rather than as a collection of specialties. At one level, Deming recognized that each specialist in an organization may be performing according to their job description even though the organization as a whole is faltering. At another level, he recognized that even if a firm and all of its constituent specialists were producing state-of-the-art quality at low cost, a well-organized and well-managed firm should be able to improve continually on its performance. Following Deming, the continuous improvement perspective goes far beyond the limited realm of problem solving that we are studying here. The more versatile and forward-looking view obviously comes from a different paradigm than the one that produced the maxim "If it ain't broke, don't fix it." While we would not expect an operating CIF to face the magnitude of quality problems exemplified in the Acme Paper example, we can legitimately ask how a CIF would do towards solving the problems.

We would expect to find Japonica organized to promote improvements. From the point of view of the continuous improvement paradigm, the more that each employee understands the broader framework within which his/her specialty fits, the more likely significant improvement will follow. For that reason, as we have seen, floor workers are rotated daily across a number of jobs, and through the various ranks of managers; individuals are promoted across departments, so that each succeeding level of the management hierarchy marks a more comprehensive perspective. The crucial point is that by virtue of the way a CIF is organized and managed, most of Japonica's employees would have in-depth knowledge of paper making as a system that encompasses many functional specialties, starting with the cutting of trees and ending with the delivery of shipments to customers. Individual members of the firm would understand how each specialty fits into the bigger picture. They would know how one work station was affected by another because they had actually worked at both. The exchanging of ideas in quality circles would probably be synergistic because participants would be "speaking the same language." The same thing would apply when middle managers meet to tackle problems. Given Japonica's continuous improvement setting, we would not be surprised that the pattern of sales and the flexibility of production allowed for "smoothing," which in turn allowed for machinery to be maintained on a regular schedule.

At Acme, each functional department may have performed its function well within the given parameters. The CEO may have demanded that the sales department get more orders, that production keep the lines moving and do something about poor quality, and that all departments keep costs down. Thus, the sales department may have had to offer special discounts and special services to good customers because of a weakened competitive position deriving from poor quality. Production may not have been able to request a fixed maintenance schedule because of long periods of overtime to meet special orders. The purchasing department may have had to buy materials from whichever suppliers submitted the lowest bids to keep costs at a minimum. The personnel department may have had to hire workers with the minimum skills needed to perform the required tasks, prepared to lay them off when sales and production declined; and training may have been limited to immediate production tasks because the firm could not be certain how long workers would remain in its employ. The personnel director may have believed in these policies as a way to keep costs down. Each department may have been doing just what it was supposed to according to the given parameters, but they were all going around in a vicious circle. No one saw the big picture, not even top management. No matter how hard they tried, the departments could not solve the firm's problems. In fact, it seems that the harder they tried the worse they did.

At Acme it is the departmental parameters that need to change, which is precisely what the respective departments cannot address. How every department goes about performing its own tasks and meeting its particular goals sets up constraints within which any other department must work. Was it the business of the sales department to know that the special services they promised customers often caused production to run overtime? And even of they did know it, the boss told them to increase sales. How was the production department to know that putting off maintenance was causing the machines to function erratically? Even if they did know it, they had to run overtime to fill the orders, especially if a lot of the output had to be scrapped for quality reasons. In that situation, who was to see that a significant factor in the quality variations of parent rolls was the fact that the sales strategy was preventing manufacturing from setting up regular maintenance schedules and forcing them into a "respond to breakdown" mode? How was purchasing to know that although its low-bid system was bringing in the proper species of wood, wide variations in molecular structure imparted other variations into the system? How was logistics to know that its inventory system was exacerbating the problems of variation in both wood structure and chemical strength? And how was personnel management to know that its training programs needed more emphasis on the importance of careful measurements in the making of pulp liquor? The point is that the solution to these types of problems is more likely to be perceived by informed generalists who can communicate across functions rather than by dedicated but isolated specialists.

The informed generalist of the CIF is a specialist in a number of jobs, and that range of specialization imparts to him/her an ability to see the larger systems that span several work stations or cross several functions. Furthermore, the statistical and other analytical techniques that facilitate the conception and implementation of improvement are taught to new employees as a normal part of learning the job, and the skills are renewed and upgraded as a normal part of regular periodic training. The fact that graduates from the public schools in Japan, Korea, and Taiwan, for example, demonstrate highly developed ability with mathematics facilitates the policy. A standard SPC manual used by floor workers in many Japanese firms would pose great difficulty for most college graduates in the United States (Ishikawa, 1990).

What we have witnessed is that if the MP/SM firm applies the SPC or any other analytical tools within the context of specialties, it will likely make some improvements, but because of the blinders these will be, on the whole, relatively small in scope. For example, maintenance may find ways to handle its job better within its parameters, but not likely that maintenance, on its own, will see the need to change those parameters or understand the possibilities for doing so. Furthermore, we have seen that the ability of the MP/SM firm to make improvements was premised on heavy investment costs in a quality department, statistical method, etc.

Beyond the Opportunity Cost Imperative

The CIF is organized and managed to make improvements as a normal part of day-to-day operations. The number and the impact of improvements are both functions of willingness and ability to gather information and act upon it. The question now posed is, does information gathering itself entail an opportunity cost? Even if no financial outlay is required to conceive and implement an improvement, must not something be lost or sacrificed for this new opportunity? Viewed through the MP/SM paradigm, we would have to say that the time spent gathering and processing information for improvements must come at the expense of some other activity.[7]

Aoki accepts the seemingly inevitable logic of opportunity cost when he says "[i]n the [continuous improvement] mode, economies of specialization of operational activities are sacrificed, for some portion of the time and effort of the operating units needs to be diverted for acquiring new information. . . ." He goes on to argue that the continuous improvement mode is justified in market environments that are "extremely volatile or uncertain." In those cases, he says, gains from improvements are more likely to outweigh the "sacrifice of economies of specialization." (Aoki 1990, 8–9) This opportunity cost argument says that if all workers put their efforts into operating the extant technology in accordance with standard procedures, and none into the conceptualization of improvements, fewer total work hours would be needed to produce any given capacity level of output. In such a case, there would be a cost associated with the conceptualization and implementation of improvements. If the same phenomena are refracted through the prism of the continuous improvement paradigm, however, a radically different perspective emerges. The CIF worker does not shut down a work station or slow down its operation when the glimmer of an idea comes into her/his head. Information gathering is a normal part of the day's activities. Its volume is enhanced by job rotation and/or cross-functional promotion, and its processing often takes place "willy nilly," on the job, while driving, during TV commercials, under almost any conditions. It is a patent misunderstanding of the human mind to think that the idea for an improvement of a production activity necessarily reduces productivity at one's normal task during its conception. Indeed, a worker whose mind is actively engaged in thinking about the production process may be more productive at that moment than one who sticks to an assigned routine specialty while daydreaming about something else entirely. Admittedly, implementation of an improvement sometimes requires a financial outlay (and sometimes not), but it is inadmissible to insist that the processing of ideas entails a significant opportunity cost.

Because workers are continually engaged in conceptualizing and implementing improvements, labor productivity, broadly conceived, rises continually. It is higher today because of improvement activities conceptualized yesterday, and it will be higher tomorrow because of improvement activities transpiring today. From that perspective, there would be a terrible opportunity cost if workers were required to forego improvement activities and concentrate on the immediate tasks of producing goods. From the continuous improvement perspective, such a decision would be foolish. It would sacrifice the firm's long-term strategic advantage for the hope of a fleeting cost reduction.

The opportunity cost argument stems from taking a static view of a process that is inherently dynamic. In fact, the automobile markets to which Aoki referred are much more volatile today than twenty years ago precisely because certain firms have acquired the ability to introduce new products quickly and to vary the output mix radically, on short notice. It is, therefore, the development of continuous improvement capacity that has produced market variability. The profusion of new styles and new models results from the CIF's flexibility that constitutes an important aspect of productivity, and which, like quality and deliverability, is difficult to quantify but critical to modern competitiveness. It is precisely the MP/SM firms, with their focus on cost, that have had great difficulty in the variable automobile markets.

Summary

Within the MP/SM paradigm, productivity is narrowly defined as output per worker and its source narrowly construed to be technological change. In the continuous improvement paradigm, however, neither product nor production process is fixed, even in the short run. Improvements emerge as a normal pert of day-to-day operations, and they pertain to all aspects of net customer value: quality, deliverability, and functional features, as well as cost of production. The concept of productivity, therefore, takes on many dimensions. Finally, it is the workforce that is the source of the CIF's emerging incremental improvements. This point is in sharp contrast to the relatively passive role assigned to labor (as opposed to management) in the MP/SM paradigm. Furthermore, the "production" of improvements is a tacit component of all job descriptions in the CIF. It is a part of business as usual and not something to be subjected automatically to benefit-cost considerations.

The CIF's approach to productivity enhancement has direct implications for the analysis of cost of production. In the following chapter, we explore those implications by building upon the standard approach to the firm's cost of production.

NOTES

1. This is interpolated from data presented in Abegglen and Stalk (1985, table 5-4, 106), which shows that one worker day is required to assemble a car in a Japanese firm, presumably Toyota and at an unamed US firm, 2.5 worker days. The two factories were said to be similar in terms of the stages and complexity of the work performed.

2. In the standard theory of the firm, the short run is defined as a period not sufficiently long to permit a change in the firm's fixed resources (e.g., productive capacity). The long run, therefore, is a period long enough to permit such a change.

3. Some would argue that improved product quality results in increased market value for the product. In such a case the money value of output per worker would rise, thereby reflecting the productivity increase. That this explanation will not suffice is illustrated by the problem of an improvement in light bulbs that doubles their useful life. (That case is taken up in chapter 7.) From the point of view of productivity, the resulting reduction in price (based on falling demand) would reflect a decline in output per worker, but the improvement might give the innovating firm a strategic advantage in the market. Surely workers whose activities result in strategic advantage are more productive than workers who do not engage in such activities. In this case, the falling market value (price) of the product goes hand-in-hand with rising productivity, broadly defined.

4. It is noted, however, that in some markets a firm may choose to produce to the right of Q^* in figure 5.1, thereby differentiating its product in terms of quality.

5. The converter may be another unit of the firm that produces the parent roll. In such case, the customer is internal rather than external.

6. The distributions shown in figure 5.4 and the analysis concerning them are greatly simplified relative to what is utilized in SPC analysis.

7. This comports with Adam Smith's (4) argument that with specialization there is a "saving of time which is commonly lost in passing from one species of work to another."

CHAPTER 6

COST AND THE ECONOMIES OF FLEXIBILITY

The improvements that constitute technological change in the CIF as pictured in the earlier chapters develop in two stages: conceptualization and implementation. With reference to conceptualization, we have argued that there is little if any opportunity cost. On the other hand, we have conceded that some cost will likely be involved in implementation. Taking the single minute exchange of dies (SMED) as an example, we noticed some need for construction (i.e., for tables to preset the dies), but it was minimal considering the magnitude of technological change involved.[1] Admittedly, then, if the improvement involves reconfiguration of work layout, some implementation cost is likely to be involved.

If we compare the CIF's cost for internal technological change to the MP/SM firm's cost for changes of similar magnitude, we can appreciate the advantage enjoyed by the former. Technology costs much more in the MP/SM paradigm because it is developed externally to the production process by a specialized R&D organization.[2] When new technology is the product of an organization whose sole purpose is to provide new technology, the price tag for its acquisition covers the cost of its conceptualization as well as its development. Furthermore, the cost associated with new technology goes beyond acquisition and installation. There is a sizable period of reduced productivity associated with the initial use of new technology. First, production stops while the hard aspects of the technology are installed, and second, productivity diminishes during the period required to learn the imported technology.[3] Compared to that scenario, we have seen that the CIF has little or no such opportunity cost and installation costs often lower than those of the MP/SM firm. Furthermore, because persons intimately familiar with the process changes have conceptualized and implemented them, and because the pace of change is incremental, the magnitude of loss due to learning is minimal and often nonexistent (Schramm, 1993). Finally, there is often no down time associated with the change.

In arguing that much of the CIF's technological change is costless, Imai (1986) distinguishes between what he calls *kaizen,* or incremental improvements, and the major technological innovations often associated with radical change. He says that although the CIF does at times import technology from the outside, for which the full range of cost must be calculated similarly to that of the MP/SM firm, it is the realm of internally generated change that gains the CIF its major competitive advantage. In that regard, the reader is cautioned against thinking of the incremental improvement process as less important than major technological innovations. Indeed, it may be more accurate to think the opposite. JIT manufacturing, the epitome of continuous improvement, as seen in retrospect is a major technological breakthrough, but it is really the product of millions of internally generated improvements accumulated over several decades. It makes no sense to suggest that Toyota paid an opportunity cost for the development of JIT. What sense does it make to assign a cost to a new paradigm? Though standard mass-production firms would surely have to put up considerable investment to convert to JIT manufacturing, that is another story entirely.

The CIF's Cost of Production Curve

To illustrate the impact of emerging incremental improvements on productivity and cost, let us posit two firms that in an initial period feature identical cost functions for products that customers consider almost identical. In our scenario, we posit that both the MP/SM firm, called "A," and the CIF, called "J," began as mass producers, at which time the cost functions for each could be represented by SAC_1 in Figure 6.1.[4] When operating at optimum capacity, both feature unit costs of C_1 and output of Q_1. Now let us assume that the "J" firm receives a deus ex machina infusion of continuous improvement capability so that incremental improvements begin to emerge internally as a normal part of day-to-day operations.[5] For example, the work

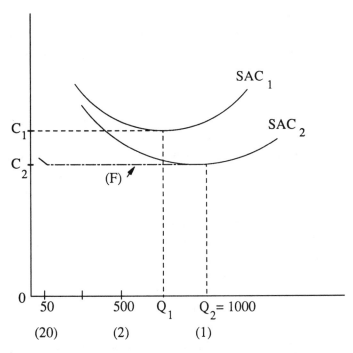

Figure 6.1. Economies of continuous improvement and economies of flexibility. Quantities in parentheses indicate number of product variations. Numbers outside parentheses indicate the quantity of units produced for each variation.

stations in the manufacturing plant implement internally generated improvements that reduce product variation in terms of conformance to engineering specifications. One result is that the associated scrap and rework are reduced. That, in turn, reduces the need for inventories. This increasing "leanness" of "J" would be reflected by a fall in unit cost, as shown in figure 6.1.

Looking at the same phenomenon from a different perspective, however, we see that because of improved quality a given batch of resources, machinery, and material throughput can now produce a larger finished goods output in a given time period. In other words, the percentage of a given amount of throughput that becomes effective product has been increased.[6] Therefore, the cost function for "J" should both fall and move to the right, as shown by SAC_2. Not only does the "J" firm now enjoy lower cost per unit than the "A" firm, but it also has simultaneously

129

increased its capacity to cater to the ensuing expansion in its market size (due to the concomitant improvement in product quality and the lower cost).[7] We should note that although cost reductions occur along an asymptotic function, the enhancement of capacity does not suffer the limitation of a prescribed upper limit.[8]

The movement of the "J" firm's cost curve to SAC_2, as shown in figure 6.1, is analogous to movements usually found with economies of scale. In other words, in standard economic theory, the simultaneous rightward and downward movement of the SAC would signify investment in a larger facility that would feature lower unit costs. The characteristics of the continuous improvement firm, however, go beyond economies of scale. The incremental improvements of production processes, and especially their accumulation into breakthrough innovations, have turned some firms' production systems into hallmarks of flexible manufacturing, or economies of flexibility. Best (1990, p. 156) says that this new system "combines the specialist advantages of a job shop for small-batch production with the scale advantages of a flow line for high volume production." Where flexibility was formerly associated with relatively small factories in such industries as machine tools, it is now found in automobile firms and electronics. Indeed, Toyota's former goal of making die changes in one minute has given way to the new goal of changing dies in seconds, putting it on the threshold of the ability to make production runs that are completely differentiated, but have the same average cost as a run of thousands of homogenous units (i.e., mass production).

What we are calling economies of flexibility may appear similar to economies of scope. It is a mistake, however, to equate the two. Sometimes termed economies of joint production, economies of scope bring the production of several products into one manufacturing organization to achieve sufficient volume to take advantage of at least some aspects of economies of scale. Chandler (1990, 25–6) refers to German dye makers who were able to invest in plants large enough to exploit economies of scale because they could produce both dyes and pharmaceuticals from the same basic raw materials and intermediate chemicals. In that case, the scope of operations promoted economies of scale. To think, however, that a CIF differentiates its output mix in order to attain economies of scale would miss the point entirely. From the point of view of economies of flexibility, the analysis begins with a volume of mass production that already enjoys economies of scale. The trick of flexibility is to increasingly differentiate output without losing the economies of scale.[9] The benefit of that flexibility is in allowing the firm to pursue marketing and production strategies that cater more and more closely to individual customer-value preferences. Flexibility, therefore, permits the CIF to carve markets into niches in which MP/SM firms have difficulty competing. The latter do lose economies of scale when they are forced to vary their output mix.

The introduction of flexibility into analysis is illustrated in figure 6.1 by the dashed line *(F),* which represents the range of product differentiation that can be produced while still enjoying the minimum cost associated with full-capacity utilization. This horizontal curve (F) would be the case if we assumed that set-up times (e.g., set-up cost) for each product changeover were zero.[10] Considering relevant situations in which die changes are made in a matter of seconds, that assumption can serve a useful instructional purpose. For example, a production run of 1,000 units may consist of 50 units each of 20 variations of the product, or it may consist of 10 units each of 100 different product configurations.[11] In each case, the differentiated runs are made at the same unit cost as in a full run of 1,000 homogenous items.[12] To the extent of any positive set-up costs, *(F)* would slope upward to the left, indicating the additional cost of increasing differentiation of production runs, which we could interpret as an opportunity cost of offering just-in-time delivery as a service to customers. Reducing the slope of the flexibility function *(F)* is certainly a goal of the CIF.

To summarize, what we are dealing with in the "J" firm of figure 6.1 may be properly termed economies of flexibility. The continuous improvement process simultaneously improves the product quality and reduces costs of production, shifting the SAC curve downward and to the right. Variation in unit costs for the CIF is a function of overall capacity utilization and not of output mix. In other words, so long as the production runs fully utilize the capacity, the degree to which output is differentiated matters little.

Lean Manufacturing

It may be useful at this point to use a popular metaphor to show how the phenomenon of declining cost in the CIF is misperceived by many MP/SM observers. Popular opinion holds that leading Japanese firms feature lean production, which we illustrate by firm "J" in figure 6.2b. The perceived leanness is in relationship to the obesity of the MP/SM firm represented by figure 6.2a, which shows itself in various types of inventories, inspection stations, scrap, and rework, each of which represents costs as personnel, material, and space.[13] At the outset, we should acknowledge that the "J" firm was fat until it developed the internal improvement process. The weight reduction regime unfolded in more or less the following manner: Statistical process controls helped identify the sources of flaws and internal improvements in task performance, and machine layout and design and product design underwent changes that resulted in fewer rejections and rework. What followed were increasingly tighter engineering specifications for the products and further improvements to meet the new specifications. Over time, as this process continued, the product had fewer problems both in production and in the hands of the customer. Consequently, the requirements for inspection, rework, and inventories declined, eventually approaching zero. Elimination of all apparent fat in figure 6.2a would require that zero defects occur in the process. The reduction in inspection, rework, and inventories reduce labor requirements as the organization becomes leaner.[14]

The impact of improvements on the costs of production may be deceptively obvious. The implication is that fewer inputs are required for a given full-capacity output (capacity of machine operations). This perspective is incomplete, however, because capacity itself is changing. Another useful point from which to understand this transformation is afforded by the concept, *work-in-process turn*, used by industrial engineers and cost accountants. Work in process (WIP) refers to all throughput beginning

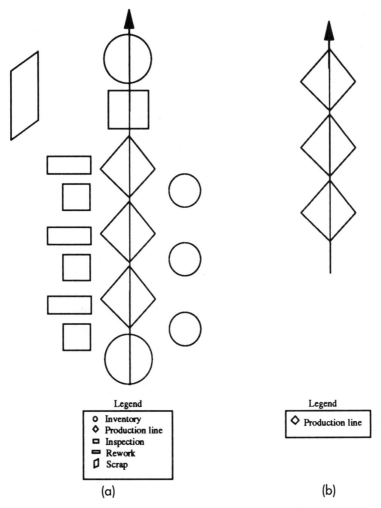

Figure 6.2. (a) Stylized "A" model. (b) Stylized "J" model.

with initial inventories of delivered components and materials, up to and including any inventory of finished product. In theory, a work-in-process turn refers to the time required to completely process all of the throughput that is in the system at some point in time. The standard measure of work-in-process-turns is

$$\text{WIP Turns} = \frac{\text{Total Annual Production}}{\text{Work in Process}}.[15]$$

133

Best (1990, 148) notes that "[in] the late 1970's when Western automobile companies had WIP turns of around 10 . . . , Toyota's WIP turn was greater than 300 per year." Whereas the perspective of figure 6.2 indicates that the "J" firm was leaner than its competition, the perspective of WIP turns suggests that it was also faster. The former perspective suggests that increased efficiency comes in the form of reduced inventory and so on. The latter perspective has it come from increased speed. Note, however, that speed, in this context, has a special meaning. Output per time period for a given mix of capital and labor is greater, even though neither the labor nor the machines in the process (e.g., the Production lines in figure 6.2) actually speed up their operations.

To understand why the operations of the CIF have in fact increased their speed, we have to focus on the driving force of the transformation from fat to lean manufacturing: the improvement in quality. The reason why the "A" firm features inspection stations is that the operations (and the suppliers) produce flawed components. If the internal improvement process takes a firm from a point where 25 percent of material throughput is lost through flaws to a point where 100 percent of throughput is effective, then the productive capacity of the facility increases. While the total volume of throughput processed in a given period remains constant, the volume of *effective* output increases. The result is as if additional equipment had been put in place or the speed of the production line had increased, neither of which occurred.

The speed-capacity can be illustrated with a real-world (but unnamed) US computer chip maker. In the early years of its operation the company was getting only about a 10 percent yield from its throughput; in other words, 90 percent of potential output was scrapped after inspection, with only 10 percent being shipped to customers. After experiencing tremendous competitive pressure from foreign firms, the company hired consultants to help it adopt some key aspects of a CIF approach to quality.[16] Eventually, it had to scrap only about 10 percent of potential output while shipping 90 percent to customers. After improvements, a given amount of material inputs, used over a given period of time, yielded 9 times more effective output than previously. If the same fixed capital arranged in the same basic layout was producing 9 times as much as previously, the operation must have speeded up. Whether we call it increased capacity, more effective throughput, or increased speed depends on the relevant context, but it is, in fact, all of those things.

There is yet another angle from which we must view the implications of the speed-capacity phenomenon. The improvements in quality of throughput not only increase the effective capacity of a given manufacturing plant; they also reduce the amount of labor required to operate the facility. As the quality of inputs and throughputs improve, the requirements for inventory, inspection, and rework reduce. This is observed in figure 6.2, where the inventory, inspection, and rework stations present in figure 6.2a are no longer found in the stylized "J" firm. The labor once associated with those work stations has also been removed. It is important to note, however, that the ability to reduce labor requirements goes beyond the straightforward elimination of inspection, rework, and inventories. The same improvement process that achieved the trimness noted in the "J" firm also eliminates some of the duties and operations performed by the line workers, as is implicit in the reduction of machine downtime and the alleviation of other work station problems. Obviously, then, the labor time required to operate each machine diminishes. If there was a ratio of one worker per machine before improvements, the continuance of that ratio would imply that each labor unit was utilized increasingly less intensively over time.

The obvious recourse for the CIF manager is a reorganization of the production layout in order to fully utilize labor time, which typically shows up as a repositioning of machines, as shown in figure 6.3.

In figure 6.3a, a work group is organized originally with four machines and four attendant workers lined up in the logical sequence of the machining operations. After a period of continuous improvement of the production processes, the group's work is reorganized as shown in figure 6.3b, which maintains the sequencing of machines but reduces the number of operators to two.[17]

This new configuration accomplishes much more than the straightforward reduction of labor costs; it enhances each worker's effectiveness as an improvement agent. Not only is each

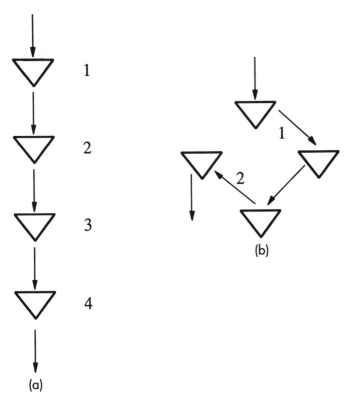

Figure 6.3. Reorganizing the shop floor. Triangles represent machines in a work group. Numerals represent workers. Arrows indicate throughput.

worker now responsible for two machines, the two work as a team to handle special problems, and they rotate assignments, thus expanding the immediate information horizon of each worker. Recalling the Ayres/Ogburn/Gilfallen approach to technological change (chapter 3), we can say that the number of improvements per worker is some function of the amount of information available to each one. Comparing the workers in figure 6.3b with those in figure 6.3a, we determine that the volume of improvements per worker will be higher in the former than the latter and probably that the average improvement coming out of the reorganized situation will have relatively more impact, because the workers now understand more of each process than they did previously.

Some observers have pointed out that when the internal improvement process leads to the reorganization of work as explained here, labor, by its own actions, is eliminating jobs. From that perspective, it would appear that labor has an incentive to resist participation in the improvement process.[18] If the market for the firm's output remained constant, the reorganization of work stations would be tantamount to downsizing the firm's labor force. The situation should be viewed, however, from a broad competitive perspective. If the CIF can expand its market by using improved quality and deliverability as its wedge, the expansion will produce offsetting employment opportunities. Therefore, permanent employment, a major cog in the continuous improvement process, can continue unabated only if there is growth in the size of markets for the CIF's products. How this imperative for growth is realized in global competition will become evident in the succeeding chapters.

Given the evolutionary development of the CIF into a lean and flexible competitor, some observers apparently and incorrectly believe that the route to lean manufacturing is through reducing the size of a firm. Instead of eliminating the *need* for inventories, for example, they would start by trying to eliminate inventories. This, of course, would be disastrous if the operations are producing throughput flaws. Likewise, they miss the point that the lean firms reduce the *need* for coordinators by becoming more effective, not vice versa. The overweight firm beginning the competitive struggle by downsizing the personnel ranks is analogous to the corpulent and sedentary man trying to become a world-class athlete through diet only, with no recourse to exercise. He may become thinner but not necessarily more competitive. It is only through the exercise of continuous improvement that a competitive leanness will be attained.

Productivity Redefined

We must reemphasize that the analysis of productivity in the CIF should go beyond the standard measures of output per worker and cost per unit. During the period when operations are being speeded up, output further differentiated, and costs reduced, the quality of the output is improving in every sense. The production process is, consequently, adding to the net customer value of the product through every channel available to it. We can better appreciate the competitive implications of the continuous improvement process when we view productivity from all of these vantage points.

NOTES

1. Some may argue that operation of the SMED system requires more labor for die changes per se than the old system does. Even if that were so, what we are talking about is an operating cost and not a cost of acquiring the new technology. In terms of operating cost, any small amount of additional labor required to have dies preset would be overwhelmingly offset by the elimination of time formerly lost while lines were down for die changes.

2. The R&D is external to the production process even in those cases where the laboratory is owned by the firm in question.

3. Schramm (1993) develops this point in the course of comparing the learning processes of the CIF with those of the MP/SM firms.

4. We may also add the assumption that both firms in this original position have fully traversed the standard learning curve appropriate to the technology in use.

5. We use the deus ex machina assumption to sidestep questions about the origin of continuous improvement capacity. The deus ex machina assumption appears to say that continuous improvement characteristics were costless. The point is certainly debatable. Some would say that the cost of carrying a permanent work force through recessionary periods should be set off against the enhanced willingness of the permanent workers to acquire firm-specific information. Others say the workers trade a guarantee of relative permanence for a relatively lower wage. Such arguments usually take the form of ex post rationalizations that overlook the fact that no explicit investment decision was made to adopt the continuous improvement mode. That mode was not a technology "on the shelf" and therefore subject to benefit-cost considerations. In fact, the emergence of continuous improvement was largely an evolutionary process that was neither initially intended nor understood. On the other hand, if a follower firm assumes that permanent employment is a necessary step toward conversion to a continuous improvement mode, it would properly include the additional cost in its benefit-cost analysis. Admittedly, certain investments had spin-offs that were instrumental in stimulating the evolutionary process. For example, the work force was taught methods of statistical quality control and other techniques for analyzing production processes. It is clear, however, that continuous improvement goes far beyond the use of these quality-control techniques. Certainly, many millions of dollars have been spent to train US workers in the area of statistical quality control, apparently without significant emergence of continuous improvement capabilities.

6. This improvement has the result of reduced input, materials, capital and labor per unit of effective throughput. The reader will appreciate that we are not referring here to the phenomenon of "economies of speed" noted by Chandler (1977, 1990) with regard to the development of mass production firms. Undoubtedly, however, the realized improvements increase the speed of the throughput in addition to the cost reducing tendencies of

shrinking input requirements. Chandler claims that the improved organization of production associated with the inception of mass production allows for more throughput per given unit of capital and/or labor. Each unit of capital and labor can accomplish more throughput without regard to its effectiveness. In the present case, more output per unit of input is obtained due to the improvement in throughput quality. Some of the improvements, however, may also increase the speed of the throughput, effectiveness given.

Mayhew and Carroll (1993, 110) refer to Chandler's "emphasis on management of throughput" in their discussion of his concept of "speed." That perspective could be extended to cover the improvements in throughput effectiveness that are developed here, although neither they nor Chandler do it.

7. Referring to Toyota, Ohmae (1982, 191) says that "[t]hroughout the past decade [1970s] [it] has maintained its employee level at about 45,000 while increasing its throughput 2.5 times." While some of the change is undoubtedly due to automation, a significant amount is due to internally generated improvements in the production process and increases in the speed of the throughput.

8. Recall that this improvement in productivity cannot be accurately interpreted with the learning curve, which assumes a given technology. What we have here is technological change, or more precisely, the CIF's peculiar form of technological change.

9. To liken economies of flexibility to economies of scope would encourage the observer to overlook the evolutionary process of some firms from the mass production mode into flexible manufacturing. Furthermore, it would obscure the dilemma of mass production firms that face competition from continuous improvement firms. The dilemma, simply put, is that the mass production firm views quality from the perspective of opportunity costs so that meeting the competition's quality will mean higher costs.

10. Although some labor cost will always be associated with the preparation of new dies for a changeover, the fact that the changeover itself happens in seconds is the crucial point. In the typical mass production plant, the production line is down for hours while the changeover is being made.

11. In practice, of course, the production runs need not be divided equally among the several product configurations.

12. We take for granted that costs may vary with costs of materials, etc. What we are depicting here is some assembly line process, such as automobiles, in which the configuration of the items moving on the line varies. The six cylinder on that line will cost more than the four cylinder and the four-door model more than the two-door, etc.

13. It is useful to assume that the "A" firm is operating at the Q' of figure 5.1.

14. The elimination of inventory of purchased inputs and finished product does require careful coordination with input suppliers and product distributors,

respectively. Nevertheless, the general reduction in supervision and management should easily eclipse the increased coordination with suppliers and distributors.

15. See Best (1990, 148). As conventionally used, WIP turns do not include a measure of finished goods inventory. There is no conceptual reason that precludes its inclusion in our illustration.

16. Of course, this US firm was experiencing cost outlays in its efforts to improve, but our point here refers to speed, not to cost of change.

17. Some critics of the CIF, especially labor union leaders commenting on Japanese subsidiaries, characterize such a reorganization of work as a "speed up." The implication is that additional productivity is being squeezed out of the workers by making them move at an unreasonably faster pace. The argument overlooks the fact that reorganization follows on the heels of process improvements that reduce the performance requirements at a given work station. Unions may have a legitimate reason to fear that MP/SM managers will misperceive what is happening in the CIF and simply reduce the size of their own labor forces as a competitive response. If that occurred in the absence of process improvements, labor would have grounds for leveling charges of exploitation.

18. Another tack taken by some union leaders is to argue that when management reorganizes the work station after the workers have initiated process improvements, it is expropriating benefits that rightfully belong to the workers. In one case, we were told, a local leader urged workers not to reveal any improvements they initiated but simply to take the benefit as extra leisure on the job.

CHAPTER 7

CUSTOMER VALUE APPROACH TO DEMAND

Value in Economics

Value is an elusive and much debated term in economics. We shall avoid some of the more esoteric aspects of the debate and concentrate on what has found its way into basic economics textbooks. There the most fundamental measures of value are *utility* and *price*. Utility refers to the satisfaction that an individual consumer realizes from the purchase and use of a good or service; the price of the good or service is an aggregate phenomenon determined by market supply and demand. The connection between an individual's utility and the market price is made in consumer demand theory via the assumption that the consumer behaves so as to maximize the total utility derived from consumption of goods and services, given a fixed amount of income. An individual consumer maximizes total utility by purchasing amounts of a good up to the point where the marginal utility of the nth unit is equal to price paid for the good, ceteris paribus. However, because of some well-recognized anomalies, such as the water-diamond paradox, economists do not maintain that market values represent intrinsic values.[1] Nevertheless, for most products, it is thought, or at least implied, that there is some reasonable association between price and value.

It is accepted, however, that total value realized by consumers is greater than the market value because the utility derived from a good or service varies among consumers, whereas the market determines a single price. In figure 7.1, for example, the forces of supply and demand have established a price of P for a marketed quantity of Q. The total market value is therefore $OPBQ$. We can see, however, that each and every customer represented by quantities less than Q was willing to pay more than P for the product – which implies that the consumers' marginal utility derived from those units was greater than P. In fact, the

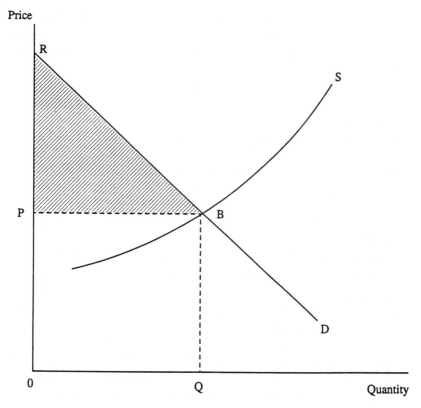

Figure 7.1. Consumer surplus.

demand curve is drawn to show the quantity that would be demanded at each possible price. The triangle *PRB* therefore represents value received by customers for which they do not compensate producers. In standard economics jargon, it is the "consumers' surplus." Total value would, therefore, be the summation of market value and the surplus value. This approach to value will serve us as a starting point.

Net Customer Value

Before continuing on with the analysis of consumer demand, we should note our preference for the term *customer* in lieu of

143

the more commonly used *consumer*. We prefer the former because it allows the analysis to be extended to competition among producers of intermediate goods as well as final goods manufacturers. While the demand for a component part derives directly from the demand for the final consumer good in the world of mixed competition, CIFs are likely to respond to consumer demand differently from MP/SM firms. Because CIFs tend to have much more stringent requirements concerning quality and timely delivery, they will discriminate between input suppliers that feature continuous improvement and those that do not. Therefore, we should gain some analytical power by broadening the scope of inquiry to include intermediate goods markets. Furthermore, the broader concept *customer* is often used in the business literature.

With figure 7.1 as our reference, we can say that total customer value is represented by the area *ORBQ*, with *OPBQ* representing the market value and *PRB* the customers' surplus. This latter term can be taken as a first approximation of the concept *net customer value,* as used in the management science literature. According to Carothers and Adams (1991, 34), pioneers in development of the concept, net customer value is the total value realized by the customer from the purchase and use of the good or service less that which must be sacrificed to obtain and use it.[2] *Net* customer value is enhanced from two basic sources: (a) an increment to customer value provided by an improvement in the product itself, and (b) a reduction in the amount of sacrifice that the customer must make to obtain and use the product. In measuring this sacrifice, price is a first approximation. As we shall see, however, the customer also bears a number of opportunity costs, but these are not reflected in figure 7.1.[3] Because of those nonprice elements of sacrifice, net customer value will be less than the consumer surplus as conventionally measured.[4] One area of competitive advantage for the CIF is in reducing those opportunity costs. For the moment, however, we will deal only with price as a first approximation of the sacrifice made by customers to purchase and use the product. We can see, then, that for a given demand function, the lower the price the greater the net customer value.[5]

A customer's choice among relatively similar products will be made on the basis of net customer value. In searching for a decision rule, we could begin by saying that between two competing products selling for the same price, a customer will always choose the one apparently offering the more value. Accordingly, of two products that are perceived to offer the same value, the customer will choose the one featuring the lower price. We are, however, unable to make the flat statement that a customer will always choose the alternative perceived to offer the highest net customer value because income constraint might preclude a customer from doing so. An individual may perceive a particular automobile, for example, as affording 120 thousand dollars of value while carrying a price tag of 90 thousand dollars or a net customer value of 30 thousand dollars (for simplicity, assume that other opportunity costs are zero). The individual, however, might be constrained by personal finances from entering that market and may pay instead 20 thousand dollars for a car perceived to yield only 20 thousand dollars in value (net customer value of zero). For that reason, our subsequent discussion of competition will compare products that are close substitutes.

Perceived value differences among competing products, therefore, serve as a basis for establishing competitive advantages or disadvantages. In such cases, it would not be an anomaly to find that the market-leading firm is charging the higher price.[6] Indeed, logic would dictate that the firm offering a product of lesser value would have to sell it for a lower price. We can say then that in the face of full and free information, the difference in price should fully reflect the difference in total value if the lower-quality producer expects to stay in the market.

The traditional economics approach to analyzing market dynamics is to take product characteristics as given and then explain competition among firms in terms of price and/or output. This is emphasized by Barney and Ouchi (1986, 18) who say, "[b]uying and selling is the fundamental process studied in economics." That perspective leads to the development of analytical models in which the short-run decisions of the firm's management are limited to volume of output and/or price. In the perfectly competitive model of standard economic theory, perfect competition results in a uniform market price. The managers of a firm in a perfectly competitive market can only alter the quantity of output in the short run, as the firm is a price taker.

In the imperfectly competitive markets (monopolistic competition and oligopolistic market models), the firms have varying degrees of market power and, thus, the managers, in the short run, simultaneously make an output and price decision.

According to the standard textbooks, decision making for the long run is less constrained. A wider range of choices opens up because the long run is defined as a period long enough to alter the amounts of all inputs (including investment in capital). Thus, the existing capital stock may be enhanced so as to provide greater economies of scale, or existing capital may be replaced by new technology. Moreover, new investment may entail producing an entirely new product or the same product as before but with improved quality. Note that in any of these cases, the change process is discontinuous and revolves around the benefit-cost considerations that precede new investment.

There is a paradox underlying this approach to the economics of the firm. Mathematical complexity requires conceptual simplicity. While the simplistic view of the world combined with complex mathematics yields important truths, it necessarily obscures others. In the context of current global competition, nothing is more obscurantist than the almost universal practice of taking the product as a given. Though this practice is in harmony with the MP/SM paradigm, it is in obvious disharmony with the continuous improvement paradigm in which products are continually changing. The competitive goal of product improvements is precisely to change the customers' valuations of the product.

In the conventional MP/SM paradigm, the price/quantity of output decision functions as the basic weapon of day-to-day and month-to-month decisions. New products and new markets are decisions for the long run, the type associated with investment.[7] Significant changes in quality are associated with the long run, too. For the CIF, however, such decisions are the essence of competition in the short run as well as in the long run. Indeed, the essence of continuous improvement is the constant enhancement of the value inherent in the product or service. Put succinctly, the CIF uses improvements in customers' valuations of its product to extract strategic advantage in the marketplace. Hence, the appropriate proxy for success in the long run would be market share. As we shall see, however, the growth of market share is likely to be accompanied by a simultaneous growth of profits.

Net Customer Value and Customer Choice

For purposes of analysis, we can say that the instrumental component of customer value derives from (a) functional features of the product, (b) product quality, and (c) timely delivery. We are intentionally omitting aesthetic design – a competitive aspect that is obviously important in many product markets but which is not instrumental in nature. With instrumental values, there would be near universal agreement that a particular change constituted an improvement. We are not saying that there would be agreement as to the value of the change, but only that most would agree on the direction of the change. Take the automobile braking system as an example of a functional feature. Instrumental measures of brake performance would include how quickly a brake system will stop a vehicle and the stability it imparts to the process of stopping. Another value feature of the braking system is reliability: How many times can one replicate the braking process without failure?[8] The design of the car, on the other hand, is more aesthetic than functional. We cannot say a priori that an aesthetic change emerging from the production process constitutes an improvement. Only the test of the market can yield that judgment. While aesthetic qualities are admittedly important considerations in the marketplace, we must omit matters of taste in the subsequent analysis.[9]

Instrumental changes are those whose effects can be evaluated objectively. Members of a firm can pursue them with a high level of assurance that once introduced into the market they will enhance the net customer value of the product. The CIF's ability to anticipate customer response has the implicit effect of adding a marketing side to the job description of each and every employee, in contrast to the MP/SM firm in which marketing is usually a specialty and an ex post or reactive approach to customer satisfaction ("do they like our product") tends to be the rule. With the CIF, on the other hand, the approach to value creation is ex ante and proactive. The reactive approach can lead a temporarily successful firm to complacency, whereas an ex ante strategy for improvements in customer value is dynamic and open-ended.

A potential automobile customer with information about the performance and reliability of the braking systems in competing models would be able to rank them according to the instrumental value they add to each automobile. Those calculations would include maintenance, repair, replacement, and other operating costs, as well as the probability of avoiding injury, death, and adverse legal action. After customers perform similar comparative calculations for other significant features of available automobiles in the relevant price range, they will have a ranking of customer value. The penultimate step is for the customer to relate customer value for each automobile to the full cost of each (price plus opportunity cost). The product chosen will be the one that offers the highest net customer value.

Is it reasonable to propose that customers actually make value estimates by mathematical calculation? At the outset, we should recall that we are holding constant the aesthetic features of the product. Other emotional factors such as patriotism and peer pressure can also be important in the decision matrix. If we leave aside these emotional factors and concentrate on the instrumental factors, it may not be too far-fetched to assume that instrumental value can be quantified in money equivalents. However, if it would be unreasonable to imagine that customers take calculator in hand and work systematically through the suggested calculations, it is sufficient for our purposes for them to confront these issues on a much less formal basis, as we believe they do. The fact that the market supports several publications, such as *Consumer Reports, Consumer Digest,* and *Consumer Guide,* which provide potential customers with objective information on the instrumental features of various consumer products is at least casual evidence that many consumers evaluate products in a manner similar to what is suggested here. Thus, the customer who purchases brand X in preference to brand Y is saying that X should give me more net customer value for my money than Y. In other words,

$$V_x - O_x - P_x > V_y - O_y - P_y,$$

where V_x, V_y are total instrumental value for X and Y, respectively, O_x, O_y are the non-price opportunity costs for X and Y, respectively, and P_x and P_y represent the respective prices.

The customer would be indifferent as between X and Y only under the following conditions:

$$V_x - O_x - P_x = V_y - O_y - P_y \quad \text{or}$$
$$(P_x - P_y) = (V_x - O_x) - (V_y - O_y).$$

In other words, the price of Y must lag the price of X enough to fully compensate for any perceived difference in the total instrumental value and non-price opportunity cost if Y is to be a viable alternative for the customer. In that case, there is no difference in net customer value offered by the respective products. What we find, then, is that the perceived difference in value constitutes a wedge between the price of the CIF's product and that of its competitor. Because the underlying motivation for employees of the CIF is the ongoing improvement of its product's customer value, the wedge tends to grow over time.

Net Customer Value and Individual Customer Demand

At this point we are in a position to trace the impact of product improvements on individual customer demand. Figure 7.2a presents a customer's indifference curve, V_1, showing the combination of good A with a bundle of goods N (representing all other goods or non-A goods), which provide the customer with a constant net customer value. The location and slope of the budget line reflect the customer's income and the relative opportunity costs of the goods ($P_N + O_N$ and $P_A + O_A$). The tangency between the indifference curve and the budget line indicates the combination of good A and good N the customer should purchase to maximize net customer value. Now assume that good A is produced by a CIF which, through the continuous improvement process, improves the product while the value associated with good N remains constant. Further assume that there is no change in the price of either product. The effect on

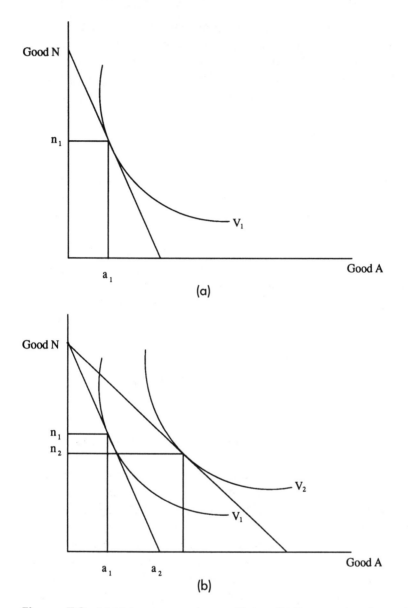

Figure 7.2. (a) Net customer value equilibrium. (b) Customer reaction to improved value.

the customer's decision making will depend on the type of improvement in the product. If the improvement results in less maintenance, repair, or other aspects that reduce the nonprice opportunity cost to the customer, the effect is to alter the slope of the budget line. The budget line becomes flatter, reflecting the reduced opportunity cost of good *A,* as shown in figure 7.2b.[10] The result is that the customer will purchase more of good *A* and less of good *N* than previously and move to a higher indifference curve reflecting an increase in net customer value.

If the improvement is not something that simply reduces nonprice opportunity costs, the analysis becomes decidedly more complicated. For example, if the improvement in good *A* takes the form of extending the life of the product, a standard graph, such as figure 7.2, would have to show a change in the slope of the indifference curve, representing a new set of tradeoffs between good *A* and good *N.*[11] What the shape and position of the new indifference curve would be cannot be determined logically. In order to pursue the impact of improvements in durability, we will follow the lead of Lancaster, as discussed in Tirole (1988, 99–100, 102), and focus the analysis on product attributes rather than on the good per se.

In the case of light bulbs, the principal attribute is light, which may be measured in lumens. In figure 7.3, therefore, the indifference curves represent constant levels of total customer value to be received from various possible combinations of lumen hours of light (provided by light bulbs) and bundles of attributes associated with good *N.* If internally generated improvements enhance the life expectancy of a given light bulb without proportionately raising the cost of producing a bulb, then the cost per lumen hour is reduced.[12] For example, if the total cost of making a given quantity of a certain size of bulb remains constant while the life expectancy of the bulb is doubled, the cost per lumen hour is cut in half.[13]

If we assume competitive markets where price equals the cost of production, a given budget would purchase twice as many lumen hours even though the price per bulb would remain constant. If the attribute/good relationship for composite good *N* does not change, we can trace the impact of said improvement by moving the budget constraint's horizontal intercept proportionately to the right. While we can expect that the income and

Attributes of
Good "N"

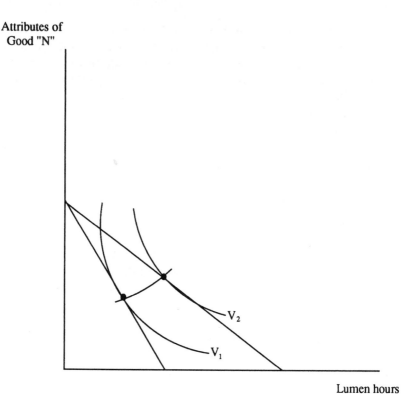

Lumen hours

Figure 7.3. Customer reaction to extension of product life.

substitution effects would lead this customer to purchase more lumen hours, we cannot say that they would also entail the purchase of more bulbs. Indeed, in the example depicted in figure 7.3, we obtain the intuitively acceptable result that while the number of lumen hours increases, the total number of bulbs purchased falls. That result is implicit in the fact that customers now take more value in the form of good N attributes than they did before, in spite of the fact that there have been no changes in the attributes associated with a unit of N.[14] Since we assume no change in the price of light bulbs or in composite good N, and no change in income, if customers purchase more of good N they necessarily purchase fewer light bulbs.

In the above example we see that some improvements may serve to reduce demand for the product. This plausible result appears to run counter to much discussion in the general or wider literature on quality. The usual assumption is that improvements in quality will expand markets. Though it is certainly plausible that a firm that offers improvements to enhance the life of the product may expand its market share, we see that such improvements may very well slow the overall growth of the market. This approach, therefore, provides a useful perspective from which to interpret recent phenomena in the US automobile market, such as the increase in the average age of automobiles in service that is implied by the increase in automobile loan-payoff times to as much as five years. Is it not likely that improvements in durability are imparting a tendency to slow the growth of demand?

Net Customer Value and Market Demand

The analysis of individual customer behavior shows that the reaction to improvements in net customer value is complex, and we face major problems in trying to sort them out. In the previous examples, improvements that increase performance reliability of the product and improvements that extend the life of the product obviously add customer value. As noted, however, those two types of improvements may have different effects on the demand for the product. The improvement in reliability would reduce the opportunity cost shifted from producer to customer. As previously discussed, the customer who pays price P for an automobile also pays for maintenance, non-warranty repairs, time foregone, and so on. Whenever a firm produces less than maintenance-free and operationally perfect products, some cost in addition to the market price reverts to the customer.

It will be useful to picture the demand function in figure 7.4 as one in which a large number of potential customers each exhibit unit demand for a product (say an automobile). The potential customers are then ranked on the basis of willingness to pay, thus yielding a negatively sloped demand curve.[15] The shift of demand to "d'" represents a reduction in shifted opportunity cost. Although we know from discussion in chapters 5 and 6 that cost of production would quite possibly fall simultaneously with

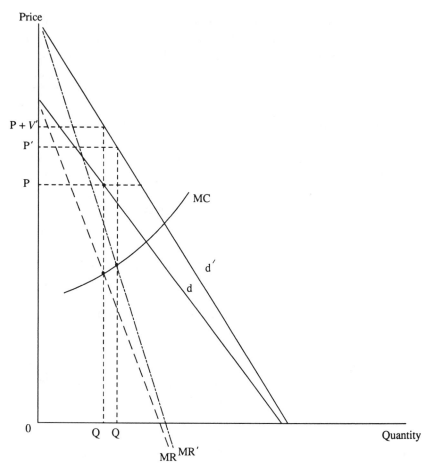

Figure 7.4. Reducing shifted opportunity costs.

improvement in the product, at this point we hold marginal cost constant to isolate the effects of the decrease in shifted opportunity cost. There is no doubt that this type of improvement would increase demand, ceteris paribus. The fact that the shift in the demand curve is disproportionately large at higher prices simply proposes that the demand for quality, by itself, features a negative slope.[16] Specifically, the shift in the demand curve indicates that customer expenditures and opportunity costs related to product shortcomings have reduced. It follows that a customer who was willing to pay a price P for an automobile that would involve an additional opportunity cost of V' would also be willing to pay $P + V'$ for an automobile that did not carry the shifted opportunity cost. Alternatively, at price P, the improvement has the same type of effect on quantity demanded as would obtain if price of the product were lowered. Hence, both total customer value and net customer value have increased.

In our other improvement example, however, in which the life of a product is extended, the effect on demand is uncertain. Imagine, for example, a case in which the life of an electric light bulb is extended from an average of one month to two months and later three months, four months, and so on. As a result, the slope of the demand curve will change in an indeterminate manner. One possible result is shown in figure 7.5 in which the demand has shifted from d to d'' as a result of the longer product life. In this hypothetical case, the product improvement should lead to an increase in the total value (market value plus consumers surplus), as indicated by the change from $OIAQ$ to $OJCQ''$.

Continuing our example, if the improved bulb burns twice as long as the unimproved one (nuisance of changing bulbs = 0), we can see that an informed customer would equate one improved bulb with two unimproved bulbs. The price of the unimproved bulb, therefore, would have to be one-half that of the improved one. Obviously, a firm that could double the life of a light bulb without doubling the cost of production, could become the market leader based on the provision of greater net customer value.

Though we cannot logically determine the market results when net customer value and market value go in the opposite directions, the net customer value concept is a powerful tool for explaining competition among firms. We can say that the price differential between two products with similar end uses will always reflect the difference between the respective instrumental customer values and the nonprice opportunity costs of the two products.[17] Though improvements in durability have the downside of reducing market demand, they should give the innovating firm the potential for a decisive competitive advantage. Thus,

155

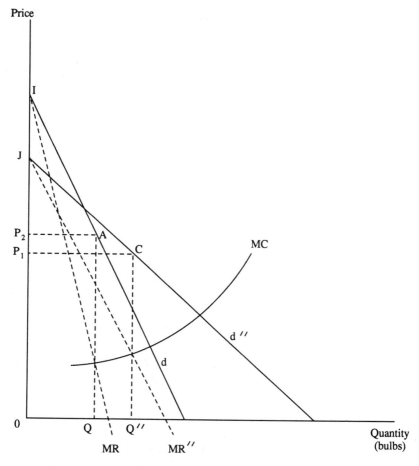

Figure 7.5. Demand and improvements in durability.

improvements may reduce overall market size while simultaneously increasing the market share of the innovator and, of course
squeezing that of the noninnovator.

Customer Demand within the CIF Paradigm

Where the traditional textbook approach takes product characteristics as fixed and then models buying and selling behavior,
mixed competition starts with perceived product differences, es-

pecially in product quality. In the preceding exercises, we assumed the market featured two brands with similar uses in the customer's view, the crucial difference being in quality. It is important to recognize, however, that the competitive advantages of the CIF go far beyond simple differences in product quality. They involve the ability of the firm to discriminate between customers on the basis of individual wants. We have seen, for example, that a major feature of the CIF is flexibility in terms of output mix. Best (1990, 156) maintains that this new system "combines the specialist advantages of a job shop for small batch production with the scale advantages of a flow line for high volume production." Such flexibility was formerly associated with small-scale factories in such industries as machine tools; now it is found in leading Japanese automobile firms and other industries. The so-called "single minute exchange of dies" (SMED) is a prime example of a series of process improvements that promote flexibility. Given that many of the same improvements that increase product quality and add to flexibility also reduce unit cost, we can appreciate that the CIF loses absolutely no competitive advantage by differentiating its output mix. Indeed, the continuous improvement process is geared to improving all aspects of net customer value simultaneously.

The logic of the just-in-time manufacturing system is to produce what individual customers want when they want it. Customer orders are quickly communicated back through the system to the initial input suppliers who begin the movement forward of the components to be machined and assembled to meet that demand.[18] Though customization is the ultimate goal, the currently effective customer for CIF automobile manufacturers is the retail dealer who initiates orders based on the most recent sales experience. In the MP/SM paradigm, by way of contrast, the producer must forecast the estimated demand mix at least a year or more in advance. Because the MP/SM firm needs long runs of identical models and styles in order to achieve conventional economies of scale, it builds up huge inventories which the firm pushes forward to dealers who in turn hope that future market demand lives up to forecasts. It is precisely this difference in approach to demand that accounts for the vast difference in the amount of real estate used by US automobile dealerships as compared to their Japanese counterparts operating in the United States.

The CIF's ability to produce on a flexible basis also promotes the proliferation of styles. We have seen such a proliferation in the automobile industry to the extent that some manufacturers are trying to divide the market into many small niches. If the ultimate goal of continuous improvement is indeed complete customization of the market, the firms that survive will be those that give customers the greatest leeway and assistance in designing their own products with the highest quality and deliver them cheaply, as quickly as possible. That a number of product markets are moving in this direction seems obvious, and nothing could make the eventual demise of the MP/SM paradigm clearer. The implications for the traditional approach to the study of demand are equally ominous. What is the future of an approach that takes the characteristics of the product as given when actual market trends point toward eventual customization?

The situation in which the perfectly flexible CIF is a monopolist has each unit priced to absorb all potential consumer surplus. That is to say, the firm would attempt to engage in perfect price discrimination, producing for individual customers exactly what they want and charging them exactly what they are willing to pay.[19] In the real world, however, the CIF does not find itself in such a monopoly situation; mixed competition between CIFs and MP/SM firms is the order of the day. In the mixed competition setting, the CIF's ability to constantly improve on net customer value is the competitive weapon that forces the MP/SM firm to be a follower. It is to that form of competition that we now turn.

NOTES

1. This paradox is discussed fully in many places including Hirschlifer 1980, 213–14).

2. This approach to the concept of customer value is based upon the work of Carothers and Adams (1991, pp. 33ff). The term "customer value" also appears in Hayes, Wheelwright, and Clark (1988, p. 342), but it is not subjected to formal development, as in the previously mentioned work.

3. These other measures of sacrifice include financial outlays and time lost to provide maintenance, repair, and other operating costs.

4. The concept of customer value is generally compatible with a utility approach. Note, however, that when the focus is on customer value, analytic capabilities broaden. With the utility approach, price and quantity are the relevant variables for decisions that involve the short run. The customer value approach is useful in developing the implications for strategic behavior based upon the internal generation of continuous improvements in the several relevant product attributes. Later we will see that the analysis can focus upon specific sources of value improvement and that in some of those cases value can be measured.

5. We cannot draw the straightforward inference that the net customer value is the total value received less the price. As we shall see, we may have to consider other costs, especially those associated with low quality.

6. In the standard textbook models, the way to get more market share is to feature a lower price relative to rivals.

7. It is, of course, an exaggeration to say that MP/SM firms do not make some product changes and market shifts in the short run. The MP/SM firm should avoid such changes whenever possible because they detract from the ability to gain maximum operating economies. On the other hand, such changes are the basis of the CIF's strength.

8. An implicit element of reliability is consistency, e.g., the absence of noticeable variation in performance. For example, an average distance required for a stop at a given speed may be 100 feet, but the range might vary from 50 feet to 200 feet. This lack of consistency in performance would surely be disconcerting. That a consistent performance would receive a higher value rating should therefore be obvious.

9. The authors recognize the difficulty of separating the instrumental from the aesthetic. There is something aesthetic and something instrumental about a smooth ride or a crisp acceleration. Nevertheless, we ask the reader's forbearance so that we may pursue some interesting implications that otherwise get lost in the tangle of interrelationships.

10. With a given amount of income, the customer can purchase a greater quantity of good A at the lower total opportunity cost $(P_A + O_A)$.

11. The slope of the indifference curve changes because the perceived trade-offs of good A for good N will be different if good A comes to have greater total instrumental value to the customer.

12. Economics textbooks usually assume that production costs increase proportionately as a particular attribute improves. Tirole (1988, 102) says "[u]nit production cost naturally rises with quality."

13. It is usual to think of an attribute improvement arising within the context of R&D expenditures. What happens within the context of total quality management, however, is that the average life of a light bulb can be extended by improving the existing production processes to reduce variation so that the existing equipment-labor combination can produce bulbs to tighter engineering specifications.

14. In Tirole's treatment of the light bulb improvement case (1988, 102), he makes the standard assumption that costs increase parri passu with improvement in the number of lumen/hours per bulb. Hence, consumers are found to be indifferent between one bulb with $2x$ lumen/hours and two bulbs with x lumen/hours.

15. Tirole (1988, 100) uses a similar assumption about demand for his discussion of quality, one which takes place within the context of a trade-off between quality and cost.

16. In order to work with smooth functions, we are making the additional assumption that across customers, the price per unit of quality varies directly with the market price for the product.

17. This statement holds if we assume equal aesthetic value and make the common assumption of perfect and costless information.

18. As we have seen, if the production process is working flawlessly, there will be no need for inspection, inventory, or rework.

19. The validity of this statement rests upon the assumption that no two customers want similar products. If they did, there would still be room for the generation of some consumer surplus.

CHAPTER 8

THE CIF IN MIXED COMPETITION

The term *mixed competition* refers to head-to-head competition in global markets between mass production-scientific management firms and continuous improvement firms. Based upon features described earlier, the CIF has the ability to persistently improve the net customer value associated with its product. Because its improvements emerge on a day-to-day basis, the economist's distinction between the so-called short run and the long run does not apply to it.[1] In a market characterized by mixed competition, the MP/SM firm has no short-term response, other than price reductions, to counteract the growing customer-value content of the CIF's product.

The fact that the CIF's product provides more net customer value establishes it as the market leader. The logic leading to this eventuality is clear. Because of the perceived value difference between the two products, the price charged by the MP/SM firm must lag that of the CIF by an amount that fully reflects the perceived difference in net customer value. The price difference always reflects the value wedge, which itself tends to grow in size over time. The following analysis will show that the existence of this value wedge puts the MP/SM firm at the mercy of the CIF's strategy. If the CIF chooses to maximize its profits, the MP/SM can retain all or most of its market share, but it will suffer reduced profits or incur losses. If the CIF chooses to maximize its market share, the MP/SM firm will find itself in an even more precarious position. It will lose a significant portion of its market share and perhaps incur losses that could eventually force it out of the market.

Mixed Competition

Because of differences in product value and cost and because of paradigmatic differences in outlook, we cannot devise a unique model that logically determines market clearing. It is possible, however, to develop plausible heuristic models that replicate in general some of the recent history of mixed competition.

We can illustrate the impact of value on competition by focusing on ceteris paribus improvements in product quality. From the perspective of the old paradigm, when products with similar functions or end uses differ substantially in terms of quality, for example, they would be analyzed as if sold in separate markets.[2] We must reject that artifice if we are to strengthen our understanding of probably the most important form of business rivalry in our time, interparadigmatic competition or mixed competition. In order to isolate the role of factors other than price, we assume that the market can be initially depicted by a duopoly situation in which two MP/SM firms, labeled "A" and "J," respectively, sell virtually identical products and feature identical cost functions. In such a case, figure 8.1 would depict an initial long-run equilibrium in which quantity $0Q$ and price P reflect a profit maximization situation if each firm's traditional demand is represented by D and cost by MC.

This equilibrium may have been achieved through naive Cournot behavior or through collusion.[3] Note, however, that the customers who pay a price P for quantity $0Q$ of automobiles, for example, also pay for maintenance, non-warranty repairs, and time foregone because of product downtime and/or time spent facilitating repairs, whether or not they are covered by a manufacturer's warranty.[4] Whenever a firm produces less than maintenance-free and operationally perfect products, some opportunity cost in addition to the market price is shifted to the customer, as we discussed earlier with reference to the shift of demand as represented in figure 7.4.[5] There, the shift reflected a reduction in the total opportunity costs as currently perceived by customers, including the prices they are willing to pay plus the present value of expected additional costs resulting from future maintenance and product imperfections, for various quantities of output, ceteris paribus. In that case, for quantity $0Q$ we represented the shifted cost as $[(P + V') - P]$ or V'.

Let us now assume that the "J" firm attains a deus ex machina continuous improvement capability and achieves

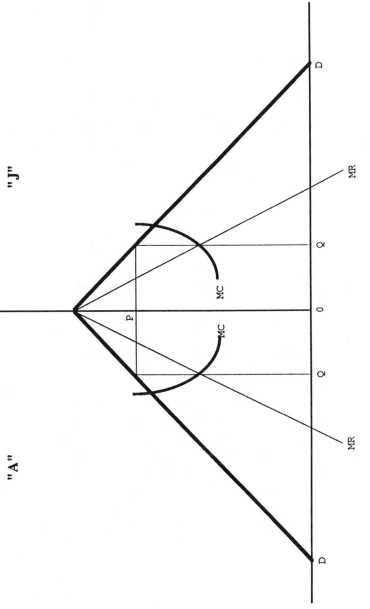

Figure 8.1. The duopoly situation.

elimination of enough product imperfections to reduce the shifted opportunity cost significantly.[6] Assuming that the products of the two firms remain virtually identical in all other respects, the "J" firm's effective demand curve shifts to D_j', as shown in figure 8.2, which represents an increase in the customers' valuation of the product. Furthermore, because the transformation is achieved by the continuous improvement process, unit costs for the "J" firm are reduced and production capacity increased, as reflected in the shift to MC'. Of overriding importance is the fact that the increased net customer value now embedded in its product endows the "J" firm with the role of market leader because at any given price the "J" firm's product provides more net customer value than that of the "A" firm. When the products of the two firms had virtually identical attributes, customers perceived no net comparative difference between them. As the "J" firm improves one or more of its product's attributes, a competitive gap opens up that fully reflects the difference in customer value. That gap is reflected in the distance between D_j and D_j' in figure 8.1, a quantity we shall call V'. The parallel shift requires the simplifying assumption that the improvement in the quality of the product for "J" carries the same value for each potential customer.[7]

We make the simplifying assumption that "J" adopts a profit maximization decision rule – a useful assumption because it helps us illustrate that the success of the CIF does not depend upon such strategies as forsaking profits for market share or such market maneuvers as "dumping," as some have alleged. To maximize its profits the "J" firm would now produce a quantity of output $0Q_j$ offered at price P_j. The "A" firm must now lower its price to $P_j - V'$ in order to provide its customers with an equal net customer value. At any higher price for the product for "A," customers would choose to purchase from the "J" firm because they would receive a higher net customer value. In essence, at any price above $P_j - V'$ the quantity demanded is zero for "A," implying that the "A" firm's demand curve becomes horizontal at the price $P_j - V'$ until it intersects the original demand curve at point G, where it becomes downward sloping. The horizontal portion of its demand curve also represents its marginal revenue curve, which now has a discontinuous segment

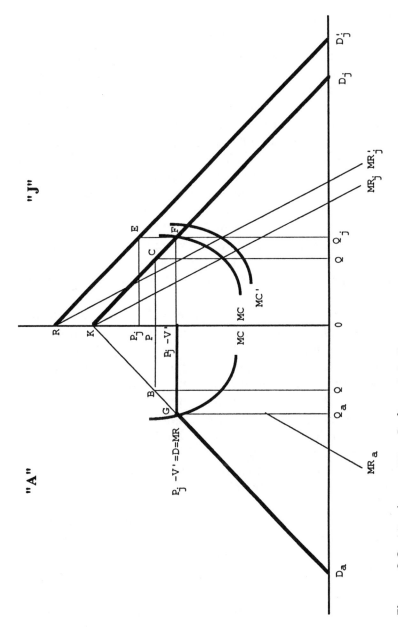

Figure 8.2. Mixed competition: Profit maximization.

between the horizontal and downward-sloping portions.[8] The "A" firm will maximize its profits by producing the quantity Q_a and, as a result, it will retain its 50 percent market share.[9]

An important point to note is that market size, as measured by total quantity, has increased because of an increase in *net customer value*.[10] The nature of the leader-follower relationship results in the MP/SM firm being forced to increase the net customer value of its product, although it has done nothing to improve its inherent value. The only way to accomplish this in the short run is by reducing price. Assuming full and free information, "A" would not find a single customer unless the price differential reflected the full value difference, or V'. Furthermore, if "A" selects a price of $P_j - V'$, all customers are indifferent between the products of the respective firms. Therefore, at prices P_j and $P_j - V'$, market shares are equal at $0Q_j = 0Q_a$, and all potential customers will be indifferent about the market's alternatives.

We should note that net customer value (consumer surplus) has increased (the triangle $P_jRE > PKC$) for the "J" firm's product. At the same time, the "J" firm has increased its price. Because "J" achieves the product improvements simultaneously with cost reductions, the amount of profit is also increasing. Furthermore, "A" offers the same increased net customer value, despite the fact that the "A" firm graph shows no consumer surplus at the price $P_j - V'$. In other words, although A has done nothing to improve the intrinsic value of its product, it has been forced to increase net customer value by GBP ($P_j - V'$). The increase in net customer value, therefore, results in a profit reduction for the "A" firm.

Note also that in the case depicted in figure 8.2, the "J" firm is sharing the increase in customer value with its customers. Furthermore, the internal improvement process of "J" has resulted in a total net customer value increase of $GBCF$ for all customers in the market. In other words, the competitive force of the CIF produces positive externalities in the form of net customer value.

Since many analysts believe the leading Japanese firms pursue greater market share rather than profit maximization, it should be instructive to look at the logic of mixed competition when the CIF chooses to maximize market share subject to a minimally acceptable profit rate (i.e., normal profit). In figure 8.3, we have two firms that began with the same initial situation depicted in figure 8.1, in which they shared the market equally at profit maximizing quantities OQ, with identical product characteristics and costs. "J" then becomes the market leader by "magically" acquiring continuous improvement capabilities. In the present case, the "J" firm decides to use its improved net customer value as a wedge with which to increase market share, as illustrated in figure 8.3 by "J's" choice of price P_j and marketed quantity $0Q_j$, which passes along to customers as much of the value increase as is consistent with covering the average cost of production. This choice forces "A" into a position where its price cannot exceed $P_j - V'$. With its marginal revenue determined by its competitor's price minus the value differential $(P_j - V')$, "A" would face a loss-minimizing quantity of $0Q_a$ and a market-share protection quantity of $0Q_a'$. Given the structure of cost, "A" clearly cannot protect its market share and would have to reduce its output to minimize its losses in the short run.

At this juncture, a shortage would exist in the market equal to the difference between $0Q_a' - 0Q_a$. Therefore, this equilibrium is not stable, and customers can be expected to shift to "J" firm's product. Because the "J" firm's demand curve will shift outward so long as a shortage exists, the new equilibrium will occur at price P_j', where "J" maximizes market share and "A" firm's marginal cost equals marginal revenue ($P_j' - V'$) at the kink. Thus, the stable equilibrium will occur with "J" producing the quantity $0Q_j'$ at price P_j', and the "A" producing $0Q_a''$ at the price $P_j' - V'$. Note, however, that this action results in "J" firm's demand increasing to D_j'', while "A" firm's demand falls to D_a' in our example. Clearly, in such a scenario, "J" has translated its market power into significant gains in market share. In the long run, "A" faces the necessity of reducing its cost of production or leaving the market. If "A" chooses to compete only by reducing cost, e.g., to become lean through diet, it's CIF competition undoubtedly will engage in persistent efforts to further widen the customer-value wedge between the respective products.

Some may say that what we see here is perhaps no more than the segmentation of a market as usually discussed. It is customary to talk about automobiles, for example, as segmented

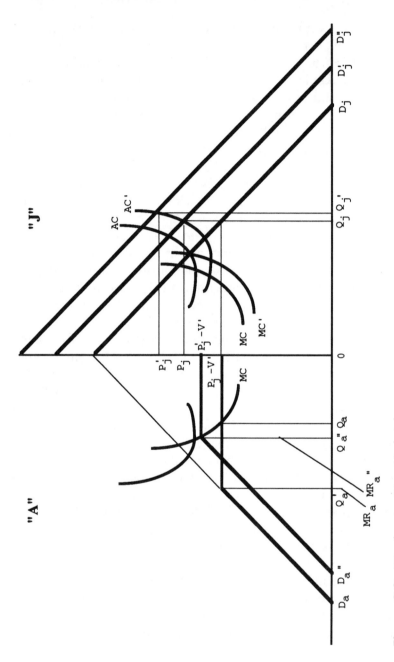

Figure 8.3. Mixed competition: Market share.

into high-priced and low-priced submarkets. The foregoing scenario depicts much more than that, however. The standard view of market segmentation may be exemplified by comparing Mercedes Benz with the Ford Escort. The expensive auto reflects higher performance, more and better features, better materials, and so on. The higher-priced car obviously costs more to manufacture and hence carries a higher price tag. In our mixed competition example, on the other hand, we have stipulated that the respective vehicles are identical except in terms of reliability; the "J" product requires fewer repairs and less maintenance. We have stipulated that there is no discernible difference in terms of performance and features. Furthermore, because of the synergism between quality improvements and cost improvements, "J" offers lower cost per unit, not higher. Therefore, we must recognize this scenario as one in which the high-cost producer must accept the low-priced market segment. In that regard a significant aspect of real-world mixed competition is reflected in figure 8.3.

CIF's Goal Is Market Differentiation

Because value is based ultimately on personal characteristics and individual perceptions, an obvious goal for a flexible CIF is development of the capability to allow each customer to order a customized product. In the case of a monopoly CIF, the firm's efforts might be to design for each customer a product so differentiated that it could levy a price to eliminate all consumer surplus. (Customers, of course, might look for ways to conceal their true valuations, in which case intricate bargaining strategies could result.) In the case of mixed competition, the greater the consumer surplus derived from improvements of any kind, the lower the rival's price must be. In the case where competition is between CIFs, each firm would try to offer each potential customer more net customer value than the rival firms, by some combination of product improvement and price reduction. In this form of competition, the CIF with the product that provides the greatest net customer value would be the market leader, and it would force the rival CIF to feature a price discount.

Expanding the Analysis

It might appear that once the "J" firm reduced its shifted opportunity costs to zero, the only remaining economic role for continuous improvement would be the attempt to reduce the cost of production. It should be noted, however, that the functional design of the product should also have room for improvements that could result in financial and opportunity-cost savings not previously captured in the net-customer-value calculations.[11] For example, an increase in the number of miles an automobile can travel between tune-ups or a reduction in the need to lubricate parts can raise the product's value to the customer. The impact can be illustrated by reference to figure 8.3. If the "J" firm provides state-of-the-art functional design improvements, its demand (D_j and D_j') would shift to the right.[12] Accordingly, the value gap V' would increase for the "A" firm, indicating a potential loss of market share.

If we limit our analysis to market efficiency and focus on the activity of the "J" firm as portrayed in the foregoing exercises, we may tend to be critical of the welfare implications of continuous improvement. With market price and cost as measuring rods, we see that "J's" price has risen while its costs have fallen and marketed quantity remains less than optimum. From a net-customer-value perspective, however, the total cost to customers (price plus opportunity cost) has fallen. Both firms, therefore, provide an increase in net customer value. Thus, market power and net customer value have increased together, with the latter paving the way for the former. One could argue that if the market were supplied by many small competitors, an efficient outcome would result, passing all of the increased net customer value (V plus cost reductions) to customers. It would be necessary, however, to include the stipulation that such firms have the ability to simultaneously reduce the cost of production and remove the opportunity costs that had been shifted to customers.

Application beyond Consumer Goods Markets

The competitive behavior just portrayed is not limited to firms in consumer-goods markets. Considerations of product quality and timely delivery now call into question the usefulness of the standard distinction made between differentiated and non-differentiated products. Clearly, aspects of net customer value beyond price are pertinent for products heretofore considered nondifferentiated, such as sheet steel, plate glass, and bulk newsprint. In the case of sheet steel, the ability to produce very close to engineering specifications is a measure of quality. Significant variation in thickness may mean "thin spots" in the roll that lead to tearing and stoppages in the customer's operations unless the production line slows to accommodate them. In any event, costs are driven up by the characteristics of the input.[13] Therefore, the steel manufacturer that can reduce variation to a minimum will succeed in reducing the operating costs of its downstream customers.

Moreover, with the increasing importance of "just-in-time" manufacturing, the steel firm that can deliver its product precisely when needed gains a competitive advantage. This ability is a hallmark of the CIF and serves to differentiate its product from that of the MP/SM firm. Like improved quality, it provides additional value to the input user by reducing its operating costs. The competitive implications of timely delivery and improved input quality are illustrated in figure 8.3, where, for the "J" firm, the difference between D and D' is now taken to represent reductions in customer's inventory carrying costs and cost reductions deriving from the elimination of downtime and slow runs associated with quality variations. The ensuing analysis would then demonstrate the same type of leader-follower relationship that we saw resulting from reliability improvements.

Conclusion

In the new global economy, competitive advantage derives from improvements in net customer value associated with the

171

product. So long as there are perceived differences in the value provided by the respective products of the CIF and the MP/SM firm, there will be a wedge between their prices, the size of which will tend to grow over time.

The CIF produces improvements in customer value as part and parcel of its normal operations, often without an investment cost. Indeed, the improvements in customer value are often accompanied by falling unit cost. The MP/SM firm, on the other hand, associates product improvements with new technology. In its view, both the new (improved) product and the processes that make it are developed eternally to the firm's manufacturing operations (and often, externally to the firm). For the MP/SM firm, therefore, improvements always have a cost that puts it at a double disadvantage. Not only does it have to pay for improvements that the CIF can have without cost; its need to adapt externally produced technology places the MP/SM in a time lag behind the CIF. In more ways than one, the MP/SM firm is the follower in the new global competition.

NOTES

1. In the standard theory of the firm, changes in the productive capacity of a firm or changes in technology require investment. The long run is a period of time sufficient to change the amounts of all inputs, including technology and productive capacity. The short run is any period shorter than that. The distinction is purely conceptual.

2. The degree of substitutability between the two products would then be reflected in the slopes of the respective demand curves.

3. In this initial position, plant size, cost functions, and product characteristics are all identical. Therefore, we have an a priori reason for assuming that the two firms would initially collude to set price and share markets.

4. If the product were a television or stereo, the loss could be measured in terms of time spent and utility foregone. In any case, the proposition that the consumer would view maintenance and poor product quality as an opportunity cost should fit comfortably with economic doctrine.

5. "Perfect" product would be defined in relation to the state of the art. The 'state of the art' may change over time and affect demand. For example, a firm's improvements in the manufacturing of its automobile engines that extend the average mileage before a major overhaul enhances the state of the art for automobiles.

6. The deus ex machina assumption begs the question of how an MP/SM firm becomes a CIF. Toyota's journey from mass production to continuous improvement was an internally generated evolutionary trip that took about two decades. Past experience is not necessarily binding on other firms, however. Some may opt for revolutionary change that would involve investment in the soft technologies of continuous improvement. We discuss this type of innovational approach in chapter 10. Also, see note 5 of chapter 6 for additional treatment of the deus ex machina assumption.

7. As noted in chapter 7, there is reason to believe that the gap between D_j and D_j' would decrease as the demand curve moves downward and to the right. See note 16 in chapter 7 and the attendant discussion.

8. The relationship between the demand and MR curves is similar to that found in the kinked-demand curve model sometimes used to depict oligopoly behavior in standard economic theory.

9. Should the "A" firm's MC curve intersect its MR within the horizontal portion, its profit-maximizing quantity would represent less than a 50 percent market share. Such a solution would also create a shortage in the market equal to the difference between Q_a and the profit-maximizing output, thus creating a dilemma for the "J" firm. The "J" firm would either have to raise its price or increase its output to satisfy the excess quantity demanded. If the "J" firm raises its price, it will rise until the "A" firm's MC intersects MR (p_j' − V) exactly at the kink creating a stable solution, but the "J" firm will no longer be maximizing its profits. If the "J" firm chooses to increase

output to satisfy the excess demand, its demand curve would effectively shift further to the right, and the "A" firm's demand curve would shift to the left until the kink was at the intersection of its *MR* curve. Alternatively, if the "J" firm does nothing, secondary markets would develop in which the product would sell at a premium over the "J" firm's price.

10. The increase in market size is not dependent upon an increase in total market demand or a reduction in average market price. Neither of those things occur in this case.

11. This functional design aspect is of little importance in basic intermediate industries such as paper, steel, and chemicals.

12. For purposes of developing our argument, we ignore the likelihood that some design improvements may have aesthetic dimensions that would also impact demand.

13. Moreover, the greater the spread of variation in the width of rolls produced by the supplier, the wider on average the rolls must be in order to meet the critical minimum specification on all rolls. Wider average also means higher cost.

A CONTRADICTORY WORLD OF
COMPETING PARADIGMS

Throughout the book we have made comparisons between the CIF and the mass production/scientific management firm, sometimes as Weberian ideal types and other times as descriptions of real firms competing in real markets. Several of the characteristics of the CIF and MP/SM firms that we have discussed in earlier chapters will be revisited here with an emphasis on their relationships to the respective paradigms. The point here is to show how characteristics of the CIF that appear to be contradictory when refracted through the prism of the MP/SM paradigm are logical when viewed from the framework of the CIF paradigm. We also argue that the MP/SM paradigm has become a set of blinders for Western managers confronted with the CIF in global markets, making it more difficult for them to respond to this new form of competition. The actions of the new firms make sense only when their study is directed through the lens of the new paradigm.

The concept of paradigm used here is that explained by Thomas S. Kuhn in *The Structure of Scientific Revolutions* (1970). Kuhn applies the term paradigm to achievements that share the following two characteristics: (a) the "achievement was sufficiently unprecedented to attract an enduring group of adherents away from competing modes of scientific activity," and (b) "it was sufficiently open-ended to leave all sorts of problems for the redefined group of practitioners to resolve." (10) Kuhn explains his choice of the term paradigm "to suggest that some accepted examples of actual scientific practice . . . provide models from which spring particular coherent traditions of scientific research." He goes on to identify some implications for practitioners of a discipline who have accepted a paradigm. He states, "[t]he study of paradigms . . . is what mainly prepares the student for membership in the particular scientific community with which he will later practice. Because he there joins men who learned the bases of their field from the same concrete models, his subsequent practice will seldom evoke overt disagreement over fundamentals." (10–11)

The use of the term paradigm throughout this book is meant to suggest similar implications for MP/SM firms and CIFs. The vast majority of owners and managers of Western firms were prepared for entry into the field of business through indoctrination in standard economic theory and/or the business disciplines that are grounded in standard economic theory. As a result, there is little disagreement over the fundamental beliefs that the primary objective of the firm is to maximize the net present value of the firm, that competitive markets result in an efficient allocation of resources, that specialization of the labor force improves economic efficiency, that economies of scale reduce costs of production and give a firm a competitive advantage, that top-down management is necessary to overcome the principal-agent problem, and that quality improvements always have opportunity costs. On the other hand, after World War II the owners and managers of Japanese firms developed their own paradigm, based on the notion of continuous improvement as taught by Deming, Juran, and others. They, too, have a set of fundamental beliefs over which there is little disagreement. Because these beliefs, when viewed through the lens of the mass production/scientific management paradigm, appear to be contradictions, the decisions engendered by them appear to be wrong-headed and counterproductive. In this chapter we will review some of the characteristic beliefs of the CIF and show them to be logically consistent when viewed through the context of the continuous improvement paradigm.

Contradictory Attributes

Some of the beliefs embedded in the continuous improvement paradigm that may be perceived as contradictory when viewed from the perspective of the mass production paradigm, include:

1. The firm first should seek to continuously provide customer value and use it to earn increased profits.

2. Economies of scale and economies of flexibility are complementary sources of competitive advantage.
3. Top-down and bottom-up decision making are necessary for the prosperity of the firm.
4. Specialization of tasks must be combined with a generalization of the labor force.
5. An efficient allocation of resources requires a combination of competition, cooperation, and some barriers to enter into domestic markets.

Producer Value and Customer Value

Standard economic theory emphasizes the importance of profit maximization and price competition which in perfectly competitive markets, it is argued, results in allocative and productive efficiency. The implication is that the stockholders' interest in maximizing profits should be given priority because it will be consistent with society's interests in an efficient allocation of resources, as demonstrated in the static analysis of standard price theory. In practice the emphasis placed on pursuing shareholders' interests in the MP/SM firm results in a management philosophy driven by the need for the firm to continuously earn adequate profits in the short run to avoid adverse effects on the price of the firm's stock. Within this system, a failure to show adequate profits can result in a precipitant decline in the price of the corporation's stock, which, in turn, can result in either a takeover of the firm, in which management is likely to be replaced, or stockholder pressure on the board of directors to remove the managers responsible for the decline in the share price. Standard economic theory assumes that the firm maximizes profits (i.e., producer value) in the short run, requiring the firm to minimize its costs of production. Within the MP/SM paradigm, because higher product quality results in higher costs, an inverse relationship exists between customer value and producer value, ceteris paribus. Typically, the MP/SM firm settles for a significant level of flawed production because the additional cost of removing the remaining defects often exceeds the additional revenue that would be gained from doing so. Thus, the MP/SM firm's objective of maximizing profits in the short run contradicts the pursuit of product perfection and, in general, the provision of increased customer value only becomes the MP/SM firm's pursuit when it will quickly increase its profit.

Within the CIF paradigm, the stockholders' interests do not predominate but instead balance against the interests of other corporate stakeholders (e.g., customers, suppliers, employees). The financial institutions, as the primary stockholders, prefer reinvestment of profits for long-term growth and stability rather than short-term increases in dividends and capital gains. This policy is reflected in the CIF's organizational objectives, which "emphasize growth objectives, such as increased market share and new product ratio . . ." (Kagano et al. 1984, 36), and in its strategy, which tends toward long-term resource accumulation and a pattern of only slowly withdrawing from disappointing markets (40–1). As a result, corporate management is free to pursue the corporation's long-term development without interference from the stockholders unless confronted with a crisis. Consequently, increased emphasis is placed on the interests of other stakeholders. As noted, the labor force is largely immobile and the employees' interests are closely tied to those of the firm. The CIF management generally takes a paternalistic attitude toward the employees' interests and places them on a par with the stockholders' interests.

The CIF is also influenced by the interests of stakeholders outside the firm, for instance the maintenance of close long-term relationships with its suppliers. The Japanese CIF primarily maintains these relationships within the *kereitsu,* which requires that it take actions necessary to fulfill its obligations to the member firms. In summarizing the attitude of the CIFs toward these long-term relationships Kagano et al. (1984, 35) state, "Japanese firms emphasize 'relationship' itself and try to build and maintain good relationships with exchange partners even when the relationships create more constraints than benefits."

The stakeholder toward whom the CIF shows its greatest concern, however, is the customer. The CIF begins with the goal of continuously improving net customer value (see chapter 7) and as a result expects to further the interests of all other stakeholders. As an example of this priority, the CIF strives for 100 percent perfection in the production process. This approach enables the CIF to develop flexible manufacturing, which has the prerequisite of zero or near zero defects. As discussed in chapters 5 and 6, economies of flexibility are achieved when small batch production is possible at mass production costs. In its ideal version it produces single units of output without inventories of intermediate inputs in response to customer demand. In a less perfect mode, small lots of output are produced with very little inventory in anticipation of customer demand over the very short run. In such a scenario, there is a direct, rather than inverse, relationship between customer value (e.g., product quality) and producer value (i.e., profits), ceteris paribus.

The direct relationship between customer value and producer value can be illustrated with reference to the Toyota's just-in-time production system. JIT is based on a pulling system (*kanban*) and a sequence schedule. As explained in greater detail in chapter 3, the sequence schedule specifies the order in which the variety of products come through the assembly lines, with the sequence timed so that one unit is completed as the next unit on the schedule is introduced to the line. When the final assembly of a product begins, each worker goes to the immediately preceding process to withdraw a part. In each case, the *kanban* system signals for a replacement for the withdrawn part in an ongoing process that takes place throughout the CIF's and supplier's plant for all parts, subassemblies, and final assembly.

Within this system, defects in parts or products are costly because they cannot be immediately replaced out of inventory. If a worker goes to the preceding process for a needed input and upon returning to the assembly position determines that the part is defective, the line must stop while the worker returns to the preceding process to have the defect corrected or wait for a replacement part to be produced. However, not only does the flow of that particular process and its preceding process have to stop, but so does the entire production line. The continuation of the other operations would put scheduled production out of synchronization, and at the end of the day some parts would be produced in excessive amounts and others in deficient amounts. Such a production process cannot operate at a rate of 90 or 95 percent of perfection. To do so would cause the production process to shut down repeatedly. The result would be increased costs of production to the detriment of profits and producer value. Therefore, for the CIF, the higher the customer value (i.e., product quality) the lower the cost of production and the greater the producer value (i.e., profitability).

The emphasis on customer value also serves the interests of other stakeholders (e.g., management, workers, and suppliers), because it promotes the growth of the firm and increases the CIF's market share. Improved customer value attracts more sales over time, which requires increased production (see chapter 8) and probably leads to greater employment opportunities for the workers (and/or greater job security), an increase in the number of management positions as the firm grows, and increased demand for supplier inputs. Each of these outcomes appeals to the varied interests of the firm's stakeholders, rather than primarily serving the interests of the stockholders, as profit maximization does.

Note also that the customer-value approach enables the employees to internalize the firm's goal. They can directly relate the quality of their work to value perceptions of the customers. In other words, most of the improvements generated within the CIF have an instrumental value that allows employees to know ex ante that customers will appreciate the changes ex post. In addition, the worker can perform these responsibilities enthusiastically because they are consistent with the employee's interest in job security and wage growth. By contrast, in the profit-maximizing MP/SM firm the employee cannot relate directly to the firm's goal. Higher profits within the MP/SM paradigm are consistent with reducing costs of production, which includes employees' wages. Workers typically perceive the speeding up of the production process and improvements in the production process that reduce labor requirements, to be consistent with the firm's profit-maximization goal, but inconsistent with their own interests.

Thus, the belief that the firm should continuously improve customer value seems contradictory when viewed from the perspective of the profit-maximizing MP/SM firm. When viewed from the perspective of the CIF, which is organized to serve the interests of all stakeholders, customer-value priority has evolved precisely because it is consistent with the interests of all the CIF's stakeholders.

Top-Down and Bottom-Up Decision Making

A second fundamental belief held by adherents to the CIF paradigm relates to the locus of decision-making authority of the firm. The CIF is organized to take advantage of both top-down and bottom-up decision making, which from the perspective of the MP/SM paradigm appears contradictory. The MP/SM paradigm holds that the firm is a hierarchical organization within which control emanates downward from owners through management to the level of the operators. In standard economics, agency theory explicitly reflects this viewpoint. In the joint-stock firm, absentee stockholders are considered principals and the professional managers their agents, who in turn, hire workers as their agents. The emphasis in agency theory is on creating effective financial controls and incentives to ensure that the stockholders' interests prevail over the interests of managers and workers. Thus, decisions made by the stockholders determine the actions to be carried out by management and labor.

The CIF paradigm, however, combines top-down decision making with bottom-up decision making, which in part reflects the diminished importance of stockholders' interests and the correspondingly enhanced importance of other stakeholders' interests. Matsumoto's analysis of stock cross-holding among Japanese firms shows the extent to which stockholders' interest are diminished in the CIF. He states, "[a]ny influence [stockholders] do exert . . . is based more on their role as a financial institution or the stability of their business relationship with the corporation in question." (Matsumoto January 1982, 33) The CIF functions to serve a much more diverse set of interests than the single purpose of short-term maximization of the firm's net present value on behalf of the stockholders. Aoki refers to this as "The Third Duality Principle." He states, "[t]he corporate management decisions of Japanese firms are subject to the dual control (influence) of financial interests (ownership) and employees' interests rather than to unilateral control in the interests of ownership." (Aoki, 20)

Within the CIF top management exerts top-down decision

making by establishing the strategic vision of the firm through sharing values and information. In a comparison of Japanese and Western corporations, Hamel and Prahalad argue that CIF managers "approach strategy from a perspective that is fundamentally different from that which underpins Western management thought." (Hamel and Prahalad 1985, 63) They identify the role of top Japanese managers as determining the "strategic intent" of the corporation.

> [S]trategic intent envisions a desired leadership position and establishes the criterion the organization will use to chart its progress. . . . The concept also encompasses an active management process that includes: focusing the organization's attention on the essence of winning; motivating people by communicating the value of the target; leaving room for individual and team contributions; sustaining enthusiasm by providing new operational definitions as circumstances change; and using intent consistently to guide resource allocations (64).

Their research indicates that companies that rose to positions of global leadership over the past 20 years were obsessed with strategic intent.

This top-down decision making in the CIF is combined with bottom-up decision making, in which conflict is resolved through broad consultation (see chapter 3 on *ringi* and *nemawashi*). This policy places great decision-making responsibilities on middle- and lower-level managers, who must work closely with employees at all levels discussing problems, communicating decisions, and coordinating activities. Managers are, as a result, intimately involved in all aspects of the production process. They participate in product design, where "[i]nterminable discussions among engineering, production, quality assurance, and sales personnel take place before the design is made final." (Hayes 1981, 62) Once production begins, they work closely with production workers, "training [them] to deliver consistently high-quality products while developing in them expectations of producing high quality." (62) Lower-level managers, too, are a key link between labor and upper management. Matsumoto states, "[t]he major role of the Japanese foreman, rather than to manage the workplace, is to function as a personal leader within the workplace, to guide the work teams and to convey the feelings of the people in the factory to the management." (Matsumoto March 1982, 41) The middle- and lower-level managers, thus, play a crucial role in the horizontal communications network that is so important to the effective functioning of the CIF.

Production workers similarly have a wide range of decision-making responsibilities. They not only perform the typical production tasks, but in conjunction with management, they also help plan and organize production, ensure quality control, maintain equipment, and initiate suggestions for process and product improvements. In line with their extensive responsibilities, the production workers in the CIF also have adequate decision-making authority to carry them out.

Because extensive involvement of production workers, along with upper- middle- and lower-level managers, makes decision making in the CIF more complicated than it is in a MP/SM firm, a widespread system of joint labor-management conferences has evolved in the Japanese CIF. "In this system, problems of all sizes common to both employees and management are worked out by means of consultation between employees and management. Such problems include: rearrangement of production lines, new factory installations, moves into overseas markets, work environments, safety measures, and welfare policies." (Matsumoto January 1982, 34) In reference to Japanese firms, Matsumoto concludes, "[w]hether a decision is made at the top or the bottom of the corporate ladder depends on the type of decision to be made and whether it is best resolved by employees or management." (34) The upshot is that in the CIF, top management establishes the firm's vision and values and shares information rather than instituting financial controls to influence employee behavior, allowing those at lower levels greater authority and responsibility to make decisions with important ramifications for the well-being of the firm. While this approach would be contradictory within the context of the profit-maximizing MP/SM firm, it is wholly consistent with the diverse objectives of the CIF.

Economies of Scale and Flexible Production

A third tenet of the CIF paradigm, to simultaneously achieve economies of scale and flexible production, has given the CIF a strong competitive presence in a wide range of markets. Since the introduction of mass-production technology, economies of scale have driven the MP/SM firm to seek larger and larger production runs. Yet, to achieve the volume of production that would provide the maximum benefits from economies of scale, the MP/SM firm's production has been limited to the styles or types of each product for which a mass market exists.

The CIF likewise enjoys economies of scale that derive from capital investment in production facilities with high capacity of output. The continuous improvement process, however, has allowed the CIF to go beyond economies of scale to achieve economies of flexibility (see chapter 6). As noted throughout this book, the management and organizational structure of the CIF is particularly adept at incremental change. Over time, the incremental and breakthrough improvements alter the system to such an extent that a view of the present operation would look like a major internal innovation when compared with a "snapshot" of the operation several years earlier. In addition to improvement in the effectiveness of the throughput, breakthrough improvements, such as rapid die changes, *kanban,* and *poka-yoke,* have allowed the CIF to develop innovative production systems that feature:

(a) extremely flexible product design and product mix
(b) rapid response to changes in market demand
(c) greater control, accuracy, and repeatability of processes for better quality
(d) reduced changeover costs
(e) greater information
(f) faster throughput

This phenomenon is described in chapter 6 as economies of flexibility.

The ultimate goal of flexible manufacturing (in the ideal type) is to produce in lot sizes of one unit at an average cost equal to that of lot sizes equal to plant capacity, which means almost an infinite variety of products. Though the ideal has not been reached, some CIFs have been able to compete in a large number of specialized market niches while producing at the low unit costs associated with economies of scale. Furthermore, traditional economies of scale derived from nonproduction activities (e.g., marketing) are important to the CIF. CIFs typically acquire access to economies of scale in nonproduction activities through their relationships with other firms, as reflected in the following statement by Kuniyasu Sakai:

> Japan's giant industrial combines . . . do not develop all of their product line, nor do they manufacture it. In reality, these huge businesses are more like "trading companies." That is, rather than design and manufacture their own goods, they actually coordinate a complex design and manufacturing process that involves thousands of smaller companies. The goods you buy with a famous maker's name inscribed on the case are seldom the product of that company's factory – and often not even the product of its own research. Someone else designed it, someone else put it in a box with the famous maker's name on it and then shipped it to its distributors (Sakai 1990, 39).

Thus, the CIF, like the MP/SM firm enjoys economies of scale in its production and nonproduction activities. Within the MP/SM paradigm, mass production is the antithesis of flexible production, limited to small-scale producers who forego economies of scale. Within the CIF paradigm, however, flexible manufacturing is an extension of mass production. By taking advantage of economies of flexibility rather than settling for the traditional economies of scale in production activities the CIF gains strategic advantages over its MP/SM rival. The CIF can compete in a wider variety of markets or market niches, respond more quickly to changes in consumer demand without large losses resulting from obsolete inventories, produce better quality products at costs comparable with (or lower than) those of mass-production firms, and, possibly of greatest importance, take advantage of an increased flow of information to generate organizational learning for the continuous improvement of products and production processes.

Specialization and Generalization

A fourth attribute of the CIF paradigm relates to the type of work force that is best suited to achieve the potential benefits of continuous improvement. The CIF fosters a work force of generalists rather than the specialists found in the MP/SM firm. The traditional approach to organizing manpower within the MP/SM paradigm is based on the principles of scientific management pioneered by Frederick Taylor at the turn of the century. The basic principle of scientific management is the separation of planning (the prerogative of management) from doing (the workers' realm). Managers plan and organize the activities of every worker based, in principle, on time-and-motion studies to objectively determine the most efficient method of production. This approach has resulted in the intricate coordination by management of a labor force in which each person specializes in one production task. As discussed in chapter 2, Adam Smith first espoused the idea of specialization of labor, and it has been incorporated into the MP/SM paradigm as an important source of economies of scale.

The concept of specialization has survived in the CIF paradigm as an important source of economies of scale. Tasks are specialized. That is, production breaks down into the manufacture of component parts which, in turn, break down into tasks and subtasks, as in the MP/SM firm. As a result the CIF obtains the same economies of scale in production as the MP/SM firm does. Scientific management, however, is ineffective in the CIF because the continuous improvement process is based upon an interdependence, rather than a separation, of planning and doing. Thus, the requirement of the continuous improvement process and economies of flexibility mandate the type of work force needed by the CIF, a work force of generalists who help to plan the specialized tasks in addition to carrying them out.

Not only must the workers be generalists to deal with the exigencies of the CIF production process; they must also be highly educated, skilled, and dedicated. Production workers are hired upon graduation from secondary school or a technical college in which they have shown to be both literate and mathematically competent. Management trainees are hired upon graduation from the university well-versed in advanced mathematics, engineering, and/or natural sciences. The CIF seeks to leverage this well-educated work force's knowledge of theoretical principles by supplementing it with extensive training (see chapter 4).

The CIF also employs job-rotation schemes to instill in all employees a comprehensive understanding of the production process. The worker further develops into a generalist through quality-control groups whose members share useful insights while seeking to improve the product and production process (see chapter 4). As a result, the CIF's production workers are skilled at all the production tasks within their departments and are familiar with the production process beyond their own departments. Likewise, managers of the CIF are experienced in all the functional divisions of the firm, enabling them to understand the firm's interrelated operations and to successfully guide the improvement process.

The labor force's dedication to improving the products and production processes in the Japanese CIF is entailed by the lifetime employment system in which the future success of the employees is intimately tied to that of the firm. The surest way for them to increase their standard of living and ensure their continued employment is to contribute to the improvement of the firm's products and production processes.

In addition to an educated and dedicated labor force, extensive training, and job rotation are necessary to achieve continuous improvement. If the workers are to use their autonomy effectively to solve problems and improve products, the firm must also give the workers the authority and responsibility to plan their production activities. We noted earlier how the workers in the CIF, in conjunction with management, plan the production tasks they are to carry out. In order for this to be done effectively, the CIF provides employees with access to information and an understanding of how each task fits into the overall production process. Information-sharing among all employees has thus become routine in the CIF.

Thus, the MP/SM firm, which separates the planning of production from the doing, is best able to achieve economies of scale and efficiency through the employment of specialists. The CIF, on the other hand, achieves the efficiencies associated with economies of scale by dividing the production process into cialized tasks, but it does not extend this specialization to the work force. The work force is one of generalists who add an additional element of efficiency associated with economies of flexibility. The specialist workers of the MP/SM firm are much less effective at contributing to the improvement process because they lack a comprehensive understanding of production beyond their own work stations and because they have insufficient information and authority upon which to base suggestions.

Competition, Cooperation, Barriers to Entry, and Efficiency

In standard economic theory, freedom of entry into markets is directly related to the efficiency of the market. Freedom of entry ensures that markets remain competitive and that the benefits of innovation accrue not only to the firm but also to the consumer. Product and production process innovations can generate economic profits for the firm in the short run, but those economic profits create the incentive for new firms to enter the market in the absence of barriers to entry. With the entry of new firms into the market, prices fall to the level of average and marginal costs of production. The decrease in price benefits the consumers and eliminates economic profits in the long run. Thus, the analysis concludes that freedom of entry is necessary to ensure competition and the efficient allocation of resources. If there are barriers to entry, the profit-maximizing innovator will keep the price of the product above average and marginal costs of production, and the economic profits will continue indefinitely, with an implicit inefficient allocation of resources.

In a wide array of Japan's domestic markets, however, various barriers to entry present difficulties for new firms. Outsiders see these barriers to entry as inefficient and unfair, especially to Western firms, and we hear frequent demands for a "levelling of the playing field" through their removal. Within the Japanese version of the CIF paradigm, however, barriers to entry and the firm's efficiency are consistent. As discussed throughout, efficiency in the CIF results from the continuous improvement process based on the lifetime employment system and the firm's concern for the interests of all its stakeholders. Freedom of entry can represent a threat to these features of the CIF.

Consider a scenario in which a new product gives a firm a competitive advantage in a market. If the demand for its product is adequate, the MP/SM firm will set the price to maximize economic profits in the short run. In the absence of barriers to entry, new firms will have incentives to enter this market until the economic profits have been eliminated. Notwithstanding the assumptions of standard price theory, firms in the real world do not have perfect information about consumer demand. In many instances the existence of economic profits encourages new entrants beyond the optimum level, creating excess productive capacity in the market and putting downward pressure on the price of the product. Eventually some, or all, of the firms will begin to suffer losses, which sooner or later will force those firms to reduce productive capacity, terminate some employees, and alter contracts with resource suppliers.

An alternative scenario begins in the same manner: A firm develops a new product giving it a competitive advantage in the market. In the face of barriers to entry, new firms cannot quickly enter the market. Given an adequate market demand, the growth-oriented CIF will set a price for the product that enables it to increase the volume of production over time, subject to some profit constraint. It does this so as to increase its employment opportunities, expand its purchases of inputs from suppliers, and assure the profitability and long-term survival of the firm. The interests of the firm's stakeholders are met and the lifetime employment system remains intact. Further improvements in both product and production processes will result in greater production efficiencies and possible price reductions in the future.

As discussed in chapter 3, the typical Japanese manufacturer operates within an environment dominated by industrial groups, or *kereitsu*. The *kereitsu* elicits a loyalty among the firms that makes it difficult for outsiders to enter a market, particularly firms selling intermediate goods, because the potential buyers have already established long-term relationships with other suppliers. But firms selling consumer goods can also find it difficult to purchase intermediate goods from the established firms within the *kereitsus* and, therefore, must find alternative sources. As previously argued, the CIF puts a greater emphasis on corporate growth and market share than on earning profits in the short run, although profits are necessary in the long run for the survival of the firm. Competition is a driving force in the pursuit of these objectives. Competition, however, is not limited to nor centered on price competition. Competition primarily takes place on the floor of the manufacturing facility – a Schumpeterian-type competition. The basis for competition is found in the continuous improvement process. The CIF attempts to achieve a competitive advantage over its rivals through improvements in the production processes that allow it to provide a high-quality product at a competitive price. Product improvements and flexible manufacturing systems also give the CIF a dynamic competitive advantage in both shaping consumer preferences and otherwise responding to changes in demand. Abernathy, Clark and Kantrow make the point in stating, "The primary sources of this advantage are found . . . in the Japanese producers' mastery of . . . a well-designed strategy based on the shrewd use of manufacturing excellence." (Abernathy, Clark, & Kantrow 1981, 74) Also, Kagano et al. state, "Japanese firms stress finding their 'niche' and strategies of product differentiation in order to gain competitive advantage." (Kagano et al. 1984, 41)

The intense Schumpeterian-type competition among the CIFs is, however, coupled with cooperation or coordination among firms, suppliers, and customers. Interfirm cooperation with suppliers includes the exchange of ideas as well as material orders, money, and products within the context of a long-term relationship. The long-term reciprocal relationships, seen within the MP/SM paradigm as barriers to entry, are viewed within the CIF as a means to facilitate investment in highly specialized activities and components and to spur the development of innovations. The most obvious example of such cooperation is the *keiretsu,* which holds "regular meetings of the chief executives, [through which] the core bank and trading company coordinate activities among the member firms and promote the collective marketing and financial interests of the group." (Best 1990, 179) This is not to imply, however, an absence of competition among the *kereitsu* firms; each party exerts long-term pricing pressures in addition to the expectation of a stream of innovations to promote its growth and expand its market share. It does mean that firms try to avoid short-term exploitation of market conditions that may have long-term deleterious effects on other member firms. Cooperation or coordination among direct competitors also exists. It is facilitated by "a variety of inter-firm practices and extra-firm agencies such as trade associations, apprenticeship programs, labor education facilities, joint marketing arrangements and regulatory commissions. . . ." (Best 1990, 17) These sectorial institutions facilitate cooperation among what are otherwise competing firms to provide common services, shape complementary investment strategies, and determine the rules of the game. Thus, the adherents to the CIF paradigm recognize that competition is vital, particularly in the area of product and process improvement, but they also recognize that interfirm cooperation and coordination are sources of short-term market stability. Peter Drucker summarizes this attribute of Japanese firms, stating that

> competition tends to be ruthless between companies in the same field and between groups of companies-for example, between Sony and Panasonic or between Mitsui Bank and Fuji Bank. But whenever there has to be a continuing relationship with an opponent, the Japanese tend to seek common ground. . . . Great care is taken by all parties that there be no damage done to common interests. Great care is also taken that there be no final victory over the individuals or groups with whom one has to live and work (Drucker 1981, 88).

But, one might ask, what about the interests of the consumer? Won't there be a loss of welfare (consumers' surplus plus producers' surplus) as a result of the firm's output restriction and high price, as suggested in standard price theory? The evidence does not support this contention. Odagiri reviews the findings of a number of studies on welfare loss in the United States, United Kingdom, and Japan. He says that the evidence "clearly indicates that Japan has a smaller welfare loss under any formula. We can therefore conclude that industries are more competitive in Japan than in the USA and the UK and, consequently, the loss of welfare caused by imperfect competition is smaller." (Odagiri 1992, 214) Within the CIF paradigm, barriers to entry are not simply a means of permanently protecting the economic

nomic profits of the firm. Rather, they serve the purpose of preventing excessive increases in the market supply that can result in redundant productive capacity. Barriers alleviate the problem of forcing the firm to quickly reduce its labor force or face bankruptcy. As a result, the CIF is able to continuously improve its products and production processes to achieve dynamic efficiencies and remain competitive in the long run.

We should note, however, that the logic of the CIF paradigm suggests that the barriers to entry are not absolute. If the Schumpeterian competition and its dynamic efficiencies are to be achieved, there must be some way for firms to enter profitable markets. The need to avoid the problem of rapid adjustments in productive capacity and employment but to stimulate Schumpeterian competition can be achieved through effective barriers to entry in the short run and contestable markets in the long run. This policy is consistent with the type of barriers firms encounter in most of the Japanese markets. Western firms usually lodge complaints against the bureaucratic red tape and closed networks of Japanese firms when trying to enter their markets. Only the most persistent firms eventually succeed in entering these markets. This slow entry procedure allows the existing firms to anticipate the adjustments necessitated by new competitors and develop new innovations. Under these conditions, any adjustments to employment can be made through attrition and cut-backs in temporary employees. In the MP/SM paradigm cooperation and barriers to entry may seem impediments to achieving static efficiency in markets dominated by MP/SM firms, but in the CIF paradigm they go hand in hand with a dynamic efficiency of superior products available to consumers at prices driven down by the continual improvement of production processes.

Paradigm Blinders

A scientific theory is an interpretation of facts. Our scientific theories are necessarily simplifications of the vast array of complicated facts in the real world. As such, they help us devise strategies and formulate policies to achieve our goals. On the other hand, as we have stated, theory that has achieved the status of a paradigm may also function as a set of blinders. To the extent that a paradigm "provides models from which spring particular coherent traditions of scientific research" and "seldom evoke overt disagreement over fundamentals" as Kuhn suggests, its practitioners may not be able to see the benefits of emerging alternative approaches. As long as the adherents of the MP/SM paradigm cling to the traditional view of the firm, they will be unable to see the benefits of the CIF. As a consequence, the owners and managers of the MP/SM firms will be unable to make the adjustments necessary to effectively compete in those global markets best suited to the continuous improvement process, and their firms will inevitably decline.

Because most Western firms tended to interpret the world within the context of the MP/SM paradigm, they attributed the initial success of the Japanese firms to "cheap labor." Japan's labor costs and interest expenses were indeed lower than those in the West. Over time, however, Japan's labor costs and interest expenses caught up to and surpassed those of most North American and Western European firms. Another explanation for the success of Japanese firms was that the undervaluation of the yen gave them an unfair advantage in the global markets, but the rise in the value of the yen since the mid-1980s has undermined that explanation, too. The latest argument relies upon the existence of barriers to entry in Japan's domestic markets, which are supposed to allow the Japanese firms to earn monopoly profits to subsidize their sales in the global markets. Though some laws and governmental rules to that effect have been relaxed, the fact that many remain in place provides some justification for the persistence of this particular explanation.

Those who cling to these interpretations of the new global competition, however, respond to its threat in a manner consistent with the MP/SM paradigm. For example, when the increased competition has an adverse effect on a firm's profits, management acts so as to protect the stockholders' interests. In some cases, tariff and/or quota protections are sought for the domestic market and, in those markets where implemented, the firm is able to raise the price of the product and revive its profits. When this strategy fails, cost reductions are an alternative way to resusitate the firm's profits. This approach not only results in millions of production workers being layed off and/or accepting wage cuts, but also in multitudes of midlevel managers being given "pink slips" in an attempt to make the firm lean; and if it does not work fast enough, the firm's stock price continues to fall, making it a prospect for a takeover. In that event, management becomes the scapegoat for the firm's problems, and the new stockholders replace them.

Some MP/SM firms have responded to the global competition by investing large amounts of capital to incorporate the latest technological advances (e.g., robots) into their production process for the sake of efficiency and profits. Though individual firms are pursuing these strategies, the Western governments, at the behest of their corporate leaders, are working to eliminate the structural barriers to the Japanese markets. If they are successful, they may undercut the Japanese firms' main source of profits, forcing them to cease subsidizing their global production and level the playing field in the global markets. Opening the Japanese markets to Western firms may also increase demand for the MP/SM firms' products to help return them to profitability. Though some firms certainly have benefited and others may benefit from lower costs of production, reductions in their labor force, better capital, and reduced requirements for entry into the Japanese markets, these strategies have not, on the whole, substantially improved the long-term viability of the MP/SM firm.

At the same time, more and more Westerners are learning about the elements of the continuous improvement process, TQM, and the importance of product quality to the success of the Japanese firms. As a result, managers of some MP/SM firms are implementing quality circles, just-in-time systems, suggestion systems, reductions in the number of suppliers, and other elements of the CIF. Nevertheless, in many cases it is questionable whether these changes have been very effective. Many who have tried to implement these features have already reversed course, finding them to be less than what they had expected. Hence, "American manufacturers are discarding billions of dollars of investment they made in the 1980s to adopt Japanese manufacturing ideas." (Naj 1993, 1) What did they expect? Did

they expect immediate, lower production costs and higher profits? Yet, according to Ranganath Nayak, head of world-wide op-
erations-management practices at Arthur D. Little, Inc., which
surveyed 500 manufacturers, "Although what they learned from
the Japanese improved quality and productivity in some areas,
it 'hasn't made them really competitive' " (ibid). He adds, "Most
of them 'simply aren't improving fast enough in relation to the
competition'." (ibid.) This view is reinforced by the analysis of
Michael Dertouzous, a manufacturing expert at MIT, who
states, " 'I've talked to some 100 firms. Except for a few of
them, they're flailing away'." (ibid.)

What went wrong? Why do these techniques work for the
Japanese firms, but imperfectly or not at all for the American
firms? Is it the Japanese or Eastern culture that permits the Japanese firms to do things Western or American firms seemingly
cannot? Maybe, but that would not explain how Toyota could
take over the management of a former General Motors manufacturing plant in California, rehire many of the same union
workers, and run one of the most productive automotive
manufacturing facilities in North America (New United Motors
Manufacturing, Inc.). Nor would it explain how various Japanese transplant operations are able to compete from a number
of world-wide locations.

An alternative explanation of what went wrong is that many
of the American firms attempted to adopt the Japanese techniques without giving up the MP/SM paradigm. They adopted
the individual CIF components that seemed to be most important to the Japanese firms' successes or those aspects of which
the managers were most aware, with the hope that they would
make the US firms just as competitive. This view is supported
by James Harbour, a manufacturing specialist, who states,
"Americans adopted quality circles without upfront engineering
and thought it would generate massive improvement in quality
and productivity." (ibid.)

So we see that the MP/SM paradigm has acted as blinders in
two ways. The MP/SM paradigm has prevented the majority of
Westerners from understanding the source of competitive advantage for the Japanese firms, and it has prevented others a bit less

blinded from successfully adopting it. If Western firms are to benefit from the techniques developed by their Japanese rivals, they must first remove their blinders and understand the new CIF paradigm. In the next chapter, we will discuss some of the key issues involved in the international transfer of the continuous improvement technologies that comprise the CIF paradigm.

CHAPTER 10

INTERNATIONAL TRANSFER OF CONTINUOUS IMPROVEMENT TECHNOLOGY

Technology transfer usually refers to the movement of technology across national boundaries, while the concept of technological diffusion typically is limited to the spread of a new technology within a country. We shall see that there are elements of both diffusion and transfer when the focus is on new firms adopting the prominent features of CIFs. While many of the ideas underlying continuous improvement originated with American thinkers, they were brought to a globally competitive fruition by Japanese firms. Thus, it would appear that the appropriate focus would be the transfer of operating applications of the theoretical principles rather than the principles themselves. In the pages that follow, we will study the prospects for transfer of continuous improvement techniques developed in Japan to other countries and their adaptation to the alien environment.

The international transfer of technology has a venerable history, dating back to ancient times. In the last two centuries, however, the scale and impact of technology transfer have increased significantly. Since World War II, technology transfers have been accomplished in several ways, the most prominent of which has been through the growth of the multinational corporation. In such cases, the technology transfers as a result of direct foreign investment or joint ventures with host country firms. Alternatively, technology may be sold to unaffiliated foreign enterprises.

Because modern technology is often relatively sophisticated, its effective transfer requires much more than the simple transportation of machinery. According to Robinson (1988, 3), "One is inevitably compelled to think in terms of technology transfer 'packages'." Accordingly, a technology transfer package is said to include at least several of the following: hardware, licensing agreement, technical assistance contract, management contract, marketing agreement, and training contract. The several non-hardware aspects add ambiguity, or what Robinson (p. 2) calls "mushiness" to the technology transfer concept. In the literature of technology transfer, the "mushy" or soft aspects are almost invariably ancillary to the hardware associated with a specific product and/or machine process for producing it. This ambiguity or mushiness pales in comparison with that which surrounds the continuous improvement technologies. What we are calling the soft technologies of continuous improvement are not specific to any particular piece or pieces of hardware. Our reference is to certain characteristics of organizational form and of management systems that promote the emergence of continuous improvement of product and process on a day-to-day basis as part of normal operations. Our usage of the term *soft* is, therefore, not comparable with the standard meaning of *software,* which refers to the blueprints, manuals, or other communications – visual or oral – that pertain directly to the hardware being transferred.[1] The conceptual mushiness of organizational forms and management systems derives partly from the fact that we are dealing with the perceptions of various transfer agents, perceptions that can be colored by the paradigms within which each lives and works. A putative host's view of a particular CIF system may very well be shaped by the MP/SM paradigm, for example. Even a consultant-facilitator may see phenomena very differently from how its originator sees it.

A Taxonomy of CIF Technology

When looking at questions associated with the transfer of technology from a CIF to an overseas host, we must distinguish between several types of technology utilized by CIFs. To begin with, there is "hard" technology, in the form of plant and equipment, which is of no interest to us here. The competitive advantages that we have analyzed in this work do not derive from equipment advantages. Indeed, the CIF's equipment is sometimes dated and/or imported, as in the case of Toyota's famous Kamigo Number Nine Engine Plant.[2] Of special interest, however, are the three types of technology that are widely associated with continuous improvement: at one level, the important break-through improvements and internal innovations that have resulted from active operation of the continuous improvement process; at another level, the analytical tools used by employees of the CIF to conceptualize and implement improvements; and at the final level, the organizational characteristics and management systems that account for the emergence of a heavy volume of improvements. We will expand on the differences between these three facets of technology so that the reader will appreciate why we focus so much interest on organizational form and management systems.

It is often noted that CIFs employ analytical tools that are quite similar across firms. Among these, statistical process control (SPC), statistical design of experiments, fish-bone (cause-and-effect) diagrams, and Pareto charts are probably the best known. However, whereas the CIF has made good use of these tools in promoting continuous improvement, MP/SM firms have put them to more prosaic use. Yoshida (1989) argues that when W. Edwards Deming and others introduced the statistical tools to Japanese companies, the major benefit was a new and broader perspective for the management. These tools motivated and assisted managers to see the firm as a set of cross-functional systems instead of discrete specialties. According to Yoshida, that is precisely what happened in Japan. Although the tools were useful in solving quality problems that then plagued Japanese industry, the ultimate benefit was the reorientation they provided the management. MP/SM firms, however, more often than not, use them to solve quality problems. Furthermore, they are not utilized by managers. Instead, as we saw in the case of Acme Paper (chapter 5), a new functional specialty is created in the form of a quality department. We can see, therefore, that the transfer of these tools does not necessarily constitute a step toward the development of continuous improvement capability throughout the organization.

Breakthrough improvements and internal innovations that have emerged from the CIF are properly viewed as technology. Just-in-time manufacturing (JIT), for example, is widely considered to be an important technology developed within the context of the continuous improvement systems of Toyota. Furthermore, JIT is usually broken down into constituent technologies such as single minute exchange of dies, *kanban,* autonomation (flexible and fool-proof machines), and production smoothing (see chapter 3). In each case the technology is the culmination of a long evolutionary process involving literally millions of incremental improvements. Given that these incremental improvements were often undocumented (Washio 1986), the adoption of JIT, for example, cannot be effectuated by transferring those numerous separate improvements. That which will be transferred by the outside observer is that observer's conception of the technology. A mental snapshot, so to speak, is made of a process that is constantly evolving. The content of that snapshot is largely derived from the work of scholars and journalists who have recorded their observations of the system in operation, which consultants and others then try to put into operational terms. Because those writers take their view, for the most part, from the perspective of the MP/SM paradigm and because they are studying the results of the improvement process and not the process itself, their conceptualizations stand a good chance of operating poorly for the putative hosts. The probability that a recipient firm will use JIT as effectively as its originator is highly questionable. Note, however, that even if the host could adopt any or all of the components of JIT, it would not thereby have acquired continuous improvement capability. The firm could run up its "learning curve" for the newly installed JIT system, but beyond that, further improvement would be inhibited by the attributes of the MP/SM paradigm.[3] It would remain a follower, always in the position of having to adopt new process technologies that emerge as a matter of course from the CIFs. Furthermore, in its efforts to keep up with a moving target, the MP/SM firm would be forced to make continuous financial outlays for that which the CIFs often produce without substantial investment.

To be able to produce its own technological change in the form of continuous improvements, the host firm must necessarily adopt appropriate soft technologies, that is, the organizational structures and management systems. In other words, it will have to reorganize in such a way as to make available as much information as possible to as many persons as possible. It will have to provide for the organization of workers into quality circles, or the like, and to qualify each of them for several jobs, rotating them frequently. It should promote managers across functions or find some alternative means to provide them with a transfunctional perspective. It should augment policies of easy access to all information by such devices as open offices, a minimization of walls, and transparent machine covers where feasible. Furthermore, management will have to see that incentive systems are in place that prompt personnel to acquire firm-specific information for use in firm-specific improvements. In that regard, such values as lifetime employment, promotion from within, and suggestion systems have served the Japanese version of the CIF well. An articulated company philosophy that focuses the worker on such broad objectives as customer value is also crucial to success, coupled with a training system that imparts knowledge of the necessary analytical tools and offers incentives that reward their effective use.

If a MP/SM firm is to acquire continuous improvement capability, it cannot do so by simply taking up the use of the analytical tools used by the CIF and/or by adopting major process improvements that have emanated from it. It must do nothing short of remodeling its organizational structure and the key management systems associated with it. In cases where the structures, systems, or philosophy of the CIF appear to be inappropriate for the hosts firm's cultural setting, it must design suitable counterparts that accomplish similar results. And, equally important, if not more so, it must adopt a customer-value philosophy and inculcate it into its employees' behavior at all levels of the organization. In short, it must effect the transformation that we call here an international transfer of the soft technologies of continuous improvement.

International Subsidiaries of the CIF

A major share of experience in transferring continuous improvement technology across national borders resides in the Japanese continuous improvement firms themselves. For that reason we will discuss their experiences prior to directly tackling the question of transforming the MP/SM firm. To begin with, it might seem that the CIF would have an easier job of transferring these technologies internationally than would potential foreign hosts. For one reason, the CIF's managers and technicians who served as transfer agents would be intimately familiar with the operation of the technology. For another, their understanding is rooted in the context of the continuous improvement paradigm. Even so, we shall see that the matter is not so straightforward. Indeed, we shall report circumstances in which the CIF has not attempted to develop continuous improvement capabilities in its subsidiaries.

The facts that muddy the water are three significant problems associated with the operation of a network of subsidiaries and the maintenance of a continuous improvement strategy. Those problems which can be viewed as basic contradictions are:

1. Each time a part of a CIF is moved overseas, there is an addition to the cost of maintaining standardized processes.
2. Each time a part of a CIF is moved overseas, there is a reduction in the rate of improvement due to some loss of synergism.
3. Because parent and subsidiary focus on different customers, some improvements that enhance customer value in one market may be inappropriate for the other market, especially when the subsidiary is located in a developing country.

The discussion that follows assumes that the CIF is evaluating the feasibility of developing overseas subsidiaries to operate as an integrated part of a global continuous improvement strategy. This strategy requires that all three levels of CIF technology be transferred to them: analytical tools, improvements per se, and the soft technologies associated with organizational structure and management systems. With regard to the analytical tools and the soft technologies that impart continuous improvement capability, we can think of a one-time transfer with attendant learning curves. What may not be readily apparent is that the emerging improvements per se must be transferred both ways between home and subsidiary operations on a more or less continuous basis.

In chapter 3, we developed the argument that standardization of processes is a fundamental requirement for the operation of a continuous improvement strategy. As a matter of policy, the management of a CIF must ensure that the employees at all similar work stations are dealing with the same core information by standardizing across all work stations any improvement inaugurated at any one station. Thus, there is always a common core of basic information consisting of the product itself and the technology that accomplishes the work station's part of its production. If work stations are close to each other and the improvement is straightforward, diffusion of the new improvement takes place with little or no cost. For example, line supervisors or the workers themselves may pass by the station that initiated the improvement to observe the change. Then, interested parties may discuss the change informally during breaks or lunch. If the improvement is complicated, a seminar or training session for first line supervisors or selected quality circle members may be advisable, and for the occasional breakthrough improvement, formal worker training classes. Only this latter program would involve significant cost, either in terms of financial outlay or opportunity cost.

If global political and/or economic concerns prompt the movement of one or more production lines to an overseas setting, there will obviously be an increment to the cost of transferring improvements to and from the subsidiaries. No longer could standardization be maintained by supervisors or workers walking by the newly improved work stations. At the very least, written documentation would have to be provided. In some cases, documents would require translation into the working language of the subsidiary work force. Recall, however, the words of Washio (1986) who argues that many of the incremental improvements are never documented and that many of them are undocumentable.[4] In many cases, individual engineers would have to travel internationally as transfer agents, obviously adding to cost, not only in the form of cash outlays for air travel and subsistence, but also of opportunity cost for the technicians' time.

In figure 10.1a, we begin with the assumption that the basic manufacturing facilities of the CIF consist of 20 similar production lines that are all located in the home country within close proximity to each other. Let C represent the cost of in-house diffusion, that is, the cost of keeping the systems standardized through the diffusion of each workplace improvement to all other similar workplaces. As already noted, the magnitude of C is relatively small. Figure 10.1b assumes that for political and economic reasons, half of the CIF's ongoing operations have to move to one overseas location. Thus, now half of new improvements are generated at home and half in the subsidiary, and the cost of in-house diffusion of improvements is the same for the subsidiary as for the home operations.[5] In such case, the value of C is unchanged ($C = C_1 + C_2$).

The additional cost comes in the form of expenses and opportunity cost to transfer to the subsidiary those improvements adopted in the home operations and to transfer home those improvements originating overseas. For reasons already discussed, the cost of this transfer (C') undoubtedly is significantly higher than the cost of internal diffusion of the same improvements. Not only is C' greater than C, it represents a net increment to cost. The total cost of maintaining standardized processes is therefore $C + C'$, where $C' > C$.

In figure 10.1c, we assume that ten of the production lines have been moved to ten different countries, which emulates the history of global diffusion of subsidiaries in response to the protection afforded by import-substitution policies. If we continue with our assumption that each work station will initiate as many improvements as when they were all located together, as in figure 10.1a, then we see that half of the improvements occur overseas. The matter has become much more complicated, however, than in the case represented by figure 10.1b. If a fully integrated global CIF is to be maintained, an improvement originated by firm number 15, for example, would have to be communicated to the home operations and the nine other subsidiaries. If each international transfer costs the same in the context of figure

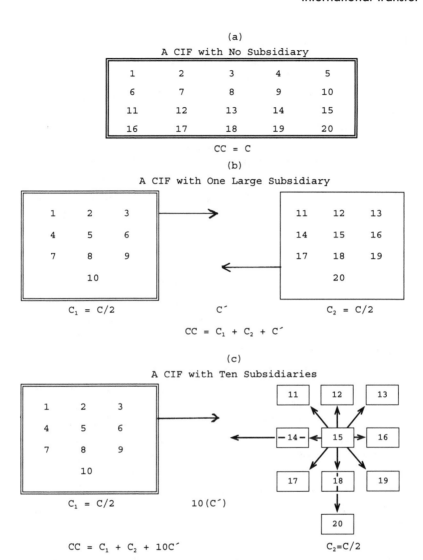

Figure 10.1. Cost of implementing and standardizing improvements in alternative organizational forms. (a) A CIF with no subsidiary. (b) A CIF with one large subsidiary. (c) A CIF with ten subsidiaries. Arrows show international transfer of improvements. Each number represents a full production line. Double-bordered box signifies home country operations. Single-bordered box represents foreign subsidiaries. C represents cost of domestic diffusion of improvements. C' represents cost of international transfer of improvements. CC is the total cost of diffusion plus international transfer.

10.1c as it does in the case of (b), total cost of transfer will be ten times higher in the current case; in other words, $C + 10$ (C').[6] It is obvious, therefore, that ceteris paribus, the parceling out to foreign locations of some of the CIF's operations tends to reduce its competitiveness by raising its costs.[7]

There are other problems, possibly more severe, that derive from a CIF's establishment of subsidiaries. In the foregoing discussion, we made the assumption that the rate of improvement generation remained constant without regard to the location of operations. There are reasons, however, that lead us to doubt that this would be the case. A large literature argues that the social and political setting of Japan and possibly some other Asian countries is especially suitable for the operation of a continuous improvement strategy. We will take up this question shortly. For the moment, however, we will trace the argument that, cultural differences notwithstanding, the proliferation of subsidiaries tends to reduce the rate of improvement generation.

This decrease in improvement rate occurs because a proliferation of subsidiaries tends to diminish the creative synergism of the CIF's personnel. We explained the importance of this synergism in chapter 3 under the topic of economies of scale of improvement generation. The problem of reduced synergism is rooted in the fact that the establishment of a subsidiary isolates the employees of the two organizational components from each other. This isolation may have somewhat less impact at the level of line workers who tend to interact more intensively with others in their immediate vicinity. Moving up the hierarchy of the CIF, however, we would expect to find increasingly more interaction across production lines and across factories, in the form of meetings, seminars, team assignments, and less formal activities such as lunch, dinner, golf, fishing, and other social activities. In all cases the interaction expands the information horizon of the participants. With the establishment of overseas subsidiaries, few managers and technicians, except those at the most important subsidiaries, would participate as members of product-development teams or multiplant problem-solving teams, and so the information available to both the teams and the subsidiaries would be constrained. The decision to transplant part of the organization via subsidiaries seems likely to entail a reduction in the amount of synergism surrounding the continuous improvement process.[8]

In figure 10.2, we replicate the three scenarios depicted in figure 10.1. In (a) there are 20 production lines located in close proximity to each other. Each work station has 19 counterparts. Ceteris paribus, there should certainly be more interaction in terms of ideas than if there were only one work station. We cannot say, however, that there should be 20 times as many interactions because there may well be some element of diminishing returns, but we can say something concrete about the number of initial perceptions for each of the process components. If we compare the situations in (a) and (b) at a point in time, we see twice as many initial perceptions of each process component in (a) as in either the home operations or the subsidiary depicted in (b). Employees exchange their views about the workplace in many ways, both formal and informal – at quality circle meetings, lunch, or other social engagements. Often, the impact of seeing things through someone else's eyes pushes one's thinking to new thresholds. In Ayres/Ogburn/Gilfallen terms (see chapter 3), the exchange provides new tools or allows fragments of information to be recombined in new and more effective ways. Given that each person's perception is influenced by non-work factors, the importance of this synergism is difficult to exaggerate. If we make the simplifying assumption that for each work station in figure 10.2a, there is one employee, and that each interacts once with the other 19, then 380 exchanges of views take place in addition to the initial 20 personal views. If we then look at the situation in (b) we find 10 workers interacting in the home operations and 10 interacting in the subsidiary. In that case there will be 10 initial views and 90 initial interactions in each format for a total of 20 initial personal views and 180 interactions. In other words, there are twice as many interactions in (a) as in (b). While we cannot allege that there would be twice as many improvements in the former situation than in the latter, we can hardly imagine that there would not be significantly more. The specific ratios given in this simple example are not intended to suggest that the process of idea generation can be distilled to some mathematical formula. There is too much of a serendipitous element involved to permit such an approach.

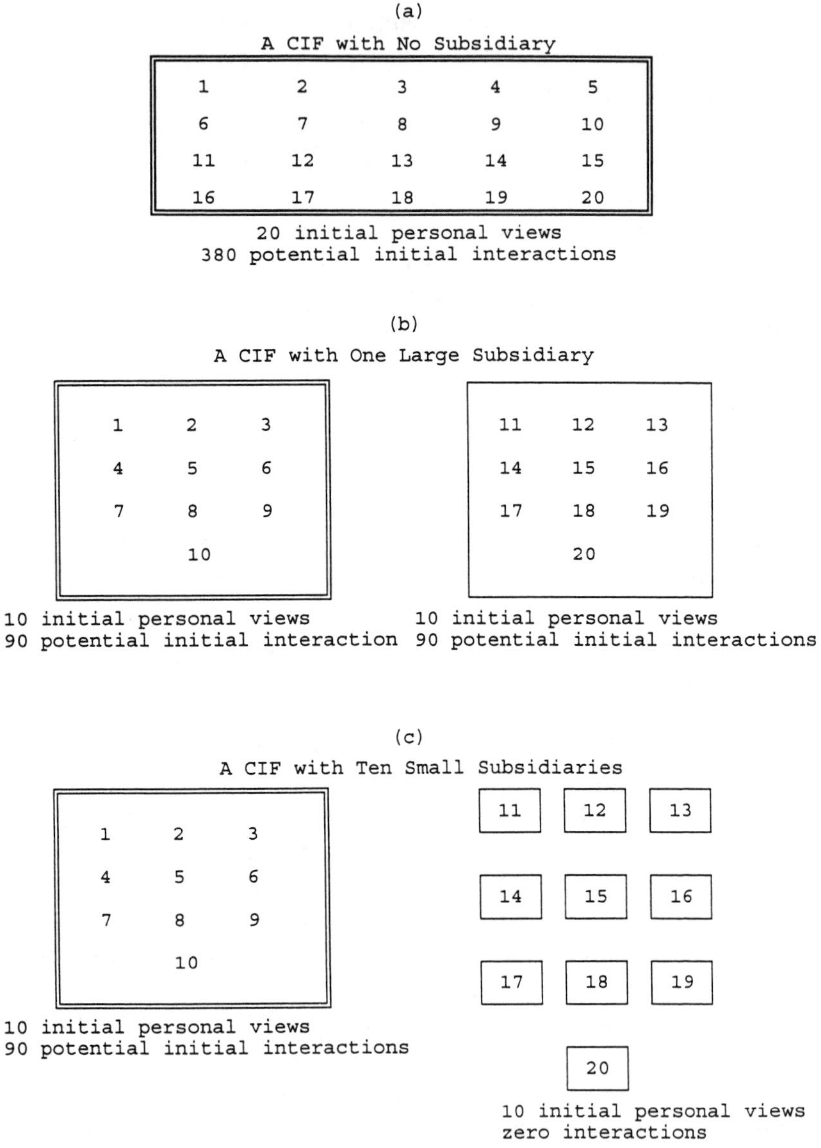

(a)
A CIF with No Subsidiary

1	2	3	4	5
6	7	8	9	10
11	12	13	14	15
16	17	18	19	20

20 initial personal views
380 potential initial interactions

(b)
A CIF with One Large Subsidiary

1	2	3
4	5	6
7	8	9
	10	

11	12	13
14	15	16
17	18	19
	20	

10 initial personal views   10 initial personal views
90 potential initial interaction   90 potential initial interactions

(c)
A CIF with Ten Small Subsidiaries

1	2	3
4	5	6
7	8	9
	10	

11	12	13
14	15	16
17	18	19

| 20 |

10 initial personal views
90 potential initial interactions

10 initial personal views
zero interactions

Figure 10.2. Synergism in the generation of information for improvements. (a) A CIF with no subsidiary. (b) A CIF with one large subsidiary. (c) A CIF with ten small subsidiaries. Each discrete operation on the production line has one work station, and each work station has one worker. Any international transfer of perceptions is in the form of an improvement: i.e., it is ex post. Each number represents a full production line. Double-bordered box signifies home country operations. Single-bordered box represents foreign subsidiaries.

Nevertheless, the foregoing numbers do tell us something about the potential for information generation, other relevant factors constant.

If we keep the same assumptions and look at the situation in figure 10.2c, we see that the level of potential synergism is further reduced, and drastically. While there would be 90 initial interactions in the home operations, there would be no interactions in the subsidiary setting. Recalling the relatively higher cost of maintaining standardized processes across many international subsidiaries, we can see that an organization featuring many small subsidiaries may be inimical to a global continuous improvement strategy.

Finally, the third contradiction between the use of subsidiaries and a continuous improvement strategy derives from the fact that some of the improvements of the home operations and of the subsidiaries will be specific to the customer mix served by the respective organizations. When improvements are directed toward aspects of customer value closely associated with particular levels of economic well-being or unique cultural attributes, they may not be appropriate for transfer to other settings. This can be an especially thorny problem when the home operations are in an industrialized country and the subsidiary is in a developing country (or vice versa). The addition of automatic icemakers to a refrigerator, for example, may be sensible in one market but not in another. The installation of airbags is appropriate to one culture but not necessarily to another, where the approach to death is radically different. This contradiction has potential long-run implications for viability of a continuous improvement strategy. Given the necessity of maintaining standardized processes as a foundation of the improvement process, the nature of the dilemma is apparent: If some changes are inappropriate for transfer to other operations because of customer-value associations, then standardization cannot be maintained. On the other hand, if inappropriate improvements are transferred, competitiveness will be compromised. (We discuss the value of the external information set that employees of an overseas subsidiary bring to the CIF's understanding of their domestic market presently.)

An obvious advantage of global standardization is that the firm may evolve in a fully integrated fashion, with organizational components always using similar processes to produce similar products, thus allowing the firm to move management and technicians without the need to also move up a learning curve. Such movement of personnel, itself, adds a synergistic element to information flows and helps standardize all processes from the manufacturing lines to the conceptualization of customer value and corporate philosophy. All of these processes, however, will be in a state of evolution.

The alternative, to let the subsidiary operate as an independent continuous improvement firm, keeping its improvements to itself and remaining isolated from many of the improvements of the home operations, also avoids the high cost of international transfer but forfeits any economies of scale of improvement creation. Operation of the subsidiary as an independent CIF has the advantage of focusing its complete attention on the customer-value considerations of the host country market (assuming that production is largely for local consumption). The fundamental disadvantage, however, is that improvements are generated internally and are based upon locally available information. Thus, the nature of the product and production processes (e.g., organizational layout, machine operations) in each facility could evolve along independent vectors. For this reason, the ability of the parent and subsidiary to usefully interact would diminish over time.

If we picture the decision to establish a subsidiary that involves half of the production operations, we can let the (b) sections of figures 10.1 and 10.2 serve as the basis for our discussion. In such a case there would be two separate continuous improvement operations, each having one-half of the improvement potential of the firm before dispersal [as depicted in (a) sections]. While there would be no international cost factor for the standardization of processes, it would still cost considerably more to standardize two unique portfolios of improvements across two sets of ten firms each than to standardize one set of improvements across 20 domestic production lines. It should not be a stretch of the imagination to say that it would cost almost twice as much.[9] Therefore, we can appreciate that if a significant proportion of the CIF's home operations were to be dispersed in this fashion, the competitiveness of the parent operation would be somewhat compromised. This situation provides a cautionary signal to CIFs that plan to parcel out factories to take advantage of low wages or reduced transportation costs. They might be trading their long-run competitive advantage in customer-value creation for a one-shot reduction in cost.

The independent CIF subsidiary may be an attractive alternative in the case of a developing country with a relatively large domestic market. It would help to counter the often-heard charge that multinational corporations produce inappropriate products with inappropriate techniques. That advantage would have to be balanced against the disadvantage of a diminished rate of improvement creation at home.

A third option available to a global CIF would be to develop the subsidiary as a host only in the improvement process, that is, to install only those improvements initiated elsewhere that are deemed necessary and appropriate for the subsidiary. The subsidiary benefits from the improvement process that operates elsewhere, but does not itself contribute to it. There would be a cost for bringing improvements to the subsidiary, but no cost for transferring improvements from it. This mode of operation may be the best one where the size of the subsidiary is relatively small or where the local economic, institutional, and cultural features do not support continuous improvement.

The foregoing arguments are not based upon research of actual costs or rates of improvement creation but upon extrapolations of the logic of the continuous improvement process. If technological change is endogenous to the firm, then it emerges independently and indeterminately throughout the organization. The greater the geographic separation, the more difficult it is for the members of the organizational components to communicate with each other about the potential for or the implementation of change. This subject surely deserves serious research if we are to know something about the magnitudes involved or their significance.

We can summarize the foregoing discussion as follows:

1. The global CIF has three basic choices concerning the status of its subsidiaries relative to continuous improvement.
   (a) The parent organization could integrate the subsidiary as a full, continuous improvement partner. This

policy would entail the transfer of analytical tools, soft technologies, and all improvements implemented elsewhere to the subsidiary.

(b) The subsidiary could operate as an independent CIF. This alternative would entail the initial transfer of the analytical tools and the soft technologies of continuous improvement but would not require that improvements be standardized between parent and subsidiary.

(c) The subsidiary could operate on a noncontinuous-improvement basis, locked into the global system as a sometime host only for improvements generated in the parent operations. Some of the analytical tools would be transferred for use in "on the spot" problem solving. Parent operation improvements deemed useful for the subsidiary might be transferred on an ad hoc basis.

2. A continuous-improvement strategy is most effective when all production activities take place in relatively close proximity to each other, and the products are destined for the same general market, especially in terms of economic development.

When political and/or economic factors apply pressure on the CIF to split the production facilities into a number of global operations, the rate of improvement creation will suffer, and the cost of maintaining standardized processes will increase.

The Japanese Experience

International politics, as much as anything, dictates the decision to establish a subsidiary overseas. It was the threat of protection more than market considerations that spurred Japanese automobile manufacturers to build factories in the United States. Likewise, we can account for the presence of Sony, Matsushita, and others in Brazil, for example, as a reaction to the implementation of import substitution policies. Although politics may force the decision to establish a subsidiary, the economic considerations summarized in figures 10.1 and 10.2 probably play a strong role in determining how that subsidiary is integrated into the system. To illustrate the point, we will briefly highlight the experiences of several Japanese industries, automobiles in the United States, electronics in Brazil, and various industries in Mexico.

Japanese Automakers in the United States

The automobile industry has long been a mainstay of the Japanese economy, featuring high wages and high value. The initial reasons for moving some operations to the United States were largely political. "Made in the USA" protectionism has been most visible in that industry. The political pressure was the direct result of Japanese marketing successes in the US market during the 1970s when the escalating price of petroleum gave the small and relatively fuel-efficient Japanese automobiles a decided boost. It was not long, however, before those products earned a reputation for high quality as much as fuel economy. In 1981 the US government responded to domestic pressure by extracting from the Japanese a voluntary restraint agreement to limit automobile exports to the US. The agreement meant that any significant growth in the Japanese share of the US market would have to be based upon locating subsidiary production facilities within the United States.

The major Japanese automakers, Toyota, Nissan, and Honda, responded to the protectionist moves by establishing production facilities in the United States. Less well-known but solid firms, such as Mazda, Mitsubishi, and Isuzu, also moved in. In some cases, the new facilities were joint ventures with Big Three automobile companies, but Toyota, Nissan, and Honda also owned subsidiaries themselves.

Because Toyota is usually taken as the prototype for continuous improvement, its intentions and its experience should be of special interest to us. In 1984 Toyota tested the waters in a joint venture with General Motors (GM) known as New United Motor Manufacturing, Inc. (NUMMI).[10] The joint venture utilized a previously closed GM plant in California and an idled work force that renewed its association with the United Automobile Workers.[11] The venture produced one basic automobile, marketed by Toyota under its model name Corolla and by GM under the name Nova. Though the GM version of the product was a market failure, the experiment was enough of a success to stimulate Toyota to build a major full-fledged subsidiary.[12]

In the NUMMI experiment Toyota had attempted to transfer all levels of its CIF technologies (i.e., analytical tools, improvements per se, and organizational architecture and management systems). A major finding was that US production workers could successfully make the paradigm shift from MP/SM to continuous improvement. Quality circles were a success and job rotation became popular and useful. The generalization of the work force is evident in the fact that NUMMI operated with only four basic job descriptions, whereas GM previously had used 80 (Kenney and Florida 1993, 104). Some US makers of autoparts learned that with considerable effort they could convert to continuous improvement, too.[13] On the other hand, significant difficulties were encountered with middle managers who had spent their careers in US automobile firms and had great difficulty in trying to shake off the effects of the MP/SM paradigm.[14]

In its 1988 move to Kentucky, Toyota established a large wholly owned subsidiary. It was a "greenfield" location where most workers and lowerlevel managers had no experience in the US automobile industry. Nor would the United Automobile Workers labor union be involved in the subsidiary. The intention was to fully integrate it with the Japanese production facilities at Toyota City. Informal statements from Toyota officials indicate that though the level of improvement generation is not yet as high in Kentucky as in Japan, they are pleased at the rate of progress made to date.[15] If we review the situation depicted earlier in figure 10.2, we can surmise that the total rate of improvement generation should decline somewhat based upon the reduced opportunities for interaction. This reduction should occur even in the case where the US-based labor force is as effective as its Japanese counterpart. Furthermore, the logic of the analysis summarized in figure 10.1 tells us that the establishment of a large subsidiary should have added something to the cost of maintaining the firm as an integrated continuous operation.

Toyota was not, however, the first of the Japanese auto manufacturers to establish a wholly owned subsidiary in the United

States. The pioneering move was made by Honda Motor Company. It should not be surprising that Honda was the first company to respond to the politics of protection. Honda had only a small share of the Japanese automobile market; the bulk of its sales were in the US market. It if were to stand much of a chance of growing in the future, it had to seriously contemplate establishing a US subsidiary. The first was established in Marysville, Ohio, and began production in 1982. That the motivation was political and not economic is attested by the fact that Honda's own feasibility studies had earlier predicted financial losses from such a subsidiary (Kenney and Florida 1993, 97). Given that the bulk of its automobile operations would likely become located in the United States, Honda was left with little choice but to establish the subsidiary as a continuous improvement firm. Apparently, it is expected to be an integrated component of a global, continuous-improvement automobile firm. This is attested to by the fact that improvements made in Marysville in the product and in the production process are transferred to the operations in Japan. The Honda subsidiary operates three R&D facilities in the United States, two in Ohio and one in California, two of which work with product design and one with production equipment (Kenney and Florida 1993, 121). This is strong indication that the customer-value focus of the improvement technologies is the US consumer market. However, because both the Japanese and US markets are relatively affluent, many customer-value improvements should transfer easily from one market to the other. In establishing the Ohio-based subsidiary, Honda transferred all three types of continuous-improvement technology, and they all seem to work successfully, although no definitive studies allow us to compare Honda's rate of improvement generation at the subsidiary with that in Japan.

Nonetheless, the Japanese automotive manufacturing experiences in the United States have not been universally successful in terms of technology transfer. In 1985 Mazda built a stamping and assembly plant in Flat Rock, Michigan. At that time Mazda was the third Japanese automotive manufacturer to set up production in the United States. Mazda's intention was to transfer the continuous improvement system to the US. In doing so, Mazda broke ranks with Nissan and Honda, which had preceded them, by forming an association with the United Auto Workers. Fucini and Fucini (1990) have documented the mutual disenchantment of workers and Japanese managers with the evolution of the organizational culture. Mistrust flows both ways. The result is an organization in which work is accomplished by teams, but teams that apparently do not produce continuous improvements. Based on the foregoing analysis of the ideal CIF paradigm, we suspect that Mazda will encounter difficulties trying to compete in markets that become increasingly volatile, requiring greater and greater flexibility.

Those who believe that the success of continuous improvement in Japan is based upon unique features of Japanese culture point to Mazda as their proof. The apparent success of Honda and Toyota, on the other hand, appear to support the opposite contention. The contradictory experiences of the Japanese auto manufacturers in the United States suggest that something other than culture may be the determining factor in the successful tranfer of the CIF technology, namely, the paradigmatic view. The problem with middle managers at NUMMI was not that they were American, but that they interpreted the world through the lens of the MP/SM paradigm. Likewise, the union workers at Mazda interpreted labor relations within the context of MP/SM organizations. On the other hand, American workers at the Honda plant did not have to overcome previous experiences within the MP/SM paradigm. But what about the NUMMI workers who appeared to have addapted so well? First, a great deal of effort was put into the selection and training of the workers in the Toyota CIF soft technologies. In addition, since the workers had already experienced the closing of the GM plant and were well aware that the NUMMI experiment would be their last chance to work in the auto industry, they had strong motives for letting go of the MP/SM paradigm that had previously failed them. In the final analysis, however, it should not be a surprise that some subsidiaries are better at continuous improvement than others. That is also the case in Japan.

Japanese Subsidiaries in the Third World

Many Japanese subsidiaries in the Third World were located as a response to import-substitution policies adopted by many of those countries. The choice offered to the firms was straightforward; either build a local facility or effectively forfeit participation in the local market. Attention to the (c) sections of figures 10.1 and 10.2 shows a representative situation. A large number of relatively small operations have been established behind protective walls in developing countries. Recent research in Brazil shows that Japanese firms there made minimal effort to transfer their CIF technologies to those subsidiaries (Bos and Cole 1993). The firms, members of the Brazilian electronics sector, were all using statistical process control, which, as we noted already, can be used for problem solving in either a mass-production or a continuous improvement process, but none had transferred JIT manufacturing, although each of them utilized that technology in their home operations. In terms of the soft technologies of continuous improvement, two-thirds used quality circles and employee suggestion systems. Only one-quarter, however, reported that they had developed special programs with suppliers.

One particularly negative finding in the Brazil research is that all CEOs and top managers in the subsidiaries were Japanese. The companies' policy to reserve those positions for Japanese nationals served as a vehicle for accomplishing a relatively steady one-way transfer of technology from Japan to Brazil. The practice of limiting promotion possibilities for Brazilian middle managers led to high turnover rates in those ranks, which necessarily has had negative consequences for the development of continuous improvement capabilities. The evidence appears strong that in the case of the Brazilian electronics sector, Japanese firms have set up subsidiaries that they do not expect to be integrated into a global continuous improvement system. As suggested by the analysis in figures 10.1 and 10.2, the expected benefits of integration to the company as a whole would be relatively small and the costs relatively high. Thus, the firms have chosen to establish the subsidiaries as an occasional host facility for improvements generated in the home operation.

A companion research project carried out in the Maquiladora zone of Mexico is reported by Wilson (1992).[16] The sample contained firms from a number of countries and from a wide range of industries, especially including electronics and autoparts suppliers. The results were much the same as reported for Brazil. JIT was not transferred to Japanese subsidiaries, management positions were reserved for Japanese nationals and, in general, continuous improvement was not expected. Japanese managers reported that JIT could not be implemented because Mexican suppliers were assumed to be incapable of effectively participating in such a system. Though Mexican workers were seen as conscientious, high rates of turnover apparently led Japanese managers to conclude that it was not feasible to try to engage them in continuous improvement. Again, for economic reasons, it appears that the firms chose to set up these subsidiaries only as host facilities for improvements generated in the home operations.

US Firms and the Transfer of Continuous Improvement Technology

The success of the continuous improvement firm in Japan and the apparent success of major subsidiaries of Toyota and Honda have not gone unnoticed by MP/SM firms in the United States. Indeed, topics such as quality and employee involvement have been at the top of reading and discussion agenda for business professionals and academics alike for a couple of decades. Bookstores and libraries are devoting increasingly more shelf space to those and related issues. Probably nothing exemplifies this push for change more than the introduction of the Malcomb Baldridge Award, which is given annually in a White House ceremony to US firms deemed to have made commendable advances in the areas of total quality management.

Two of the more popular technologies for transfer attempts are statistical process control (SPC) and JIT manufacturing. Consulting firms, special institutes, and college evening programs have sprouted up all over the country to teach SPC techniques. Most large American companies, many medium-sized companies, and even a significant number of small ones utilize SPC with varying levels of intensity and sophistication. For the larger companies, the typical approach has been to create a quality department and give it the responsibility for deploying SPC. Far from promoting the development of continuous improvement, such a move has served to strengthen the hold of the MP/SM paradigm by sending the signal that quality is just another specialization.

Probably the second most popular CIF technology has been JIT manufacturing which, of course, is composed of improvements per se, and, therefore, is not a technology that necessarily promotes further improvements. Viewing JIT through the lens of the MP/SM paradigm, many US firms attempting its transfer see it primarily as a tool for reducing inventories and the carrying costs associated with them. While it is that, it can also be much more. For the CIF it is a component of flexible manufacturing, and both of these aspects depend upon a manufacturing system whose processes produce at a rate of near zero defects. The bottom line is that an MP/SM firm can adopt such tools as SPC and improvements as JIT for its own purposes and still continue to operate as a relatively rigid mass producer. Its CIF rivals, however, will be using those technologies in another and more competitively effective milieu.

Some American firms, however, have realized the importance of making a total paradigm shift. Harley-Davidson, for example, is a textbook case of a firm on the brink of competitive destruction that survived by remaking itself. The firm made a comprehensive effort to transfer all three levels of CIF technology. According to Reid (1990, 145 ff.), what Harley-Davidson called its "productivity triad" consisted of SPC, JIT manufacturing, and employee involvement. Although it had to make financial outlays and pay opportunity costs for things that its Japanese rivals had developed largely as a matter of everyday operations, it put itself in the business of producing its own future improvements. By perfecting the productivity triad, Harley-Davidson has shed its follower role and become a leader in the new world of Schumpeterian competition.

Hewlett-Packard is another US firm that understands JIT for what it is, a demand pull system that links customer orders to the cross-functional productive system all the way back to parts suppliers.[17] It utilized the full tool kit of CIF technologies to redesign itself, including statistical process control, employee involvement, and some significant redesign of internal organizational and managerial systems to manifest the important latent, but heretofore unmanaged, cross-functional systems. Xerox, a recipient of the Baldridge award for quality, has made at least a partial transition from mass production to continuous improvement by remodeling its operations on the best practices of so-called "benchmark" firms – not only its Japanese competitors but also Western firms with good reputations for certain practices.[18]

The Saturn Corporation, a domestic subsidiary of General Motors, is undoubtedly the most comprehensive attempt by a US company to transfer the totality of the CIF technologies. Saturn, however, is at a certain disadvantage compared with Toyota or Honda. Although located in Tennessee, it is not exactly a "greenfield" operation. The initial employees were all formerly employed elsewhere in GM, and the United Auto Workers, although apparently much more cooperative here than with Mazda, is still involved. Another potential weakness is the fact that Saturn produces a larger fraction of parts in house than is the case for Japanese firms. Evidently, Saturn wants to get away from dependence on GM subsidiaries as suppliers as much as possible because it may be difficult to get some of the old-line GM subsidiaries to develop into dependable suppliers for a firm that needs zero defects in parts that have to be delivered just-in-time. The fact that so many parts are produced in house makes it difficult to balance processes in a way that fully utilizes all relevant capacities. That, of course, tends to push up cost. Moreover, one organizational feature of Saturn mitigates against its complete development of a continuous improvement firm. Top management and design engineers successfully resisted efforts to house the entire operation at or near the production facility so that they could remain behind in Detroit. That decision may be regrettable, given that a major factor in the CIF's quick response to market changes through flexible production is easy and ongoing communication between manufacturing, product design, and marketing. Not only the awkwardness imparted to communications but also the social distinction implied by this bifurcation may militate somewhat against continuous improvement.

Finally, the recent teamsters strike that paralyzed the Saturn operations reenforces the questions that have been posed elsewhere about the appropriateness of JIT manufacturing in the US socio-political setting.[19] Saturn is too young to allow a decisive judgment of its continuous improvement capabilities. Its products are selling well at the moment, but costs are reportedly high.[20]

US Subsidiaries in the Third World

Because many US firms are attempting some level of transfer of CIF technologies, it should not be surprising to find that their subsidiaries are also inclined to do so. The research in Brazil reported by Bos and Cole (1994) indicates that all US subsidiaries in the Brazilian electronics sector are attempting to adopt some forms of those technologies. A glaring difference between the US and Japanese electronics firms in Brazil is that the nationality of the CEOs for the US firms were all Brazilian, as were most top managers. This is promising for the long-term prospects for continuous improvement. Lower and middle managers of Brazilian nationality can contemplate the likelihood that they will be promoted to higher ranks within the company. The incentive for them to gather and utilize cross-functional, firm-specific information is therefore enhanced.

Interestingly, all US firms in the Brazilian electronics sector were employing SPC at some level of sophistication and 60 percent of them were attempting to adopt JIT manufacturing systems. This latter data is especially puzzling in view of the fact that no Japanese firm in the same sector was using JIT. As a complement to the JIT efforts, 60 percent of the US firms were cultivating close supplier relations. Furthermore, 60 percent utilized quality circles, and 80 percent had employee-suggestion programs. Plant visits gave no indication that the US firms were using any of the various programs less intensively or usefully than the Japanese firms that were also actively adopting the technology. One possible explanation for these differences is that the Japanese view it as costly to maintain a small subsidiary as an integrated CIF, while the US firms are not seriously practicing continuous improvement at home and therefore are not concerned about the costs of integration. The US firms with no CIF capabilities in the home operations may view these subsidiaries as a testing ground for the CIF paradigm.

The companion study in the Maquiladora zone of Mexico (Wilson 1992) again had results similar to the Brazilian findings. US firms were using CIF technologies – SPC, worker-suggestion systems, JIT, and supplier programs – much more than Japanese subsidiaries. That they were being used effectively is indicated by the fact that 96 percent of the subsidiaries reported having increased their work-in-process turns. Ninety-five percent reported having reduced production lead times and 47 percent said that they had developed improvements in their operations that they had transferred back to domestic facilities in the United States. One US subsidiary that had qualified as a supplier to NUMMI reported that a well-known Japanese manufacturer had sent engineers to them to document improvements that might be taken back to its own operations in Japan.

Another perspective for comparison emerged from the Mexico study. A comparison of continuous improvement practices of US subsidiaries with similar operations of the same companies in the United States revealed in many cases that the US subsidiary was significantly ahead of home operations in the use of continuous improvement technologies. Wilson (1992) accounts for this apparent relative success of US subsidiaries by the fact that they are operating on an industrial frontier that has removed local management from the close scrutiny of the home office. For the most part, the management put in charge was relatively young, given to making such statements as, "We know what to do, but back home no one will let us do it." They were sent to the Maquiladora zone to produce cheaply with low-wage labor and apparently as long as they shipped back their products with a low cost tag, they could manage however they liked. Sitting in their offices in the Mexican industrial park, they are a stone's throw from the big-name Japanese firms, and they enjoy taking up the challenge of competing on the basis of "best practices." Interestingly, if they got inside the factories of those vaunted Japanese companies, they would not find many of those Japanese-style "best practices" in use.

Is Culture a Barrier to the Transfer of CIF Technologies?

A major issue to consider in evaluating the prospects for transferring CIF technologies is the importance of the cultural milieu to the crucial soft technologies of the CIF. There is a running controversy in the literature regarding the extent to which culture has played a role in the success of the Japanese CIFs. According to Aoki (1988, 300ff), it is a matter of "culturalists versus rationalists." The culturalist school is epitomized by Abegglen (1958) who argued that Japanese business firms should not be considered as having assimilated the Western model. Instead, he argued, the emerging Japanese system has been a matter of adapting Western factory technology into an organizational context that was consistent with traditional Japanese customs and social relations. Numerous others have added the view that the particulars of the CIF, such as permanent employment, group responsibility and action, and the subjugation of individual goals to those of the organization are particularly Japanese (see, for example, Cooney 1989; Crosby 1979; Ford and Honeycutt 1992).

In their research on the influence of culture on economics Hofstede and Bond (1988, 20) conclude that, "Eastern thinking is synthetic." Similarly De Mente (1981, 34) has referred to the Japanese businessman's use of "logic that is cyclic, or elastic; not absolute." Decision making by Japanese managers is, DeMenthe says, "[i]n general terms, . . . intuitive instead of logical." The cultural tendency toward synthetic thinking implies a bringing together of all the parts, which, of course, is a hallmark of the CIF, reflected in such attributes as close relationships with suppliers, close and sustained contact with customers, consensual decision making, and an emphasis on interpersonal skills in the promotion of managers. Lest we forget, job rotation and cross-functional promotions serve to give the employee a synthetic viewpoint.

Hofstede and Bond's (ibid.) research, on the other hand, indicates that "a concern for the Truth," which they label "uncertainty avoidance," is much stronger in Western cultures. As a result, the Western way of thinking is said to be analytical, prompting American managers to break down an organization into its constituent parts and pursue specialization, and limiting its association with suppliers and customers to short-term market relationships. This view also suggests that Americans are predisposed to scientific management with its hierarchical organization, a reliance of top management upon objective means of evaluation and control of subordinates, and the concentration of decision making within the ranks of experts.

One fact that would seem to come down on the side of the culturalists is the checkered experience of US and other Western firms in trying to adopt at least some of the major features of the CIF. The general opinion seems to be that a lot of effort has been put forward to try to transfer the soft technologies of continuous improvement without much to show for it in the marketplace. In many instances, analytical tools such as statistical process control were put to use within the context of MP/SM paradigm in a new specialized quality department to assist in the discovery of quality problems, but not really to establish a continuous improvement system. In that context, SPC can help improve quality, but without simultaneously helping to reduce costs or improve deliverability or reduce development – cycle time.

Another example of limited transfer is the appointment of ad hoc teams to function within an otherwise MP/SM context. In discussions with managers from various industries, it is not at all unusual to encounter arguments to the effect that the crucial soft technologies such as permanent employment and job rotation are simply not feasible in the Western cultural context. Permanent employment, it is said, would reduce the incentive to perform well, but more importantly, it would not allow management to attend to the needs of the principal stakeholder, the owner. Moreover, some Western firms have used JIT primarily as a means of reducing inventory costs rather than as an important breakthrough improvement to be achieved through a series of incremental improvements to reduce product defects to near zero. In these cases costs may decrease (or often simply revert to suppliers), but quality improvements and other aspects of net customer value remain unaffected.

In an interesting approach to the question of cultural relativism, Goonatilake (1984) argues that scientific management was shaped and energized by the peculiar cultural features of the US economy during the time of Frederick Taylor and Henry Ford. The MP/SM system developed to fit into a society in which class distinctions played an overwhelming role. References to this emphasis on class distinctions appear in the writings of that time, for example, in Veblen's *Theory of the Leisure Class* (1934) and Edith Wharton's *The Age of Innocence* (1920). Another cultural feature of that time was the preponderance of non-English speaking immigrants in the labor force of the US Midwest, where both mass production and scientific management were developed. The language problem helped make a necessity what classism prompted. Top-down control of workers who were given menial and clearly delineated assignments made eminent sense in that context.

If we apply the Goonatilake approach to the CIF paradigm, we see it as probable that the Japanese culture (and Eastern culture, in general) has been open to and supportive of it, thus giving it an advantage in the development of certain technologies. For example, the Japanese *keiretsu,* which is an institutional manifestion of Japanese culture, has made it easier for the Japanese CIF to cooperate in long-term relationships with suppliers and customers. Western firms have no historical precedent for such an institution, which may put them at a disadvantage in the development of the CIF technologies.

The culture issue does not have to be a one-way street. While MP/SM was appropriate to the US of a century ago, have not major contradictions emerged in the interim? Has classism in the US not declined from the level of a century ago when those with money tried to emulate British aristocracy? Are democratic tendencies not a strong underlying value in the American social milieu? Has education not reduced the differences in ability to communicate that supported scientific management? While some cultural issues may continue to act as as impediments to some cultural issues may continue to act as as impediments to the adoption of the CIF technologies, are not other strong cultural currents in the West potentially fertile ground for nurturing the growth of CIF-type organizations? The important question, therefore, is whether the CIF system may be more appropriate than the MP/SM paradigm for the United States at the threshold of the twenty-first century. We will not know whether the cultural changes have been sufficient unless and until concerted efforts are made to shed old forms and take on new ones. In this chapter we cited several cases of US firms that have made comprehensive efforts to change. So long as the examples of significant and continuing success are few, they may remain in popular thought as exceptions that prove the rule. Until the new paradigm makes significant inroads into the turf of MP/SM, the presumption of many will be that change is impossible.

The rationalists view of the matter may be represented by Aoki (1988) and Koike (in Aoki 1984). After noting that small groups are the robust core of the CIF, Aoki challenges the widely held view that the group orientation is unique to Japan. Specifically, he argues that "[g]roupism is not a sufficient condition for the competitive performance of the J-firm, . . . [and] it is not a necessary condition either." (1988, 299) He goes on to argue that because the Japanese organizational constructs were a rational reaction to market conditions, at least some of them may be usefully adopted by Western firms.

A not unreasonable position to take on the matter of culture would be that it has played a role but not one that is immutable. We would like to go a step beyond culture, however. What this volume has strongly suggested is that the paradigm view itself is a major hindrance to the successful transfer of CIF features to Western firms. So long as the ones who purport to study the CIF look at it through the lens of MP/SM, they will never understand it. The first step in successful transfer is gaining an understanding of just what the MP/SM paradigm is and how pervasive it is in shaping (and warping) our thinking. The next step is to understand the CIF paradigm. Probably the most useful approach is to study the two paradigms simultaneously. The upshot is that we have to see both forms as paradigms that shape the way their adherents see the world. Once the features of the CIF are seen in the context of its paradigm, it becomes obvious, for example, that none of the features work well in the absence of a customer-value focus. There is no way to understand the customer-value focus while using the MP/SM perspective. The closest we can get is the customer-satisfaction approach of the standard marketing function, and that is a long way off the mark. The former is proactive; the latter is merely responsive. The task may appear monumental because it means changing the way all employees of the firm believe the world works in the arena of manufacturing.

NOTES

1. This usage of the term *soft technology* and its distinction from the normal usage of *software* was developed earlier in Cole and Sanders (1983) and Cole and Mogab (1987).

2. Schonberger (1986) described this plant as "the most efficient in the world," noting that it was equipped with American machinery that was then more than 20 years old.

3. One reason it is unlikely that an MP/SM firm could operate JIT as effectively as a CIF is that the production process must be producing at a rate of near zero in terms of defects.

4. Washio (1886) recalls a case in which an effort to detail a CIF-technology transfer resulted in a stack of computer printouts literally two meters thick.

5. Some would argue that because of cultural differences, it is unlikely, ceteris paribus, that the rate of improvement generation would be as great in the context of subsidiaries as it would be in context home operations.

6. Of course, the transfer costs to the various susidiaries will differ somewhat depending on distance and other factors. It is possible, that there be some economies of scale in standardization across subsidiaries as the number of subsidiaries increases. The assumption of equal additional transfer costs for each subsidary is a simplification made here for explanatory purposes that does not invalidate the basic argument that the cost of standardization will be greater with overseas subsidiaries than without them.

7. Some economies of transfer may develop in such a way that costs may increase at a decreasing rate as new subsidiaries are created.

8. Possibly there will be some gains from the establishment of subsidiaries in the form of the external information that the employees bring to the workplace setting. For example, the employees of Toyota's plant in Kentucky certainly bring to the workplace a different external information set than that of Toyota City workers.

9. If the output of the home operations is reduced by one-half while the cost of standardizing processes remains the same, the impact will be to raise the cost per unit.

10. According to Kenney and Florida (1993, 98), "Toyota's purpose in agreeing to the joint venture was to test the feasibility of transferring the Toyota system to the United States."

11. According to Kenney and Florida (1993, 114), about 85 percent of the NUMMI work force was recruited from the ranks of former GM employees who had been laid off when the plant shut down.

12. According to Rubenstein (1991, 125), the GM version failed because the Nova name had been used years earlier on a car that proved very unpopular. The GM "twin" is currently marketed as the Geo Prizm.

13. A step-by-step account of the conversion of some Packard Electric facilities to continuous improvement in an effort to qualify as NUMMI suppliers is found in Walker (1988).

14. These views are reflected in statements by NUMMI workers, as reported in Kenney and Florida (1993, 117–18).

15. Personal communication at the site in Georgetown, KY (Sept. 1991).

16. The Maquiladora industry was born in the 1960s based upon agreements between the US and Mexican governments and upon special provisions of the US tariff code. Accordingly, transnational plants import duty-free inputs and export relatively duty-free output into the US market. The duty paid upon entry to the United States is only on the value added by Mexican labor.

17. The successful recent history of the Hewlett-Packard plant in Vancouver, Washington is explored by Hayes, Wheelwright, and Clark (1988, 363–4).

18. For example, XEROX adopted L.L. Bean as its benchmark for logistics and distribution (Hayes, Wheelwright, and Clark 1988, 157–8).

19. In a number of US industries, the practice of carrying larger inventories than strictly required by technical considerations has developed precisely to avoid shutdowns during strikes at suppliers or by the teamsters.

20. Information in this paragraph is based upon personal observations and discussions with Saturn and GM personnel, both in Michigan and Tennessee.

CHAPTER 11

THE FUTURE OF TQM

The continuous improvement firm harnesses the minds of the members of the work force at all levels of the organization and directs that substantial resource toward the improvement of net customer value on a day-to-day basis. It is the combination of employee involvement and customer-value orientation that produces the value wedge that constitutes the CIF's competitive advantage. By internally generating a stream of technological change and delinking it from capital investment, the CIF is able to simultaneously reduce the cost of production and improve all aspects of net customer value. Its advantage over the MP/SM firm appears sufficiently great to allow us to say, ceteris paribus the continuous improvement approach is superior to the mass production/scientific management approach. Hypothetical superiority, however, does not always translate into marketplace superiority. It is appropriate, therefore, to explore the long-term prospects for the CIF paradigm in the real world where *ceteris paribus* does not hold.

It is generally conceded that political actions have the potential to thwart economic efficiency trends and thereby give an outdated system a new lease on life. We have already noted that protectionist efforts, both in the West and in developing countries, have placed Japanese CIFs in the position of having to establish foreign subsidiaries. In such cases, the rate of improvement creation decreases and the cost of the improvement process increases. The result, in short, is a diminution in the size of the value wedge that separates the product of the CIF from its competitors' offerings. Further efforts to save domestic firms from foreign CIfs can be expected to include various forms of protection, whether through regional groupings or old-fashioned national barriers. While the CIF paradigm may provide a system that is superior in theory, its progenitors continue to find themselves somewhat hobbled by the political rules of the game.

Nor should our real-world concerns be limited to political factors. Because the CIF phenomenon is relatively new and its success has taken place during a period of exuberant economic growth, we should be somewhat circumspect about the prospects for long-term success. Should we not speculate, at least, about the prospects for continued success as markets and firms mature? Will the CIF develop bureaucratic lethargy with the passage of time? Will the CIF be able to maintain the vigor of the improvement processes over time? To pursue answers to these questions, we will look at some implications that the Schumpeterian development-cycle concept and the product life-cycle hypothesis may have for the CIF paradigm.

Schumpeterian Capitalist Development and the CIF

It is exhilarating to refract the current mixed competition between the CIF and the MP/SM firm through the prism of Schumpeter's (1962) dynamic theory of capitalist development. For Schumpeter, capitalist development takes place through the process of creative destruction. He saw the entrepreneur-innovator as the driving force of that process. In explaining the role of innovation, he said "The fundamental impulse that sets and keeps the capitalist engine in motion comes from the new consumers' goods, the new methods of production or transportation, the new markets, the new forms of industrial organization that capitalist enterprise creates." (83) The new innovative mode replaces the old in a "perennial gale of creative destruction." (84) The competition that counts, according to Schumpeter, is that which "commands decisive cost or quality advantage and which strikes not at the margins of the profits and the outputs of existing firms but at their foundations and their very lives." (84) At this point, it is difficult not to reflect on the fate of the consumer electronics industry in the United States. It was, in effect, blown away by the CIFs' "perennial gale," and the automobile industry, which lost much ground in its effort to weather the storm.

In Schumpeter's view, a new wave of development is initiated by a bold innovator-entrepreneur, and it is subsequently dispersed by imitators whose risk-averse nature relegates them to the role of following a leader. Eventually, the profit margins associated with the innovation begin to fall. In the case at hand, we can view the emergence of the CIFs as creative destruction on a grander scale than anything anticipated by Schumpeter. It is not simply a matter of a new product replacing an existing one, or of a new transportation mode supplanting an older form. It is no less than the triumph of one comprehensive paradigm over another; it is the destruction of a vision of the way firms and economies operate. That it is "creative" and progressive, has been amply validated by the market.

Paradoxically, however, if we analyze the long-term prospects of the CIF within the context of Schumpeter's vision, certain troubling questions immediately emerge. Specifically, Schumpeter believed that the modern corporation with its feature of professional management could *not* be a source of innovation, as he states succinctly in the following passage: "[T]he modern businessman . . . is of the executive type. From the logic of his position he acquires something of the psychology of the salaried employee working in the bureaucratic organization. Wheather stockholder or not, his will to fight and to hold on is not and cannot be what it was with the man who knew ownership in the full blooded sense of those words." (156) In other words, the recent corporate capitalism of the West is a degenerate form that increasingly loses the dynamic qualities associated with entrepreneurial capitalism. With that in mind, it is interesting to note that such giants among Japanese CIFs as Sony, Matsushita (Panasonic), Honda, and Toyota were pioneered by innovator-entrepreneurs.[1] It might not be farfetched to take these four corporations as responsible for the wave of creative destruction. Of course, the innovation to which we refer is the new form of organization, continuous improvement or total quality management.

The question suggested by Schumpeter is, Can the CIFs continue to operate as innovators after their innovator-entrepreneurs have passed from the scene?[2] If the institution of the continuous improvement organizational form was the original innovation, can we expect more innovations from those organizations, or should we anticipate that the bureaucratic arteriosclerosis described by Schumpeter will also afflict the CIFs? The quick and ready answer might be that we can expect more innovation. In a very real sense, the continuous improvement organization endogenizes innovation. That is what Best (1990, 137 ff) means when he uses the phrase "the entrepreneurial firm in Japan" as a chapter title. The ability to persistently manifest new levels of quality, new features, enhanced ability to deliver to tighter and tighter schedules, and reduced cost of production are all contributions to a firm's competitiveness. Furthermore, while these changes often emerge in incremental form, in accumulation they add up to innovation, as in the case of just-in-time manufacturing. If the process that produces change remains intact, we could well expect further hallmark innovations to emerge.

The endogenization of the ability to produce innovations is, therefore, a megainnovation. Are we, therefore, looking at a phenomenon, an organizational form, that has moved us beyond Schumpeter's fear that the demise of the entrepreneur-innovator would deplete the innovative potential from capitalism? Before attempting a definitive answer to the potential for loss of organizational dynamics, we will pursue questions associated with the life cycle of the product and possible consequences. At that point we will revisit the topic, possibly having new perspectives from which to view the bureaucratization of the firm.

A Life-Cycle Approach to the CIF

The widely used concept of product life cycle may hold implications for the life of the firm producing the product, especially if the firm is a CIF. As explained by Dicken (1992, 11), "the essence of the product life-cycle is that the growth of sales of a product follows a systematic path from initial innovation through a series of stages: early development, growth, maturity and obsolescence." In the early development and growth stages, demand for the product increases at an increasing rate, but market demand for the product slackens during maturity and thereafter declines. The length of the periods and precise shape of the development curve varies from industry to industry, but supposedly all are subject eventually to its iron logic. Forms left in the market during the latter stages fight over the remains. As a product market experiences diminishing growth rates and eventual shrinkage, some firms contract in size and others drop out altogether.

There are a couple of safety valves that, if utilized, can allow for extended growth of the firm. One way for a firm to escape its foretold demise is to innovate another product, as happened when audiocassette tapes and tape players came to market along side of vinyl records and record players. That innovation was followed by compact disc technology, and the sequence of innovations has allowed several major Japanese electronics firms to continue to experience increased demand for their products. In each case, diffusion of the innovative product followed the logic of the life-cycle sequence.

Another escape mechanism is expansion into a new market. Whereas the domestic demand for automobiles had probably moved to somewhere between growth and maturity (slow growth) approximately a decade or so ago, the Japanese CIFs that produced automobiles were able to shift their long-term base for growth into established foreign markets previously served only by domestic MP/SM firms. More recently, we have seen a proliferation of specialized automobiles that has served to expand the market by opening new niches. Nevertheless, even in the case of automobiles, as with other products, the overall market size and overall market-growth rate eventually must place binding constraints on the ability of the firms to grow. In the case of the MP/SM firm, downsizing and relocating to countries where wages are low may provide for greater efficiency, narrowly measured in terms of cost. For many, such a move exhausts the prescription list for long-term survival. For the CIF, however, downsizing forebodes dire consequences. Specifically, if downsizing were to entail dropping such incentive policies as permanent employment and promotion from within, then it would appear to threaten the very soul of the CIF and its identifying mark, the ability to continuously improve net customer value of the product.

To pursue the implications of the product life cycle for the future of the CIF, we will first review the sources of productivity improvement, broadly defined, within the CIF and then ask how each of these is related to the firm's ability to grow. We have seen that the dynamism of continuous improvement depends upon the willingness of employees at all levels to obtain firm-specific cross-functional information and utilize it to introduce improvements that increase the perceived value of the product. Several conditions serve as a foundation for the establishment of continuous improvement systems, and several conditions enhance the operation of such systems. First, successful operation of a CIF requires that management create among the workers a clear understanding that the firm's success depends upon its ability to offer net customer value equal to or greater than that available from competing firms. Profits, market share, and the capacity to maintain a permanent well-paid work force all tend to go to the firms with products or services that offer the highest net customer value. In the Japanese CIF, this customer-value orientation is partly a matter of indoctrination into the company's philosophy and partly a matter of formal and informal training. The bottom line is that the employees come to understand that they hold the key to competitiveness through an ability to improve the production processes and the product.[3] The absence of such understanding tends to promote actions that give priority to the interests of other stakeholders rather than the customers (e.g., shareholders), which detract from the creation of customer value, thereby eroding the CIF's competitive advantage.

Another necessary condition for operation as a CIF is the clear indentification by employees of the strong connection between market performance and their own economic future. In Japanese firms, this linkage underlies the provision of permanent employment. The expectation of permanent employment causes employees to indentify their fate with that of the firm. If they help the firm succeed, they thereby further their own security. With this association firmly established, management sees an economic advantage in providing employees with training and access to information. From everyone's point of view, employees at all levels of the firm come to be seen as fixed capital rather than agents.

Another sign of the link between performance of the firm and performance of the individual is reward for engendering improvements. In the Japanese firm promotions in the managerial ranks are always internal, and effectiveness in the improvement process is an important consideration for such promotions. At the operator level, social recognition, cash rewards for significant improvements, and some form of bonus participation in profits are useful incentives, as is the prospect for promotion to supervisory ranks and even occasionally to managerial positions.

A condition that enhances operation is the provision to the employee of as much information as possible, except information directly related to market secrets. Beyond that, work space is organized so that each employee is afforded both a broad vision of the implicit cross-functional systems and the details of operations immediately upstream and downstream from his/her station.[4] Visits by CIF personnel,including operators, to suppliers expand the range of crucial information available. Comparable visits to the CIF by supplier personnel are also important sources of information for both firms. Furthermore, there should be some direct interaction between customers and employees at all levels. Yet another source of operational efficiency is the training in analytical techniques that employees get to relate their work to customer value.

That a direct relationship exists between the net customer value associated with a firm's product and its competitive position is documentable and teachable, as is the relationship that exists between the firm's internal operations and net customer value. It is therefore possible to convince employees that their specific actions count and thereby enhance the competitive position of the firm. Ensuring that these matters receive their due is a primary responibility of the firm's management

The demonstration of the direct relationship between the firm's success and the employee's personal success is not so directly managed, however. Nevertheless, it is crucial that employees feel that their actions to improve customer value directly redound to their personal benefit. The crux of the matter is that the strength of the incentives that link customer value and employee welfare necessarily depend upon the firm's ability to grow.[5] Furthermore, the more effective the firm is at promoting internal improvements, the greater is the imperative for growth. If output per worker is growing, total output must grow if employment is to be held constant. Therefore, because continuous improvement depends upon relatively permanent employment, the improvement process itself imparts pressure for substantial output growth over time. More specifically, the minimum growth performance required to support permanent employment lies between two basic constraints. From one perspective, if output growth is enough to offset labor productivity growth (output per worker), a steady level of employment can be maintained. From another perspective, the rate of normal worker attrition may be factored in with productivity growth to determine the minimum growth rate that would support permanent employment, but at declining levels. For example, if the rate of normal attrition were 5 percent per year, productivity (output per worker) could grow at a rate of 5.26 percent within the overall context of zero growth of output. On the other hand, if the attrition rate were 4 percent and productivity grew at 6 percent, output would have to grow at a rate of 1.8 percent to avoid a decision between redundancy or layoffs. If competitive factors preclude the sufficient growth of output in such a case, the company would have to decide between the cost of redundancy and the loss of long-run competitiveness implied by the inability to ensure permanent employment.

The policy to promote from within the ranks as an incentive also has implications for the growth of output. The incentive to operate in an improvement mode, especially for the managerial ranks and technicians, depends to some significant degree on the prospects for promotion. If the current base of the employment pyramid were to move to the top, however, output obviously would have to grow in order to avoid bureaucratic redundancy. Moreover, if growth were to create the need for more managers, the probability of promotion obviously would increase.

We should recognize that if promotion were a certainty and followed a more or less set schedule, incentives would be weak because competition among managers to initiate improvements would not be seen as a factor in promotion. At the other end of the scale, that is, a low rate of promotion, incentives would also be very weak. If the promotion coefficient is the fraction of new employees in the professional-technical ranks who can expect to become top managers, then the ideal ratio would be well above zero and significantly below one. Certainly, no one ratio would fit every time and every place, but even without specific data, we should be able to say something significant about the implications of this factor for growth.

Take the pyramid in figure 11.1a as representative of a certain CIF. For purposes of analysis we will assume that, on the average, this CIF's middle managers have ten-year planning horizon and that the promotion coefficient of 0.5 will facilitate maximum improvement generation. If all initial top managers retire during the period, and if no attrition occurs in the other ranks, 14 of 28 middle managers should move to the top, and 84 persons must move up from the ranks of first-line managers in order to maintain the same ratio of middle to top managers.[6] The result is shown in figure 11.1b. If we assume no change in the operating ratio of first-line managers to middle managers, some 686 of the latter also would be employed. Note that the improvement process might possibly increase this ratio, but the number of first-line managers is not crucial to this example. Our focus is the maintenance of a promotion coefficient of 0.5 for movement into the top two ranks. If the ratio of managers to output (managerial productivity) remains constant, then output would have to grow by a factor of 3.5 to support the increase in the management ranks. Finally, assuming that all productivity gains are realized at the level of floor operations (regardless of where they were initiated), a 40 percent productivity improvement over the decade would allow for a 3.5-fold increase in output to be produced by 5,000 operators. (This would imply that the ratio of managers to operators is increasing.)

Because the above scenario involves such an overwhelming requirment for growth as to be unrealistic, we should explore a less stringent case. What kind of promotion coefficient could we expect from the doubling of output over the period of a decade? With no changes in the manager-to-sales ratio or in the level-to-level ratios among managerial ranks, a doubling of output would result in eight persons moving to the top, assuming complete attrition among those initially in that rank. Furthermore, 56 per-

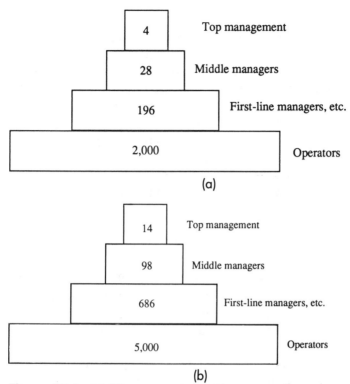

Figure 11.1. (a) CIF corporate hierarchy. (b) Internal promotion and corporate growth.

sons would move to the middle ranks. In this case, the promotion coefficient for middle manger (to top) would be 8/28 or 0.285. Because 20 middle managers were not promoted, only 36 could move up from the first-line ranks, yielding a first-line manager promotion coefficient of only 0.18 (36/196). The promotion coefficients in both of these instances are certainly not high, and yet a reasonably high annual output-growth rate of seven percent per year is required to achieve them.

The foregoing excercises are not meant to suggest that any definitive knowledge is to be gained from the numbers; the conclusions are strictly hypothetical. What is demonstrated, however, is the point that, for a given CIF, there is some specific relationship, albeit unknown, between the firm's ability to grow and the willingness of its employees to participate in the improvement process. The strength of the relationship in undoubtedly idiosyncratic to the individual firm.

From what we have seen, the necessity of maintaining permanent employment and of promoting from within the managerial ranks together generate an imperative for the CIF to grow. The pressures emanating from the promotion requirement, however, appear to be greater. If so, the ability to sustain a continuous improvement strategy over a significant period of time is intimately related to the product life cycle. In the early stages of a product's life, market growth is explosive, making it easier to maintain the promise of permanent employment and to promote rapidly; but after the product has been fully diffused, rapid growth by one firm can come only at the expense of others. If its competitors are MP/SM firms, the ability to win in mixed competition and the resulting increased market share will sustain the CIF's growth for some time after the product has been fully diffused. Nevertheless, for a given CIF in a given market, the time comes when a product's growth potential no longer supports either permanent employment or an effective promotion coefficient. The ability to generate continuous improvements then suffers because of the firm's inability to guarantee permanent employment or to promote its personnel. We can think of this scenario as the "life-cycle hypothesis" for the CIF.

Because the original development of a continuous improvement strategy is evidence of a proven ability to find new opportunities, and because continuous improvement itself disposes managers to search for ways to improve the firm's condition, we would not expect CIF managers to stand by while their competitive advantage withered away within one generation. We would indeed expect them to look for new products and new markets, or some other form of organizational innovation. Consequently, top management must take strategic action if the continuous improvement capability of the firm is to be salvaged over the long run. Operation as a continuous improvement firm might be possible through the development of additional product lines, especially ones new to the market; or the CIF might move into a foreign market, especially ones in which it could withdraw market share from existing MP/SM firms. Failing that, it will be unable to operate as a full-blown CIF. That eventuality brings up the possibility that the firm might become a modified version of a CIF by designating a significant fraction of the work force as permanent and employing the remainder on the basis of need. Most Japanese CIF's already operate in this mode, with a sizable fraction of workers employed temporarily only as needed. It follows logically from our assumptions about the role of incentives that the smaller the cadre of permanent employees, the lower the rate of improvement generation. Within managerial ranks, some might be chosen early for an elite promotion track and others left with severely reduced chances for promotion. Early retirement among the latter group might also open up positions for those on the elite track below. Again, the smaller the fraction of managers placed on the elite track, the lower the rate of improvement generation.[6]

When the CIF moves into a new market and starts with a relatively small share, its early growth can be rapid, especially if its principal competitors operate within the MP/SM paradigm. If the CIF were to absorb all or most of that market, however, its own growth would then be constrained by the growth of the market. In the case of entirely new products, the growth of the market itself should be rapid for an extended period of time. With established products in mature markets, such as the automobile, however, the rate of growth of the market will be relatively slow and probably never enough in any given country to sustain relatively high promotion coefficients.

When the CIF moves into an established foreign market served by MP/SM firms, a realistic view is that the growth of its market share will slow down long before the CIF has absorbed all or most of the market. Political factors, if nothing else, will step in to put a stop to the loss of an entire domestic industry. For example, although US firms lost the entire VCR market to foreign competition, there is no chance that the government would allow the US automobile market to experience the same fate. Furthermore, follower firms might attempt to copy some of the CIF's methods long before all of the market were gone.

One area of potential growth for the mature CIF is in those LDCs that are experiencing, or can be expected to experience, rapid economic growth. Excellent examples are the so-called "Asian tigers," with whom the Japanese CIFs are already closely working. A problem with LDCs as the basis for CIF production growth is that most of them do not wish to be mere export drops for Japanese CIFs; they want to create part of the value added themselves. In some cases, import substitution policies require that the manufactured good be at least assembled in the host country. We have already seen, however, that the proliferation of subsidiaries greatly increases the cost of standardizing processes and reduces the rate of improvement creation.

In its search for external markets, the CIF would do well to look for a very large LDC that is expected to grow significantly over the coming decades. China, for example, is an excellent candidate, having a potentially huge market for a full range of manufactured goods. Apparently, Japanese firms have already recognized that potential and have made hundreds of investments there to date. The obviously desirable mode for operation would be to arrive at an internal division of labor on the basis of comparative advantage, with final assembly and manufacture of simpler components taking place in China and design and the manufacture of more sophisticated (higher value-added) components taking place in Japan. The market potential is certainly large enough to justify placing continuous improvement capability in the Chinese subsidiaries. Indeed, they could even be closely coordinated with the home operations. Recall that the additional cost of operating one central subsidiary as a CIF is much less than that of operating continuous improvement in many geographically scattered subsidiary firms. Furthermore, the reduction in improvement generation capability is much less for one large subsidiary than for many smaller ones. Whereas continuous improvement subsidiaries might not have been economically justified in, say, Brazil, they very well could be in China.

The need to grow, then, may place constraints on continuous improvement capability. The need to grow at rapid rates forces a CIF to find substitutes for mature stagnant markets, for example, the development of new products for which a new lifecycle would begin or a new market that could serve as host for the rapid expansion needed. Even if the CIF is able to maintain its high growth rate, however, it is not without another potential problem. Will the CIF's growth eventually result in an organization that is so large that it is bureaucratically difficult to manage, one in which it will be difficult to foster within the minds of individual employees a close association between their actions and the fate of the organization? In short, are we left with reasons to believe that there may be built-in tendencies for the continuous improvement capability to wane?

With regard to the doubts about long-term viability of given CIF organizations, history provides us with examples of relatively few firms that endure for very long periods of time. The prospect of struggling to maintain continuous improvement capability and the definite prospect of losing it someday should not deter any firms from developing that capability as a competitive strategy. As Lord Keynes once expressed it with uncharacteristic lack of subtlety, "In the long run, we are all dead." And, given the nature of mixed competition, the CIF should enjoy a longer life than the MP/SM firm, albeit a finite one.

Is it Feasible to Develop Alternative Soft Technologies?

Are there possible continuous improvement soft technologies other than those developed by the Japanese? If so, it is possible to develop them within the context of Western culture? Put differently, might it not be possible to develop continuous improvement soft technologies that are especially appropriate to US culture. At an even more fundamental level, is it feasible or practical to look for new soft technologies that will produce internal improvements and flexibility and not entail some of the apparent drawbacks of the Japanese version? Especially useful would be forms that did not fail in the absence of rapid growth.

This approach may, in fact, be what is necessary if the United States and other Western firms are to achieve the continuous improvement capability. The Theory Z organizations, as proposed by Ouchi and Jaeger (1978, 311), suggest that at least a few Western firms may be moving in that direction. Theory Z organizations share several features with the Japanese CIF, such as long-term employment, slow evaluation and promotion, consensual decision making, implicit informal control, and a holistic concern for the employees. But there are also differences. In Theory Z organizations, responsibility is individual, performance measures are explicit, and careers are moderately specialized. In addition, as Hatvany and Pucik (1981, 20) point out, "Ouchi tells us little about communication patterns in these organizations, the role of the work group, and some other features important in the Japanese setting."

An alternative scenario for the development of a Western/US-based CIF is the prospect that employee-owned firms may choose to move in that direction. For example, the recent acquisition by United Airlines' pilots of controlling ownership rights could serve as the basis for implementing a continuous-improvement strategy if they were to become so disposed. In their role as shareholders, they will be sympathetic to the need to promote profits. In their role as employees, however, they will be interested in fostering the long-term growth of the firm as the basis of job security and promotion. Both goals are better served by focusing the organization on customer value.

We venture to say that if some Western firms successfully adopt a CIF mode, they should be able to triumph over MP/SM firms operating within the same political-economic setting. In short, if we view continuous improvement purely as a concept rather than as a concrete form, such as the Japanese firm, we see the distinct possibility that it could displace MP/SM even if protection excluded participation of the Japanese CIF in a specific market. Indeed, the trend away from the central aspects of MP/SM appears to be gaining momentum in many areas of the U.S. economy, both private and public. The movement is not limited to the highly visible firms that compete for the Malcom Baldridge award but extends even to the incipient move toward site-based management in public schools. We have noted, however, that some Western firms exhibit contradictory behavior, simultaneously developing certain continuous improvement features such as JIT while engaging in wholesale work force reductions and/or moving facilities to locations that feature low-wage labor. In those cases, something will have to give. A firm would have great difficulty operating effectively with one foot firmly in the MP/SM paradigm and the other in the TQM paradigm, each paradigm being so comprehensive that one ideal type necessarily precludes the other. And yet, an operating firm cannot change, in one swift motion, all of the principles under which it operates. It will necessarily change a few steps at a time. In that regard, the closer it comes to the ideal type, the more competitive clout it will have, that is, the larger the value wedge associated with its product will be. In this evolutionary process, the firm that adopts only enough TQM to allow it to solve problems will necessarily lag behind the firm that is proactive in promoting customer value. The fully developed CIF goes beyond problem solving to expand on the state of the art in all aspects of customer value, including quality, functional performance, and functional features. The organization that calls itself a "problem solving firm" has only traveled part of the distance required for arriving at the designation CIF.

Movement toward a Global Factory

While some Western firms have been experimenting recently with the development of continuous improvement soft technologies, there has been a simultaneous trend toward the emergence of the global factory. The global factory concept represents the "emergence of a *new global division of labour* – a change in the geographical pattern of specialization at the global scale." (Dicken 1992, 6) The transformation is said to be toward a "highly complex, kaleidoscopic structure involving the *fragmentation* of many production processes and their *geographical* relocation on a global scale which slice through national boundaries." (4) A World Bank report (1987) highlighted this trend focusing on the European version of the Ford Escort as an example. It showed that because the components of the Escort were manufactured in no less than fifteen countries, the fact that it was assembled in the United Kingdom and the Federal Republic of Germany was almost incidental. The point was that the finished product was broken down into as many components as feasible and their production disseminated globally on the basis of comparative advantage.[7] This trend has implications for the organization and operation of large complex firms as they try to enjoy the full benefits of ultraspecialization.

Another example of the trend toward the global factory is General Motors' policy of no longer guaranteeing contracts to some of its own subsidiaries that produce automobile components. Although still owned by General Motors, they cannot count on selling to GM, nor are they required to sell to GM. In other words, central management is encouraging at least some of its constituent organizations to purchase parts anywhere in the world where they can make the best deal and to sell their finished components to any company in the world where they can get the best deal.

It should be immediately apparent that this global factory movement is on a contradictory course with other important changes taking place in many leading Western firms. At the same time that Ford is fragmenting the production of Escort components to the four corners of the globe, so to speak, it is also engaged in attempts to adopt just-in-time manufacturing. The problem, of course, is that JIT requires the development and maintenance of close relations with suppliers and the delivery of purchased components on an as needed basis. Both of these goals are made difficult if not impossible to accomplish with the global fragmentation of the production process. The extreme geographical division of labor also has significant implications for the length of the product-development cycle. At a time when getting new products to the market quickly is becoming a matter of survival, the globalization trend would appear to be pushing firms in the wrong direction.

Obviously, the global factory trend is a desperate ultimate move by the MP/SM firm to achieve cost reductions. Not only is this the ultimate step in the global division of labor, it is the ultimate attempt by the MP/SM firm to compete on its own terms with CIFs. Once each component is made in the geographic location that affords the lowest possible cost for the extant technology, and assembly is carried out in the location that affords the best combination of low wages and adequate skills, the firm will have painted itself into a corner. The MP/SM firms will have made their long-term competitive weakness even worse, in that the global-factory approach will have decreased their production flexibility just at a time when market segmentation is emerging as a major competitive weapon.

The Prospects for TQM

At this point in time what can be said about the prospects for TQM? We shall look first at the prospects for further implementation of TQM principles in manufacturing, especially outside of Japan. The subsidiary problem for CIFs elaborated in chapter 10, in effect, serves as a sort of infant-industry protection for Western firms that would implement TQM. When conventional protection causes Japanese firms to locate in the United States and Europe, a derivative form of protection is provided to domestic producers. This derivative protection shows up in the CIF's reduced improvement capability and higher costs associated with the establishment of subsidiaries, both of which reduce the size of the value wedge. On the one hand, this situation may be viewed as a relaxation of the pressure on Western firms to shift to the new paradigm. More properly, however, it should be viewed as a breathing space. If the logic of the new paradigm is compelling, those Western firms that seriously go about its adoption will be the ones that remain in the chase. The customer will perceive a value wedge between their product and that of their rivals. Furthermore, the closer the firm can get to the ideal type of organization, the larger will be the value wedge and, thus, the faster its market share can grow. In a market setting where no firm has yet approached the ideal type, the leader in providing customer value still may evince many shortcomings. To maintain its leadership advantage, however, it will have to continually move toward the ideal.

At this point it may be interesting to contemplate the potential role of TQM for firms or organizations that provide services. It is often argued that the continuous improvement format is appropriate for any type of organization that has a product or service, whether it is private or public. A fundamental problem that confronts some service organizations aspiring to continuous improvement capability is identification of the customer. In the realm of many personal services, such as hair styling, for example, the customer is just as obvious as in the case of manufactured goods. In administrative services, on the other hand, who the customer is, is far from straightforward. Who are the customers of a state prison system? Of the Internal Revenue

Service? Who are the customers of a university? Are they the students? Their parents? The organization that hire graduates of the institution? Who are the customers of the public schools? Surely some would identify parents as the customers and educated students as the products. On the other hand, if hiring organizations are the customers, what then are the appropriate types of improvements for adding value? Most people, perhaps, would say that society at large is the proper customer in that, ideally, education should be a prequisite of citizenship. In any case, how do the employees of the school system discover just what things customers value?

It should be obvious that there would have to be widespread and outspoken agreement among all members of the school system as to what constitutes the output for which they are individually and collectively responsible and, whose valuations of that product are to be the central focus of all improvement efforts. It should come as no surprise that educators have differences of opinion on this subject. Some see themselves as the caretakers of educational materials. They see the presentation of that material as their responsibility toward students and toward the citizenry. In that case, whether or not students learn the material is entirely up to them. However, if the educated student is the proper outcome of a school system, the responsibility for students learning the subject material shifts to the teachers, and of course to the systems within which they work.[8] In a TQM setting, each employee would be striving to improve the system in ways that promoted learning.

The difficulty of identifying the customer is not limited to public-service companies. If one is to turn a health-insurance company, for example, into a continuous improvement firm, which group's perceived valuations give meaning to the improvements and provide the firm its competitive edge? Do members of the firm focus on generating improvements that appeal to the government offices that pay the bills for Medicare? The private and public organizations that sign up for group policies? The hospitals? The doctors? Individual policyholders as patients and potential patients? If they are all customers, how can we reconcile the contradictions that emerge when improved value for one group is considered to reduce value from the point of view of another group?

Other perspectives have to be revised when we consider the application of TQM to service industries. Some personal services put severe constraints on the ability to increase output per worker. Hair styling or teeth cleaning, for example, have a much less tractable human component than is found in manufacturing. Nevertheless, improvements are possible in other areas of customer value, such as quality and scheduling, which can help enhance the competitive position of the firm. Because of the limits on the ability to increase output per worker, the problem of maintaining permanent employment is not the overriding problem that it is in manufacturing. The promotion coefficient, however, is likely to be low, based largely on normal labor attrition. The situation is similar in restaurants, for example, where internally generated improvements can enhance the service, but probably not affect labor productivity by much. In such cases, however, the promotion coefficient can be raised if the organization clones itself to form a chain of service establishments. The customer-value orientation and internally generated improvements could serve as the strategic basis for such growth.

If we look to government services, however, we find that the potential for growth is often limited, especially in services that already saturate the market. If we can warp imagination enough to take income-tax collection as a service, we see that the entire market is covered by a monopoly. Growth is limited to the rate of increase in number of taxpayers, which is inextricably tied to the rate of population growth. It follows, therefore, that if productivity is improved at a very significant rate, work force reductions will be in order, a situation inimical to the development of continuous improvement. Both workers and managers will correctly associate improvement generation with the loss of job slots. Furthermore, the lack of room for output growth translates into a relatively low promotion coefficient, another obvious difficulty confronting efforts to introduce a full-blown continuous improvement system into such an organization. Managers will not want to instigate improvements that will reduce the number of employees that report to them, and operators will not want to make their own jobs redundant. Furthermore, the role of customer value in such a fundamental monopoly is small. Tax collectors need not offer customers value in order to engage them or retain them; "customers" only participate in the process because they are legally constrained to do so. Any external pressure for a customer orientation is indirect, operating through elected officials who have to account to voters for the actions of government agencies.

If we expect a government service provider to approach operating as an "ideal type" of continuous improvement organization, we must find a way to introduce competition and allow operating units to enhance their market share through the provision of customer value, which may not be as impossible as it sounds Witness, for example, the fledgling trend toward the use of private firms for the provision and operation of prisons or the voucher system[9] in public education that, in theory, could promote the introduction of effective continuous improvement. In such a situation permanent employment would not be guaranteed by tenure but effectuated by those organizations that provide best net customer value. We are not saying that a voucher system in public education would promote the development of continuous improvement systems, only that it would provide a fertile field in which continuous improvement systems could develop if we made a conscious effort in that direction. Without that effort, chances are good that the vouchers would be exchanged among schools that were organized and operated in a top-down, MP/SM framework.

The use of vouchers within a public school system would give direct recognition to the major role of parents (and derivatively, students) as customers. The fact that the vouchers were reserved for use within the system of public education, as opposed to private, would allow that the public in general was still reserved a customer role. Thus, within the constraints of preparing students to be good citizens, improvement efforts could be directed to producing increasingly better educated students as viewed by the parents. It might be worth noting that within the realm of private education, there would be no natural customer role for the general public.

Conclusion

At this point we are able to recapitulate the analysis to specify the key features of the ideal type continuous improvement firm. The defining feature of the CIF is the ability to continuously add to the net customer value associated with its marketed product. In the ideal type, therefore, each and every employee would exhibit willingness to search for ways to improve the net customer value of the firm's product and the organization would possess the capability of implementing them. In the CIF, employees understand the customer, the product, and the process so well that the organization is capable of anticipating the instrumental characteristics that the customer will value in the market. Indeed, in its ultimate design the CIF is can custom build each item for instant delivery. Because these emerging internally generated improvements are the source of the value wedge on which market leadership is based, the employees must be considered the firm's principle stakeholder. Rather than agents of shareholders, they represent a special form of capital whose skills and embedded knowledge are to be nurtured with permanent employment and promotion from within. The CIF form, however, also requires continuing growth if its unique abilities are to be sustained. In the ideal type CIF, therefore, management must search for new markets and new product lines to serve as the basis for growth.

The continuous improvement paradigm is in the process of superseding the mass production-scientific management paradigm – which is not to say that either economies of scale or the practice of consciously designing management systems is being displaced. The CIF enjoys economies of scale, but, in its more advanced versions, it goes far beyond mass production to encompass flexible manufacturing. Moreover, the consummate CIF takes management as a subject for study and a field to be perfected. We generally use the term *scientific management* to caricature the study and practice of management as accepted in the days of the older paradigm. Today management as a science is engaged in trying to understand the emerging new paradigm. As the change process proceeds, literally thousands of versions of the CIF or TQM have arisen, a few relatively close to the ideal type, but many of them seemingly light years away.

In evaluating progress toward the ideal, we should not expect to find a rapid or precipitous shift from the old paradigm and into the new. Through many institutional frameworks, the MP/SM paradigm continues to be accepted as the way to view the world of organizations. What makes sense and what does not depends on the logic of a particular paradigm. Outdated truths are very difficult to shake off. Thus, we can account for the slow transition partly by the fact that many who are attracted to the new paradigm do not yet understand it. Beyond that, political systems frequently offer selective protection against foreign firms that are organized on the basis of the new paradigm, and some services have difficulty adopting it for reasons just discussed.

We should not doubt, however, that over time, more and more firms will approach the ideal type CIF. The argument that the competitive edge goes to the firm that can provide best net customer value is decisive, regardless of the industry or the firm's distance from the ideal type. At any point in time, the management of any firm wants to be ahead of its competitors in the quest for value, not just somewhere on the road leading to a distant ideal. Thus, it must always be moving steadily toward the ideal. It may now suffice, in some cases, for only the managers and technical personnel to be ready and willing to generate day-to-day product improvements. Eventually competition, old or new, will force an established leading firm to engender improvement capabilities among all of the work force or to move over and let a new firm move to the head of the pack. In all cases, the leader will be the firm whose internal improvement process has produced a value wedge between its product and that of its nearest rival.

NOTES

1. The innovator-entrepreneurs were, respectively, Akio Morita, Konosuke Matsushita, Soichiro Honda, and Kiichiro Toyoda.

2. It probably strains credulity to imply that the continuous improvement mode was instituted by the respective entrepreneurs in the whole-cloth manner implied by Schumpeter's use of the term innovator. That they played important roles, however, is not to be doubted. It may be that, on the whole, they acted more as Schumpeter's entrepreneur-executive of the modern bureaucratic corporation than the entrepreneur-innovator that he cherished.

3. It is desirable that a substantial portion of this knowledge come in the form of education rather than pure indoctrination. Knowledge does not come from mere "pep talks."

4. As we have seen, open offices, job rotation, team work, and strategic layout of machines and work stations are useful in this regard. The synergism that results from the interaction of ideas is vital to the continuous improvement process. Such synergism is enhanced by work in teams, by the use of quality circles, and the use of specialized workshops. All of these promote the exchange of ideas within the CIF. New ideas from the outside, made available through specialized libraries and the attendance at professional and trade meetings by relevant CIF personnel, are also important.

5. The fact that the ideals of lifetime employment and promotion from within would place pressure on the firm to grow was noted by Leibenstein (1984, 352).

6. This situation implies a lower promotion ratio for first-line managers than the 0.5 ratio for middle managers. If the CIF felt that the promotion ratio of 0.5 was also appropriate for first-line managers, this policy would result in an increasing ratio of middle to top managers, which would seem to require that output grow by a factor of 4.0 to justify the increased number of middle managers.

7. Competition among oligopoly CIFs would push them toward collusion in regard to these decisions. If one CIF were to reduce its improvement intensity in one of the proposed manners, the other could grab its market share by retaining a greater improvement intensity so as to provide greater net customer value than the product of the former.

8. Apparently, the World Bank (1987) overlooked the fact that much, if not most, of this division of responsibilities for producing the Escort was based on political considerations. The fact that the division of responsibilities was largely limited to OECD countries is certainly suggestive that something was afoot in addition to or instead of efficiency.

9. In the university, some see publications as the major product for which members of the faculty are responsible.

10. Under a voucher system, parents are given credits or vouchers which they use to purchase education for their children. The fact that they may choose from among the several schools in a system introduces an element of competition. Within such a situation, the provision of customer value could be a useful strategic focus for school administrators and faculties.

BIBLIOGRAPHY

Abbegglen, James C. 1958. *The Japanese Factory: Aspects of Its Social Organization.* Glencoe, Ill.: The Free Press.

Abbegglen, James C. and George Stalk, Jr. 1985. *Kaisha: The Japanese Corporation.* New York: Basic Books.

Abernathy, William, Kim B. Clark, and Alan M. Kantrow. 1981. "The New Industrial Competition," *Harvard Business Review* 59(5):68 – 79.

Aoki, Masahiko, ed. 1984. *Economic Analysis of the Japanese Firm.* New York: North-Holland.

———. 1988. *Information, Incentives, and Bargaining in the Japanese Economy.* New York: Cambridge University Press.

———. 1990. "Toward an Economic Model of the Japanese Firm." *Journal of Economic Literature* 28:1 – 27.

Arrow, J. Kenneth. 1974. *The Limits of Organization.* New York: W.W. Norton & Company, Inc.

Ayres, Clarence E. 1962. *The Theory of Economic Progress.* New York: Shocken Press.

Barney, Jay B. and William G. Ouchi, eds. 1986. *Organizational Economics.* San Francisco: Jossey-Bass.

Best, Michael. 1990. *The New Competition: Institutions of Industrial Restructuring.* Cambridge, MA.: Harvard University Press.

Bijker, Wiebe and Trevor Pinch. 1984. "The Social Construction of Facts and Artifacts: Or How the Sociology of Science and the Sociology of Technology Might Benefit Each Other." *Social Studies of Science* 14(3):399 – 442.

Bos, Antonio and William Cole. 1994. "Management Systems as Technology: Japanese, US and National Firms in the Brazilian Electronics Sector," *World Development* 22(2):225 – 36.

Bowsher, Jack E. 1989. *Educating America: Lessons Learned in the Nation's Corporations.* New York: John Wiley & Sons.

Carmichael, H. Lorne and W. Bentley MacLeod. 1993. "Multiskilling, Technical Change and the Japanese Firm," *The Economic Journal* 103:142 – 60.

Carnegie Foundation for the Advancement of Teaching. 1988. *An Imperiled Generation: Saving Urban Schools.* Princeton, N.J.: Carnegie Foundation for the Advancement of Teaching.

Carothers, G. Harlan, Jr., and Mel Adams. 1991. "Competitive Advantage through Customer Value: The Role of Value-Based Strategies." In ed. M. J. Stahl and G. Bounds, 32 – 66. *Competing Globally through Customer Value: The Management of Strategic Suprasystems,* Westport, Conn.: Quorum Books.

Chandler, Alfred D. 1977. *The Visible Hand: The Managerial Revolution in American Business.* Cambridge: Harvard University Press.

———. 1990. *Scale and Scope: The Dynamics of Industrial Capitalism.* Cambridge: The Belknap University Press.

Church, George L. 1993. "Jobs in an Age of Insecurity," *Time* (November 22):32 – 9.

Cole, William and John Mogab. 1987. "The Transfer of Soft Technologies to Less-Developed Countries: Some Implications for the Technology/Ceremony Dichotomy." *Journal of Economic Issues* 21(1):309 – 20.

Cole, William and Richard Sanders. 1983. "The Transfer of Soft Technologies from the Tennessee Valley Authority to Mexico." *Papers and Proceedings of the North American Economics and Finance Association.* Mexico City.

255

Bibliography

Cooney, Barry D. 1989. "Japan and America: Culture Counts." *Training and Development Journal* (August):58 – 61.

Crosby, Phillip. 1979. *Quality is Free*. New York: McGraw-Hill.

Cummings, William K., Edward R. Beauchamp, Shogo Ichikawa, Victor Kobayashi, and Morikazu Ushiogi, eds. 1986. *Educational Policies in Crisis: Japanese and American Perspectives*. New York: Praeger.

De Mente, Boye. 1981. *The Japanese Way of Doing Business*. Englewood Cliffs, N.J.: Prentice-Hall, Inc.

Deming, W.E. 1986. *Out of the Crisis*. Cambridge: Massachusetts Institute of Technology, Center of Advanced Engineering Study.

Dicken, Peter. 1992. *Global Shift: The Internationalization of Economic Activity*. New York: The Guilford Press.

Dore, R.P. and Mari Sako. 1989. *How the Japanese Learn to Work*. London: Routledge.

do Rosario, Louise. 1992. "All Work and No Play: Cram Schools Keep Alive Education Nightmare." *Far Eastern Economic Review* 155(10):21 – 3.

Drucker, Peter. 1981. "Behind Japan's Success: Defining Rules for Managing in a Pluralist Society." *Harvard Business Review* 59(1):83 – 90.

Eisenhardt, Kathleen M. 1989. "Agency Theory: An Assessment and Review." *Academy of Management Review* 14(1):57 – 74.

Feibleman, James K. 1961. "Pure Science, Applied Science, Technology, Engineering: An Attempt at Definitions." *Technology and Culture* 2(4):305 – 17.

Ford, John B. and Earl D. Honeycutt. 1992. "Japanese National Culture as a Basis for Understanding Japanese Business Practices." *Business Horizons* (November-December):27 – 33.

Freedman, Audrey. 1982. "Learning from New US-Based Neighbors," *Journal of Japanese Trade & Industry* (September):31 – 3.

Fucini, Joseph and Suzy Fucini. 1990. *Working for the Japanese: Inside Mazda's American Auto Plant*. New York: The Free Press.

Galbraith, John K. 1971. *The New Industrial State*. Boston: Houghton Mifflin Co., 1984.

Goonatilake, Susantha. 1984. *Aborted Discovery: Science and Creativity in the Third World*. London: Zed Books, Ltd.

Hamel, G. and C. K. Prahalad. "Do You Really Have a Global Strategy." *Harvard Business Review* (July-August):139 – 48.

Hattori, Tamio. 1986. "Technology Transfer and Management Systems." *The Developing Economies* 24(4):314 – 25.

Hatvany, N. and V. Pucik. 1981. "Japanese Management Practices and Productivity," *Organizational Dynamics* (Spring):5 – 21.

Hayes, Robert H. 1981. "Why Japanese Factories Work," *Harvard Business Review* 59(4):57 – 66.

Hayes, R. H., S. Wheelright, and K. Clark. 1988. *Dynamic Manufacturing: Creating the Learning Organization*. New York: Free Press.

Hirshleifer, Jack. 1980. *Price Theory and Applications*. Englewood Cliffs, N. J.: Prentice-Hall, Inc.

Hodgson, Geoff. 1982. "Theoretical and Policy Implications of Variable Productivity." *Cambridge Journal of Economics* 6:213 – 26.

Hofstede, Geert and Michael Harris Bond. 1988. "The Confucius Connection: From Cultural Roots to Economic Growth." *Organizational Dynamics* (Spring):5 – 21.

Hounshell, David A. 1984. *From the American System to Mass Production, 1800 – 1932*. Baltimore: Johns Hopkins University Press.

Imai, Masaaki. 1986. *Kaizen – The Key to Japan's Competitive Success.* New York: McGraw-Hill.

————. 1990. "The Kaizen Wave Circles the Globe." *Tokyo Business Today* (May):44 – 8.

Imaoka, Hideki. 1989. "Japanese Corporate Employment and Personnel Systems and Their Transfer to Japanese Affiliates in Asia." *The Developing Economies* (4):407 – 26.

————. 1990. *Guide to Quality Control.* White Plains, NY: Asian Productivity Organization-Quality Resources.

Jensen, Michael C. and W.H. Meckling. 1986. "Theory of the Firm: Managerial Behavior, Agency Costs, and Ownership Structure." In *Organizational Economics,* ed. J. B. Barney and W. G. Ouchi, 205 – 98. San Francisco: Jossey-Bass.

Juran, J. M. and F. M. Gryna, Jr. 1970. *Quality Planning and Analysis,* New York: McGraw-Hill.

Kagano, T., I. A. Nonaka, K. Y. Sakakibara, and A. Sakashita. 1984. "Mechanistic vs. Organic Management Systems: A Comparative Study of Adaptive Patterns of U.S. and Japanese Firms." In *The Anatomy of Japanese Business,* ed. Sato Kazuo and Yasuo Hoshino, 27 – 61. Armonk, N.Y.: M.E. Sharpe, Inc.

Katz, Eliakim and Adrian Ziderman. 1990. "Investment in General Training: The Role of Information and Labour Mobility." *The Economic Journal* 100: 1147 – 58.

Kenney, M. and R. Florida. 1993. *Beyond Mass Production: The Japanese System and Its Transfer to the US.* New York: Oxford University Press.

Kinmouth, E.H. 1986. "Engineering Education and Its Rewards." *Comparative Education Review* 30, iii, August.

Koike, Kazuo. 1984. "Skill Formation Systems in the US and Japan: A Comparative Study." In *Economic Analysis of the Japanese Firm,* ed. M. Aoki, 47 – 75. New York: North-Holland.

Kuhn, Thomas S. 1970. *The Structure of Scientific Revolutions.* 2d ed. Chicago: University of Chicago Press.

Kunio, Yoshihara. 1986. *Japanese Economic Development: A Short Introduction.* 2d ed. Tokyo: Oxford University Press.

Leibenstein, Harvey. "The Japanese Management System: An X-Efficiency-Game Theory Analysis." In M. Aoki ed., *The Economic Analysis of the Japanese Firm,* North-Holland, New York, 1984.

Lynch, Lisa M. 1992. "Private-Sector Training and the Earnings of Young Workers." *American Economic Review* 82(1):299 – 312.

The Macmillan Guide to Correspondence Study. 1985. 2d ed. New York: Macmillan Publishing Company.

Maruta, Yoshio. 1990. The Kao Corporate Philosophy." Unpublished manuscript.

Maruyama, Magoroh. 1985. "Experience Looping, Design Looping and Concept Crossing: The Key to Successful Product Invention, Development and Adaptation." *Futures* 17(4):385 – 9.

Matsumoto, Koji. 1982a. "The Secret of Japanese Management Resulting in High Productivity." Part I. *Journal of Japanese Trade & Industry* (January):28 – 34.

————. 1982b. "The Secret of Japanese Management Resulting in High Productivity." Part II. *Journal of Japanese Trade & Industry* (March):40 – 5.

————. 1991. *The Rise of the Japanese Corporate System: The Inside View of a MITI Official.* New York: Kegan Paul International.

Maurice, S. Charles and Charles Smithson. 1988. *Managerial Economics.* Homewood, Ill.: Irwin. 1988.

Bibliography

Mayhew, Anne and Sidney Carroll. 1993. "Alfred Chandler's Speed: Monetary Transformation." *Business and Economic History* 22(1):105 – 13.

Milgrom, Paul and John Roberts. 1992. *Economics, Organization and Management.* Englewood Cliffs, N.J.: Prentice Hall.

Monden, Yasuhiro. 1983. *Toyota Production System: Practical Approach to Production Management.* Norcross, Ga: Industrial Engineering and Management Press.

Naj, Amal Kumar. 1993. "Shifting Gears: Some Manufacturers Drop Efforts to Adopt Japanese Techniques." *Wall Street Journal* (May 5):A1, A12.

New York State Education Office. 1992. "A Cross-Cultural Comparison of the American and Japanese Educational Systems." Albany: New York State Office for Planning, Research, and Support Services.

NHK Enterprises, Inc. 1987. *Anatomy of Japan: The Wellspring of Economic Power.* Videotape No. 8: "Small Companies: The True Heroes of Japanese Industry."

Odagiri, Hiroyuki. 1992. *Growth Through Competition, Competition Through Growth: Strategic Management and the Economy in Japan.* New York: Oxford University Press.

Ohmae, Kenichi. 1982. *The Mind of The Strategist: the Art of Japanese Business.* New York: McGraw Hill.

Ohno, Taiichi. 1988. *Toyota Production System: Beyond Large Scale Production.* Cambridge, Mass: Productivity Press.

Okano, Kaori and R.F.C. Claridge. 1992. "From School or University to Employment: The Japanese Way." Working Paper No. 4. New Zealand Centre for Japanese Studies, Palmerstown North, New Zealand.

Okuda, Kenji. 1983. "The Role of Engineers in Japanese Industry and Education: An Industrial Sociologist's View." *Journal of Trade and Industry* (September/October):23 – 6.

Ouchi, William G. and Alfred M. Jaeger. 1978. "Type Z Organization: Stability in the Midst of Mobility." *The Academy of Management Review* 3(2):305 – 12.

Patience, Wayne M. and Douglas R. Whitney. 1982. *What Do the GED Tests Measure?* Washington, D.C.: GED Testing Service of the American Council on Education.

Reid, Peter C. 1990. *Well Made in America: Lessons from Harley Davidson.* New York: McGraw-Hill.

Robinson, Richard D. 1988. *The International Transfer of Technology: Theory, Issues, and Practice.* Cambridge, Mass: Ballinger Publishing Company.

Rose, Robert L. 1994. "Humming Mills: Once the 'Rust Belt,' Midwest Now Boasts Revitalized Factories." *Wall Street Journal* (January 3):1, 4.

Rosenberg, Nathan, 1982. *Inside the Black Box: Technology and Economics.* Cambridge: Cambridge University Press.

Rubenstein, James. 1991. "The Impact of Japanese Investment in the United States." In *Restructuring the Global Automobile Industry,* ed. C.M. Law, New York: Routledge.

Sakai, Kuniyasu. 1990. "The Feudal World of Japanese Manufacturing." *Harvard Business Review* (November-December):38 – 49.

Schnitzer, Martin C. 1991. *Comparative Economic Systems.* Cincinnati, Ohio: South-Western Publishing Co.

Schonberger, Richard J. 1986. *World Class Manufacturing.* New York: The Free Press.

Schramm, Stella S. 1993. "The Learning Organization: The Implications of Continuous Improvement for the Theory of the Firm." Mimeograph.

Schumpeter, Joseph A. 1962. *Capitalism, Socialism and Democracy.* 3d ed. New York: Harper and Row, Publishers.

Shingo, Shigeo. 1988. *Non-Stock Production: The Shingo System for Continuous Improvement,* Cambridge, Mass.: Productivity Press, Inc.

Smith, Adam. 1957. *An Inquiry Into the Nature and Causes of the Wealth of Nations,* Chicago: Great Books of the Western World.

Smolinowski, Henryk. 1966. "The Structure of Thinking in Technology." *Technology and Culture* 7 (June):371 – 83.

Stern, Sam and Hiromitsu Muta. 1990. "The Japanese Difference." *Training and Developmental Journal* (March):74 – 82.

Tirole, Jean. 1988. *Industrial Organization.* Cambridge: The MIT Press.

US Department of Education. *Japanese Education Today.* Washington, D.C.: US Government Printing Office.

Veblen, Thorstein. 1934. *The Theory of the Leisure Class.* New York: Modern Library Edition.

Walker, James P. 1988. *A Disciplined Approach to Continuous Improvement.* Packard Electric.

Washio, Hiroaki. 1986. "The Provision of Manuals and Japanese Private Technology Transfer." *The Developing Economies* 24(4):326 – 33.

Westney, D.E. and K. Sakakibara. "The Role of Japan Based R&D in Global Technology Strategy." *Technology and Society* 7:315 – 30.

Westrum, Ron. 1991. *Technologies and Society: The Shaping of People and Things.* Belmont, Calif: Wadsworth Publishing Co.

Wharton, Edith. 1920. *The Age of Innocence.* New York: Grosset & Dunlap.

Wilson, Steven R. 1992. "Continuous Improvement and the New Competition: The Case of US, European, and Japanese Firms in the Mexican Maquiladora Industry." Ph.D. diss., University of Tennessee, Knoxville.

Womack, James P., Daniel Jones, and Daniel Roos. 1991. *The Machine That Changed the World: The Story of Lean Production.* New York: Harper Perennial.

World Bank. 1987. *World Development Report, 1987.* New York: Oxford University Press.

World Bank. 1992. *World Development Report, 1992.* New York: Oxford University Press.

Yoshida, Kosaku. 1989. "Deming Management Philosophy: Does It Work in the US as Well as in Japan?" *The Columbia Journal of World Business* 24 (3):10 – 17.

INDEX